The Ulster Unionist Party

Country before Party?

Thomas Hennessey, Máire Braniff,
James W. McAuley, Jonathan Tonge, and
Sophie A. Whiting

OXFORD
UNIVERSITY PRESS

OXFORD
UNIVERSITY PRESS

Great Clarendon Street, Oxford, OX2 6DP,
United Kingdom

Oxford University Press is a department of the University of Oxford.
It furthers the University's objective of excellence in research, scholarship,
and education by publishing worldwide. Oxford is a registered trade mark of
Oxford University Press in the UK and in certain other countries

First Edition published in 2019

Impression: 1

Published in the United States of America by Oxford University Press
198 Madison Avenue, New York, NY 10016, United States of America

British Library Cataloguing in Publication Data
Data available

Library of Congress Control Number: 2018945755

ISBN 978–0–19–879438–7

Printed and bound by
CPI Group (UK) Ltd, Croydon, CR0 4YY

Acknowledgements

We acknowledge with very grateful thanks the financial support provided by the British Academy (SG150211, Principal Investigator: Hennessey) and the University of Liverpool Knowledge Exchange programme to undertake research for this book. We are also indebted to the Economic and Social Research Council for funding the 2010, 2015, and 2017 Northern Ireland Westminster election studies (ES/H037012/1, ES/L007320/1, and ES/R005060/1 respectively: Principal Investigator: Tonge) which have assisted the profiling of Ulster Unionist Party (UUP) voters. The ESRC also kindly funded the Memory, Commemoration and Public Symbolism seminar series (ES/M001741/1 Principal Investigator: McAuley) which influenced some of the thinking in this volume around unionist collective remembering and its linkages to the identity and outlook of the UUP.

We are indebted to a large number of people within the UUP for their unstinting cooperation. We especially wish to thank Robin Swann, Mike Nesbitt, Steve Aiken, Hazel Legge, Colin McCusker, and John Moore. A party membership survey involves a great deal of effort from the party under scrutiny and party officials were invariably helpful and efficient in terms of mailshots and facilitating interviews. We are grateful to all interviewees, from party leaders and peers to grass-roots party members for their time and assistance in allowing insight into different levels of the UUP. Party members may of course profoundly disagree with some of our conclusions but we have attempted to conduct an objective study. We are extremely grateful to our Research Assistant, Josh Harwood, for undertaking hours of work preparing membership survey packs and for producing powerpoint presentations of the data.

We also wish to acknowledge our appreciation for the late Liam Clarke. An outstanding and much-missed journalist. Liam took great interest in our previous book, on the Democratic Unionist Party, serializing its findings in the *Belfast Telegraph* and was interested in this project on the other main unionist party before his untimely death. We acknowledge with thanks encouragement for the project from the journalist Alex Kane.

Finally, we offer a large thank you to Dominic Byatt and Olivia Wells at Oxford University Press, who have been very supportive throughout the research and production of both our books on unionist parties.

Contents

List of Figures

List of Tables

List of Abbreviations

APNI	Alliance Party of Northern Ireland
DSD	Downing Street Declaration
DUP	Democratic Unionist Party
GB	Great Britain
GPNI	Green Party Northern Ireland
IRA	Irish Republican Army
LAW	Loyalist Association of Workers
MEP	Member of the European Parliament
MLA	Member of the Legislative Assembly (Northern Ireland Assembly)
MP	Member of Parliament
NIO	Northern Ireland Office
NIWC	Northern Ireland Women's Coalition
OFMDFM	Office of First and Deputy First Minister
PBP	People Before Profit
PIRA	Provisional Irish Republican Army
PSNI	Police Service of Northern Ireland
PUP	Progressive Unionist Party
RUC	Royal Ulster Constabulary
SDLP	Social Democratic and Labour Party
SF	Sinn Féin
TUV	Traditional Unionist Voice
UCUNF	Ulster Conservatives and Unionists New Force
UDA	Ulster Defence Association
UDP	Ulster Democratic Party
UDR	Ulster Defence Regiment
UK	United Kingdom
UKIP	United Kingdom Independence Party

List of Abbreviations

UUUC	United Ulster Unionist Council
UVF	Ulster Volunteer Force
UWUC	Ulster Women's Unionist Council
UWC	Ulster Workers' Council
YU	Young Unionists

Authors

Máire Braniff is Director of INCORE and Senior Lecturer, University of Ulster.

Thomas Hennessey is Professor of Modern British and Irish History, Canterbury Christ Church University.

James W. McAuley is Professor of Political Sociology and Irish Studies, University of Huddersfield.

Jonathan Tonge is Professor of Politics, University of Liverpool.

Sophie A. Whiting is Lecturer in Politics, University of Bath.

Introduction

Despite the voluminous literature on Northern Ireland politics, remarkably few books have been written about the two main unionist parties. Even less has been produced about the people who belong to those two parties. We attempted to partly rectify this deficit a few years ago in writing about the Democratic Unionist Party (DUP), a study based upon an extensive membership survey. However, there is also little material about what was for decades the most significant unionist organization, the Ulster Unionist Party (UUP), which remains, in size of membership though certainly not in political influence, the larger of the main unionist political vehicles. The dearth of literature is surprising given the long period of UUP hegemony, covering the first fifty years of Northern Ireland's existence. The UUP continued to be pre-eminent within unionism for three decades thereafter, before its extraordinary and dramatic fall from favour at the beginning of this century and a struggle for relevance in recent years. As was the case with the DUP study, the authors were given unique access by the party leadership to survey the UUP membership and produce a detailed account of who those members and what constitutes their political outlook. There is much to tell.

There are very few works dedicated exclusively to analysing the UUP. Graham Walker's *A History of the Ulster Unionist Party: Protest, Pragmatism and Pessimism* offers an impressively detailed and well-researched account of the party's coalitional nature, its historical appeal to unionism across social divides, and its fracture at the time of the Belfast Agreement.[1] It ends before the current leadership took over and substantially restructured the UUP and is understandably leadership-focused. David Hume's book *The Ulster Unionist Party 1972–92*[2] is a sympathetic account of the Party under direct rule during the Troubles and yields useful organizational insights but was published before the Belfast Agreement and all the subsequent upheavals for the UUP. John Harbison's 1973 work, *The Ulster Unionist Party 1882–1973: Its Development and Organisation* is obviously even more dated.[3] Beyond these party accounts, there are profiles of the most important, if often beleaguered, UUP leader of the modern era, in Michael Kerr's 2005 book *Transforming Unionism: David Trimble and the 2005 General Election*[4] and Dean Godson's *Himself Alone: David Trimble and the Ordeal of Unionism*.[5] There are also some impressive treatments of unionism as an ideology, such as those offered over the decades by Arthur Aughey[6] and Norman Porter,[7] or of unionism's role in the peace process,[8] but they are not specific to the UUP and have inevitably become dated given the post-1998 political dispensation, notwithstanding the quality of argument. There is also an important consideration of the relationship between unionism and Orangeism offered in the fine work of Patterson and Kaufmann,[9] but that is obviously only one dimension (and of less importance than was once the case) of the UUP's ideology.

The need for a book on the UUP is pressing given all that has engulfed the organization. The party fell spectacularly from its dominant position in Northern Ireland politics within five years of the 1998 Belfast Agreement. Having held unbroken power from 1921 to 1972, the UUP was still comfortably the region's largest party throughout the Troubles and was instrumental in negotiating the Agreement. That deal proved disastrous for the UUP. As unionist confidence in the power-sharing accord drained rapidly, the UUP was eclipsed by the rival DUP, led by the fundamentalist Protestant preacher, the Reverend Ian Paisley. By 2005, the UUP had been outpolled by the DUP in all four types of election (Westminster, European, Assembly, and Council) and, in a spectacular nadir, the Party's leader, David Trimble, having enjoyed international acclaim and collected a Nobel Peace Prize, found the voters in his own patch of Upper Bann less enthused, losing his parliamentary seat. The DUP duly went on to conclude the St Andrews Agreement in 2006, agreeing to share power with Sinn Féin in a deal which sectarianized the arrangements for electing the First and Deputy First Minister that the UUP had negotiated eight years earlier. As the DUP moved decisively from being a party of protest to one of power, the UUP was side-lined. Recent years have seen various attempts to revive UUP fortunes to little obvious effect, the Party bereft of Westminster representation from 2010 to 2015 and again from 2017. The UUP quit the dysfunctional Northern Ireland Executive in 2016 and held only ten of the Northern Ireland Assembly's ninety seats following the 2017 Assembly election.

The key architects of the Agreement have failed to become significant custodians. Yet reports of the UUP's final demise may be exaggerated. The twenty-first century has been characterized by volatile politics in which fortunes may vary wildly in a short space of time—and there is electoral space for recovery. Nonetheless, the UUP has also to consider the possibility that its days as the standard bearer for unionism may never return.

The Aims of the Book

This volume charts the Troubles history of the UUP, the reasons why it supported the Belfast Agreement, the cost of that deal, and its attempts to recover ground rapidly lost. The volume then analyses the party itself. Who are its members? Why do they remain? What do they believe? It does so via extensive access to the Party, based upon a first-ever membership survey. This entailed a detailed, 69-question, survey sent to all UUP members, which elicited replies from 909 members, almost half (49 per cent) of the total membership. This survey was complemented by in-depth, semi-structured interviews with elected representatives, senior officers, and members, plus focus groups comprising samples of the party membership drawn from various parts of Northern Ireland. As such, the book yields a unique dataset of the demographics and attitudes of UUP members—the most extensive range of interviews and focus groups with UUP members and leaders yet undertaken. These membership data are complemented by electoral data, collected via the 2010, 2015, and 2017 Economic and Social Research Council Northern Ireland General Election surveys, showing the basis of UUP voting support and extent of antipathy towards the party.

The book examines the extent to which the UUP represents a more moderate, less religiously fundamentalist but constitutionally robust, organization compared to its main rival, the DUP, and assesses members' views on the key issues confronting Northern Ireland. These include institutional instability; the impact of Brexit; sectarianism and segregation; the legacy of violence; and national identity. This contemporary focus will complement the detailed exposition of why the UUP spiralled into decline—and how it has strived to revive. The book establishes the primary political, religious, and social motivations and inspirations that led to joining the UUP and staying loyal. It explores the relationships between leaders and led within the Party. Is that relationship essentially 'top down', or is the party democratic? How skewed is that membership in terms of its religious composition and gender balance and what are the implications of its demographic imbalances?

This volume also examines the perceptions of Party members and leaders concerning the extent, rationale, and desirability of the political changes undertaken by the UUP during the peace and political processes, including sharing power with Sinn Féin, the electoral collapse which followed, and the relaunching of the Party. It assesses the fundamental bases and repositories of unionism within the Party; what, for UUP members, provides the contemporary unionist core: Britishness, Northern Irishness, Protestantism, Orangeism, opposition to republicanism, or something else? The membership data and discussions are dissected to identify whether liberal, civic, or ethnic unionist tendencies dominate. The book analyses how content the UUP membership was with the performance of the power-sharing and all-island institutions agreed by their leaders in the Belfast Agreement. The book also analyses the views of UUP party members and leaders regarding prospects for unionist unity: should unionist parties unite politically or electorally and on what basis, or alternatively, are UUP members prepared to transcend the sectarian divide and support alliances with non-unionist parties? Beyond the constitutional question, do members perceive common social and political agendas, or are there strong right versus left rivalries? The book looks at future directions for the UUP. Are they still conflict-related, based upon issues of victims, truth and reconciliation, and justice; cultural, centred upon parades and flags; or socio-economic, with concerns over jobs or housing, as examples, to the fore? The degree of social liberalism on issues such as abortion and same-sex marriage is also assessed.

The Plan of the Book

The UUP's dominance of Northern Ireland from 1921 until the onset of the Troubles has been covered elsewhere[10] and is not featured in this book. Whilst UUP hegemony may have been exaggerated—there were significant external challenges from the Northern Ireland Labour Party[11]—the party remained *primus inter pares* within unionism, maintaining sufficient cross-class and interdenominational Protestant support to retain its dominance, a position consolidated by the UUP's close relationship with the Orange Order. However, the UUP lacked intellectual development, suffering complacency, impotence under direct rule, and poor internal organization, all of which would cause later problems.

We begin our volume by examining the onset of those problems, examining the UUP during the Troubles from 1969 until 1998. The era posed numerous political problems for the Party, in addition to the direct impact of violence upon many members. The collapse of the power-sharing Sunningdale Agreement, the brief period of unionist unity following the Anglo-Irish Agreement, the quiet integrationist approach of James Molyneaux, and its unravelling during the early peace process, are all considered, as is the election of David Trimble as UUP leader in 1995.

The second chapter reveals how and why the UUP took risks in negotiating the Belfast Agreement. This section documents the flaws and ambiguities which the leadership failed to resolve, notably in respect of the decommissioning of paramilitary weapons. The chapter details the rationale behind the decision of party leader David Trimble to 'jump first' into government in advance of

IRA decommissioning and assesses the fallout within the UUP. Were internal divisions and disunity inevitable and if so why?

Chapter 3 analyses the electoral consequences of the UUP's support for the Belfast Agreement. The UUP fell from its perch, suffering electoral collapse and the loss of all the party's Westminster MPs by 2010, before temporarily recovering in 2015 only to lose Westminster representation again two years later. The electoral problems of the UUP arose as unionists lost confidence in the Belfast Agreement. The UUP was engulfed by internal chaos and the DUP picked off the talent from its rival, outwitting the UUP politically and offering seemingly superior internal discipline. The DUP claimed to offer the unionist electorate a better arrangement than the deal negotiated by the UUP, a successful electoral pitch. The chapter assesses the UUP's attempts to shore up its position, via a variety of alliances—with the Conservatives in 2010, via electoral pacts with the DUP in 2015, and a cross-community pitch for nationalist vote transfers in 2017.

Our fourth chapter provides the first detailed data on the demography, geography, and viewpoints of the UUP membership. The chapter examines if the UUP is still in any way the party of 'Big House' unionism, one with a more middle-class membership than that of the DUP. The chapter profiles the party base in terms of age and income. This section assesses where the UUP, traditionally strong in middle-class areas and in rural parts of Northern Ireland, such as Fermanagh, continues to attract members. It then considers members' views of their own political positions and those of their party in terms of left–right distinctions, support for political institutions, and policy preferences.

Having profiled the UUP membership, we turn, in Chapter 5, to an analysis of UUP discourses, to understand how the Party attempts to portray itself as the superior custodian of unionist interests compared to its DUP rival. The DUP's presentation of the Belfast Agreement was primarily through a discourse of concessions to republicanism and losses to unionism, which the UUP struggled to counter. The UUP discourse has been one claiming to offer sensible and secure unionism, demonstrating that the Party secured peace and constitutional security via the Belfast Agreement. Allied to these claims has been the assertion that the DUP has played catch-up in accepting political arrangements negotiated by the UUP. Articulating this discourse, the UUP claims to be the visionary within unionism, creating civic and liberal forms of the ideology, rather than religiously derived or cultural versions. This outlook was embodied in David Trimble's assertion that he wished the Northern Ireland Assembly to operate as a 'pluralist parliament for a pluralist people', a direct repudiation of the 'Protestant parliament for a Protestant people' which governed Northern Ireland for its first five decades.[12] The chapter assesses the validity of the UUP arguments that its non-sectarian vision has helped create a shared future.

Chapter 6 assesses the basis of British identity held by UUP members. The party adapted to a devolutionary settlement, having been a party often more supportive of direct rule from Westminster during the Troubles than the regional Ulster loyalist DUP. This chapter considers whether the UUP offers a form of Britishness more closely aligned to that found elsewhere in the UK than its unionist rival. The Party has contested elections on the slogan 'Simply British'. Using the survey data and interviews, the chapter tests the extent of British identification relative to that of Northern Irishness, assessing the rival pulls of UK identity versus regionalism. The chapter also highlights the exclusiveness of identity, in terms of the degree of rejection by UUP members of a sense of Irishness.

Following the examination of how UUP members define themselves, Chapter 7 explores UUP members' attitudes towards other parties. It explores the degree to which pan-unionism is reality, or whether long-standing hostility to the DUP persists, evidenced by a frequent reluctance to offer the UUP's rival lower preference votes. The chapter also analyses attitudes towards Sinn Féin and assesses the extent of ideological proximity and distance between the UUP and other parties.

We consider the influence of Protestantism in Chapter 8. This section outlines the breadth of Protestant denominational identification within the UUP, explores the degree of religious observance, and examines the importance of Faith and Church to the Party. Whilst overwhelmingly Protestant, the UUP has always rejected the overtly fundamentalist, Free Presbyterian brand with which the DUP was associated for many years. The chapter analyses whether the Church of Ireland or Presbyterian Church provide the bulk of UUP members and assesses if there are significant political differences between those two brands of Protestant. The chapter then discusses the religiously conservative attitudes of members, assessing the extent of support for, or opposition to, the legalization of same-sex marriage and abortion, currently still prohibited (other than in exceptional cases for abortion) in Northern Ireland. The extent to which members offer support for, or opposition to, 'mixed' (Protestant–Catholic) marriages and the depth of backing for unfettered marching rights for the Orange Order, will also be examined. Are older members, politically socialized in an era of fraternal Orange–UUP relations, still more sympathetic to the Orange Order? The chapter analyses the lingering importance of Orangeism within the UUP. The survey data allow direct comparisons with the DUP.

Chapter 9 assesses the representation and roles of women in the UUP. The number of women in political life in Northern Ireland has increased considerably in the past decade. Women now represent 30 per cent of members of the Northern Ireland Assembly and 25 per cent of local councillors are now female. However, in relation to other devolved institutions, where female representation is 42 and 35 per cent in the Welsh Assembly and Scottish Parliament respectively, progress seems to have stalled in Northern Ireland. Northern Irish politics maintains a significant gender deficit, as nationality and religion tend to eclipse a gender focus. The gender deficit within unionist politics is particularly stark when compared with nationalist parties. The chapter accounts for the reasons behind the gender deficit in the UUP, where there exist low female party membership and elected representation. The chapter discusses the ways in which female participation is promoted. It examines male and female attitudes to women in the party, utilizing survey evidence on views of quotas, on whether female elected representatives can better represent women's interests and whether women have significant voice within the UUP.

We conclude by summarizing the nature of the UUP's membership, outlook, and vision and evaluate whether the party can ever again become the dominant unionist party. We summarize whether the UUP's vision of liberal and civic forms of unionism continues to differ from the cultural unionism articulated by the DUP and assess the UUP's vision of a 'shared future'. The conclusion assesses the significance of UUP internal change and modernization. It offers wider assertions concerning how ethnic parties prosper in divided political systems, considering whether it is better to operate as a 'catch-us' party, appealing to one's ethnic kin, or risk a 'catch-all' strategy, attempting to broaden political and electoral appeals beyond the communal chasm.

Notes

1. G. Walker, *A History of the Ulster Unionist Party: Protest, Pragmatism and Pessimism*, Manchester: Manchester University Press, 2004.
2. D. Hume, *The Ulster Unionist Party 1972–92*, Lurgan: Ulster Society, 1996.
3. J. Harbison, *The Ulster Unionist Party 1882–1973*, Belfast: Blackstaff, 1973.
4. M. Kerr, *Transforming Unionism: David Trimble and the 2005 General Election*, Dublin: Irish Academic Press, 2005.
5. D. Godson, *Himself Alone: David Trimble and the Ordeal of Unionism*, London: Harper Perennial, 2011.
6. A. Aughey, *Under Siege: Ulster Unionism and the Anglo-Irish Agreement*, Basingstoke: Palgrave, 1989.
7. N. Porter, *Rethinking Unionism*, Belfast: Blackstaff, 1996.
8. F. Cochrane, *Unionist Politics and the Politics of Unionism since the Anglo-Irish Agreement*, Cork; Cork University Press, 2001; C. Farrington, *Ulster Unionism and the Peace Process*, Basingstoke: Palgrave Macmillan, 2004.
9. H. Patterson and E. Kaufmann, *Unionism and Orangeism in Northern Ireland since 1945*, Manchester: Manchester University Press, 2007.

10. See especially Walker, *A History of the Ulster Unionist Party*.

11. A. Edwards, *A History of the Northern Ireland Labour Party: Democratic Socialism and Sectarianism*, Manchester: Manchester University Press, 2009; P. Bew, P. Gibbon, and H. Patterson, *Northern Ireland 1921–2001: Political Forces and Social Classes*, London: Serif, 2001.

12. J. Tonge, 'Creating Devolved Government in Northern Ireland: From Sunningdale to the Belfast Agreement', *Contemporary British History*, 14.3 (2000), 39–60.

1

The UUP during the Troubles, 1969–1998

> Our Party has done, in essence, the heavy lifting, and taken the difficult decisions when it's cost us politically. So, it would've been easier, maybe, for those who took the decisions to have done things differently, but for the good of the country, and for the good, rather than the great. The country first, as you know, is our motto, and the Party very much second.
>
> (Jo-Anne Dobson, UUP MLA 2011–17)[1]

The modern UUP is defined by its negotiation of the Belfast Agreement in 1998. The terms of that Agreement saw the Party tear itself apart and resulted in its displacement as the dominant political presence in unionism since the foundation of Northern Ireland in 1921. In its place the Democratic Unionist Party (DUP) usurped the UUP as the premier force in political Unionism, a position it has held ever since. The outbreak of the Troubles, in 1968, and the subsequent Provisional IRA insurgency, led to the collapse of the 1921 settlement and the end of unionist hegemony which had seen the UUP govern Northern Ireland continuously since partition. The mosaic of ethnic, civic, and liberal unionism had been contained within one dominant unionist party but the trauma of losing control over the levers of political power led to divisions over how unionists might, once more, secure some control over their constitutional destiny. With each attempt at reform or agreement these tensions were exposed within the UUP, culminating in the schism that polarized unionism in the aftermath of the Agreement. This chapter looks at how a generation of senior UUP figures reached political maturity in the formative years of the Troubles, explores how they reacted to key events and personalities during these tumultuous times, and focuses especially on those figures who later became key negotiators of the Belfast Agreement.

Reform, Reaction, and Retreat

Sir Reg Empey (Lord Empey of Shandon), leader of the UUP 2005–10 and the party's number two negotiator for that Agreement, came from a family with an involvement in politics: an uncle who was a UUP MP in the old Northern Ireland Parliament; another who was a UUP councillor, and another who was chairman of a constituency association: 'So, I kind of grew up around it, and I became a member, formally, when I was at university. So, that's really where I started.'[2] Lord Trimble of Lisnagarvey, leader of the UUP 1995–2005, and the man who led the Party in the 1998 negotiations, recalled how, when he was a very young child, his father placed a unionist poster on a wooden post:

> I can remember too, father being the presiding officer at a polling station and going to the polling station with him. I was shown a ballot paper and was shocked to see that there was a candidate on it whose address was given as HM Prison Belfast....I could not understand how a prisoner could be a candidate.[3]

(During the 1950s Sinn Féin commonly fielded imprisoned IRA members as election candidates.)

The Civil Rights movement of the late 1960s had a seminal impact on both future leaders. Empey recalls:

> I was at Queen's [University Belfast] at that time, and I think the concept of it [Civil Rights], I could understand, but what happened was, at the University, we could see people who we knew were clearly primarily Republicans jumping onto the bandwagon of the Civil Rights Movement. That's why that created the reaction...we felt the Civil Rights Movement had been exploited by Republicans who were using it...people to get the old battle going again, and I think that's what put off a lot of young people joining it. Because, in those days, if you weren't familiar with Londonderry, it was a far-off place of which we knew little, you know, it was that sort of a thing. Most people wouldn't have had a grasp of the demography, or the politics of the city, or anything like that. But, when you could see certain individuals getting involved, we believed that, fundamentally, it was being used as a battering ram [against Unionism], as simple as that.[4]

For Trimble, then in his mid-twenties, the situation was somewhat confusing in terms of the allegations of discrimination, particularly those centring on Derry/Londonderry:

> There was a relative—we called him, uncle, but he was a kind of cousin, who was Lord Mayor of Londonderry for four years in the late 50s, early 60s, Jack Colhoun. Consequently, when the whole civil rights thing broke in the late sixties, much of which was attacking the set-up in Londonderry, I found it difficult to reconcile with Uncle Jack who I knew to be a man of irreproachable character.[5]

Accustomed to unbridled power, the UUP was utterly unprepared for what lay ahead. Its leader was drawn from the gentry, many members comfortably off, and its support base seemingly assured in perpetuity. John Hewitt's *The Coasters* talked about permanent government sustained by regular plebiscites of loyalty from voters who never publicly displayed their fidelity to candidates often drawn from the same families, the same class of people.[6]

According to Mike Nesbitt, much later to become party leader:

> there was a kind of comfortable, unionist middle class who coasted along and ignored what was about to happen, although the signs were there and becoming ever more obvious. *The Coasters* is a very powerful exposition of that kind of comfortable, middle class unionism.[7]

If this was confusing it soon became traumatic as the Provisional Irish Republican Army (PIRA) mounted an insurgency against the British state in Northern Ireland and the UK Government effectively abolished the UUP dominated Northern Ireland Parliament at Stormont. Fears of a sell-out by the British Government took hold in the majority unionist community as unionists had lost their Government and Parliament (after more than fifty years of majority rule) in 1972; and lost control of their state security apparatus following assumption of this role by the British Army. Before Westminster imposed Direct Rule, an attempt to reform Northern Ireland under the leadership of its Prime Minister, Captain Terence O'Neill, had seen the UUP tear itself apart with pro- and anti-O'Neill factions in the 1969 Stormont 'Crossroads' election.

The Prime Minister also failed to impress the young Trimble and Empey. For Trimble,

> O'Neill did not make much of an impression. That may be because, as Prime Minister, he wasn't actually doing things, while the others were engaged in building the economy and creating jobs... O'Neill also sounded a bit distant and rather strange every time you heard him, you know, so, not impressed by him.[8]

Empey agrees that O'Neill 'didn't communicate, basically' and felt there was no engagement with the Party:

> basically, things just happened, and there was no consultation, and of course, I suppose, you know, when you're younger, the old ways people did things, a nod and a wink... Stormont gave the impression that they were just in retreat, instead of saying, 'Okay, we're prepared to have reforms. This is why we want to do them.' But that's not the way it happened.

Instead the Unionist Government 'lost the propaganda war... There was no sense of putting up a fight. They just seemed to roll over and put their paws in the air.[9]

Other UUP members formed positive impressions of O'Neill even if from a relatively young age. Ross Hussey, who went on to become a Member of the

Legislative Assembly (MLA) established by the Belfast Agreement, was born in 1959 and joined the Party when he was 18. His father and grandfather were 'B men'—members of the Ulster Special Constabulary or 'B Specials', a part time auxiliary support to the Royal Ulster Constabulary (RUC). During the Troubles his father and mother (who had also both served in the Royal Navy) joined the Ulster Defence Regiment (UDR), the successor to the 'B' Specials. The UDR was a contingent of the British Army solely recruited in Northern Ireland. Hussey also joined the police reserve and 'always was a very staunch unionist, and always supported the Unionist Party, and it was always that style of politics, going right back to Captain Terence O'Neill...So, I came into, obviously, a Presbyterian family, with security force connections. We were always unionists.' Hussey is critical of the image presented to the world by nationalists and republicans of Northern Ireland in the lead-up to the outbreak of the Troubles:

> There are people who believe that in the '60s all Catholics were treated like second class citizens, and all Protestants were much better off. Well, I came from a working-class family, and we were no better off than anybody else...my father died when I was 13. Well, my mother had to take two jobs to keep us together as a family. My mother had to sell her pension to put my brother through university. So, as a unionist, I got no silver spoon. We had no carpeting. I remember, listening one time to Gerry Adams [President of Sinn Féin] on the radio, and he said, when he was a boy, they had a table in the kitchen, and they had lino on the floor. Well, what did he think we had on the floors? A working-class Protestant was exactly the same as a working-class Catholic.
>
> You know, so, history can be cruel at times, and some people believe what they hear about people living in thatched cottages and that was sold to the Americans by Sinn Féin... that the Irish Catholic was living in a thatched cottage, with a pig in the yard, and sometimes, the pig in the house. Because, I've seen some of the videos that were showed to the Americans, and they gullibly took it all in. Then, some of the Americans arrived over here, and saw that the Irish were living in better houses than themselves. You know, so it's a wonderful thing which you can do whenever you twist the facts.[10]

Hussey retrospectively interprets the O'Neill era as:

> very modern. He was reaching out his hand to the Republic of Ireland. If you look at the original sort of principles of the foundation of the [Northern Ireland] state, there was to be a Council of Ireland. That was within the context of the [Good Friday] Agreement, in effect. It was de Valera [onetime Taoiseach of Ireland] that tore that piece up, because de Valera didn't recognize the fact that the six counties were a separate state. So, the Council of Ireland, in effect, would've have been there, and I think had those two been allowed to shake hands and move forward, if Lemass [also a previous Taoiseach] O'Neill had moved forward, we could've seen changes.[11]

However, for those who were unimpressed by O'Neill, it turned out to be more of the same, as he was replaced as Prime Minister by another Anglo-Irish Old Etonian and a distant relative of O'Neill, Major James Chichester Clark, instead of Brian Faulkner (O'Neill's casting vote for his relative resolved the tied ballot) who came from a commercial background. Reg Empey reflects:

> looking back at it, I think, the mistake then was not to put Faulkner in, because Faulkner was a Presbyterian shirt maker, maybe he didn't quite cut it with some of them, and they put in Clark, who was a decent gentleman, but he had no capacity for propaganda, whereas, Faulkner had. I suspect, had Faulkner been put in at that stage, with his ability, his communication skills, he was a hard fighter, I think that could've changed things dramatically.
>
> But, Chichester-Clark, he couldn't articulate very well, and he wasn't a TV person. He fed into all the aristocratic landowner stuff that fed into the Republican narrative, whereas Faulkner couldn't/wouldn't. He was a very successful Minister. He was articulate, he was punchy, and I think, he could've turned the thing around. But, for whatever personal reasons, they made a mistake, they chose the wrong guy, albeit a gentleman, but I think for the cut and thrust, and the street fighting politics of the time, I think, Faulkner, had he got it at that point, would've been the man.[12]

Faulkner eventually became Prime Minister in 1971 and was the last man to hold that post once Edward Heath, the British Prime Minister, prorogued Stormont in 1972, amid mounting violence. Trimble concludes that the 'old Party sort of sleepwalked into the crisis' although, 'I think, probably, even by '69, it was too late. Once you'd had the major riots, major rioting in '69, I think that's when—although we didn't realise it at the time—I think we'd gone past the point of no return in terms of the destabilisation of the existing political . . . situation.'[13]

Both Trimble and Empey were drawn to Bill Craig, the former Stormont Minister of Development and, more controversially, Minister of Home Affairs, who founded Ulster Vanguard as a pressure group within the UUP in 1972. Craig infamously stated: 'We must build up the dossiers on the men and women who are a menace to this country, because one day, ladies and gentlemen, if the politicians fail, it may be our job to liquidate the enemy.'[14] Empey also joined Vanguard and a key factor, for him, was Craig, who was President of the Young Unionists (YUs) and how they were treated: the YUs were an incubator for the next generation of potential Unionist leaders with a paid organizer in party headquarters. Empey recalls how the trigger for joining Vanguard was not only the political capital that Craig possessed at that moment but that

> headquarters, and the Party bosses at that time resented the fact that we took a different view, and they actually locked us out. So, we couldn't get at our office,

and we couldn't get at our organizer, and we couldn't get at our books, and all the official material. So, that really is what sparked off that. [...It was] a stupid thing in retrospect, but it's the way things go. So, that annoyed a lot of people, so that's how that all started...it was a petty thing.[15]

Craig was seen as one of the few Unionist leaders who generated ideas from the time he was Minister of Development and he had, for supporters, the appearance of a forward- looking modernizer. For Trimble, Bill Craig was

a person who I had formed a positive view of at that time, which I didn't subsequently change in getting to know him better. Because he was, actually, about the brightest...and he was the person who was thinking things through, and quite prepared to do things, you know, quite radical in that kind of sense.[16]

Jim Rodgers, a Belfast City Councillor and former Lord Mayor of Belfast, was also another drawn to Vanguard. Rodgers had joined the UUP in the 1960s; his father's second cousin, Dr Sam Rogers, a GP, was a Member of Parliament for Pottinger (East Belfast) at Stormont; while his mother's side of the family were members of the Northern Ireland Labour Party. Politics was, therefore, in the blood, and Rodgers was asked, through John (the late Lord) Laird and Fraser Agnew (later an Independent MLA from 1998 until 2003), if he would be interested in setting up a Young Unionist Association in Pottinger. 'So, I said, "Okay, I'll see what you can advise me about it"' recalls Rodgers: 'So, I set that up. That's how I joined the Ulster Unionist Party, Official Unionist Party as it was known in those days. So, I've been in the party a long, long time.'[17] However, the surge in violence had a profound effect on him and he later joined Vanguard because:

I thought that the Union was becoming insecure. I wasn't the type to take up guns. I detest paramilitarism, regardless whether it's from loyalists or republicans, but I just felt we had to take a stand and send a message out to our government at Westminster. I just felt that the Ulster Unionist Party were basically just getting weaker and weaker...I had become a bit disillusioned with the direction that the party seemed to be taking. I resigned as Chairman of Pottinger Young Unionists, and others quit along with me, and the Branch just disintegrated, and that was it. It was never re-formed.[18]

Danny Kennedy, who went on to become a Minister in the power-sharing Executive created by the Belfast Agreement, was also, initially, intrigued by Craig. Kennedy joined the UUP in 1974, when he was 16: he had a fascination with politics and his father had stood for election in local government in the early 1960s. As a teenager, he went to Vanguard rallies:

The final rally, I think, was at Ormeau Park where Craig famously stood up and said that he was going to extirpate people...Or, that people should be extirpated. Now, I didn't know what extirpated meant. We went home and turned on the TV and watched what Bill Craig had said, and [asked] 'What does that mean?' Then, somebody explained what it was. So, it was poor leadership really, from a unionist point of view, but that was the only leadership we had, you know, well, the alternative was Paisley. Whilst sounding attractive, there were less attractive sides to it, as well.[19]

For Kennedy, coming from a 'rural, Conservative Northern Ireland, church-going, God-fearing' community in South Armagh meant this reflected the structure of the Party there. This acted as a brake on any thoughts of support-ing the implication, by Craig, that violence might be a necessary measure against terrorists:

you see, rural Northern Ireland, it's not like Belfast, it's riveted in church and Orangeism, and County Armagh Orangeism's powerfully strong, and so, that's where our leadership came from.

  People were stopped and prevented from getting involved in paramilitaries and inviting paramilitaries in. You know, there was the opportunity, paramilitaries made it clear that they wanted to help, even in areas like South Armagh, and approaches were made at the time. But, the leadership, to be fair to them, stood firm and said, 'No, no, no, we're going to deal with this in our own way, and we'll sort this out.' Or, 'We'll give a political reaction to this.' So, I think, you can look consistently at the rural parts of Northern Ireland, where paramilitarism didn't [have a presence]...in some of the larger towns, yes, Portadown, you know, perhaps, Lurgan, and other places like that. But, generally, in the more rural settings, paramilitarism was never allowed to take root.[20]

The main charismatic alternative to Craig was the Reverend Ian Paisley, the Christian fundamentalist, who formed his own ministry, via the Free Presby-terian Church, and political party, the DUP in 1971. Paisley had been a critic of every UUP leader, from O'Neill to Faulkner, accusing them of selling out 'traditional unionism', opposing movement from an ethnic unionism and denouncing ecumenicalism. Moves to entice Catholics towards unionism and improve North–South relations were seen as treacherous by Paisley.[21] Ross Hussey recalls:

I remember Ian Paisley, when I was a boy. I remember, saying at the time, that Ian Paisley, when he was in jail [1966]...we were asked to write this wee thing at school, and I wrote that Ian Paisley's in jail and they should throw away the key. Now, that was my view as a 10-year-old boy and my attitude never changed towards him. I always felt that he was a splitter in unionism, as opposed to a uniter...I didn't like his style of unionism...He split unionism, and he split the churches as well, if we go that far. But, when Ian Paisley come out to attack Captain Terence O'Neill, I'm firmly of the view that Ian Paisley always had one goal in mind, and that was for him to be Prime Minister of Northern Ireland...His intention was to force himself onto the political field. If it meant destroying the

15

Ulster Unionist Party, or the Unionist Party, in the process, he didn't care. He wanted to be Prime Minister, and he ended up achieving what he wanted. It took a very long time, but he destroyed an awful lot of Unionism, and unionist supporters, I think, in his wake.[22]

The UUP, as a broad church of Unionist opinion, with no other significant competitors within Unionism in the 1960s and early 1970s, reflected much of the concern with reforming leaders of the Party from O'Neill to Faulkner.[23] Nevertheless for many, Paisley and what he was thought to represent was too much even for those UUP members who thought their leaders had made serious errors of judgement. As Danny Kennedy explains, the explicit religious connection between the DUP and the Free Presbyterian Church, and personified in the demagogic Paisley, was beyond the pale for mainstream Unionists:

> I think, the difference was pretty much, probably, the Free Presbyterian Church, which was a turn-off to mainstream Presbyterianism, which is where I represent . . . And the family . . . whilst we were attracted by the soundings that Paisley was making, and it was popular stuff, and it was emotional stuff to tug at your heartstrings in terms of what was going on, and who was letting Ulster down in terms of Unionism, there was a sense that you were listening to the loudest voice, rather than the best argument. But, you see, Paisley did huge damage in his early days to mainstream Unionism, establishment unionism, to the Presbyterian Church, and to even the Orange Order. Paisley had no time for the Orange Order, and because the Orange Order had rejected his early sort of intention to try and take it over or be heavily involved.

Kennedy can also see how the onset of the Troubles would rapidly change unionist politics as deference declined and the UUP had to try and respond to challenges:

> So, we were coming from, I suppose, not quite an establishment view, because we were working class, genuinely. My father was a bread server. My mother looked after us, we were a large family of seven, living in South Armagh. The thought of a nomination as an Ulster Unionist candidate was unthinkable. But, all of that was swept away with the early Troubles, and the landed gentry, and unionism being swept away in terms of what Paisley was doing, and what was happening in the country. The reaction was in the wider Unionist Party, there was a genuine sort of insurrection against the political establishment, where it seemed to have failed unionism, or was failing Unionism at the time.
>
> Now, we might look through a different lens now, with hindsight, and say, 'Well, if we'd allowed Terence O'Neill the time and the space, and listened to the argument, rather than the loudest voice, we might, actually, be in a better position.' But, at that time, through that lens, when you were watching grainy, black and white TV images in South Armagh, you know, as to what was happening within Unionism, Paisley was attractive. But, there were other voices still in the mainstream Unionist Party, who you were listening to and followed.[24]

By 1973 the UUP and unionism in general had endured political blows culminating in the effective abolition of Stormont and the end of fifty years of self-rule. For many, a British sell-out and a united Ireland was just around the corner, especially when Faulkner accepted a power-sharing arrangement with the Nationalist Social and Democratic Labour Party (SDLP). This was a difficult proposition for the UUP to accept; although the governing body of the UUP, the Ulster Unionist Council (UUC), endorsed Faulkner's position, the majority was not decisive. The split in the Party had been illustrated in the Assembly elections earlier in the year when UUP candidates had taken differing positions on the Government White Paper that outlined the power-sharing proposals.[25]

Faulkner secured support for power-sharing at the UUC but it was clear the Party was divided on the issue. He did not secure a similar outcome at the UUC when he went further, agreeing, in subsequent negotiations at Sunningdale, to a Council of Ireland involving the Irish Government. The Council of Ireland model agreed there had executive powers, possessing the ability take decisions on all-island basis, over the heads of a Northern Ireland Assembly and the Oireachtas (Irish legislature), and, in the view of many unionists, potentially becoming an embryonic all-Ireland government. Faulkner had also relented on his insistence that Articles 2 and 3 of the Irish Constitution, which claimed Northern Ireland was not part of the United Kingdom but part of the Irish nation and state, be replaced. Instead, Faulkner accepted parallel declarations by the British and Irish Governments: in the British declaration the UK Government confirmed Northern Ireland was part of the UK; but in the Irish Government declaration the constitutional status of Northern Ireland was undefined—for to do otherwise would have been to state that it was part of the Irish state and stand in direct contradiction which the British declaration.[26]

A rump of UUP members remained loyal to Faulkner but he was forced to resign as leader. Danny Kennedy opposed power-sharing and Sunningdale, describing the 1973 proposals as 'a complete sell-out', although he qualifies this with the comment that this was how 'it was sold' at that time 'and, in many ways, that's a tragedy, you know, when I look back now, thirty-plus years'. Kennedy acknowledges that 'Paisley was able to give voice to touch the nerve of that emotionalism and fundamentalism' and that expression 'wasn't that far away from where we were sitting in our Ulster Unionist Party branch in Bessbrook in South Armagh'.[27] By this stage Trimble had become involved in Vanguard. Previously he had canvassed for Basil McIvor (one of the UUP team at Sunningdale) and applied to join the UUP but 'they never came back to me'. Prior to the 1973 Assembly elections Trimble, who was by now a lecturer in the Faculty of Law at Queen's University, was approached to give an explanation of the new electoral Single Transferable Vote (STV) system to be used:

I remember chatting to people about STV, and somebody asked me, 'Would I be prepared to go to a conference to explain this?' The first one I went to was a group of Orangemen, and I went through all the details of STV. Then, one of the chaps who was at that meeting came to me a few nights later, and said, 'Would I like to go to another meeting to talk about this?' I said, 'Fine'. He said, 'Well, the meeting's on tonight' and I said, 'Oh, well, I'm not doing anything tonight, and I'm willing to do it'. I found myself then addressing the local Vanguard Association meeting.

Then they put me in into the 1973 Assembly election . . . Originally they were only going to run two candidates in North Down and then they decided to run three and put me in as the third. I remember towards the end of the campaign meeting one of the Ulster Unionist candidates, Major Brownlow, who had a Lurgan connection. Anyway, he said to me, he said, 'You know, you'll not get very many votes, but you've done very well for yourself'. Now I did not particularly like that but it turned out to be absolutely true. I got very few votes, but a few months later, I was Chairman of the North Down Association of the Vanguard, and a few months after that, I was a party officer in Vanguard.[28]

By now Reg Empey was also in Vanguard. While he was opposed to power-sharing that 'was not the issue to which most people objected . . . Dublin pushed too hard on the North/South dimension . . . it wasn't power-sharing that put Faulkner out, it was the Council of Ireland stuff that put him out . . . but it was on that issue that he lost, not on the power-sharing.'[29] This is correct: Faulkner lost a crucial UUC vote on the Sunningdale Agreement and was forced to resign as UUP leader; in his stead Harry West took over.

One of the lessons Empey drew from Sunningdale was how Faulkner and the UUP were isolated from their supporters: 'they allowed themselves to be effectively taken prisoner. They were under house arrest at Sunningdale, they couldn't communicate, they couldn't phone, they couldn't do anything. They should've been out the door.' This, he deemed, was a key factor in Faulkner and his team agreeing to the Council of Ireland: 'they were effectively incarcerated in that place . . . they no access to phones . . . Heath was a bully. That side of it was the part of it that worried me most.'[30]

Although Vanguard had originated within the UUP by 1973 it, and Bill Craig, had been forced out of the Party, so he formed his own—the Vanguard Unionist Progressive Party. Trimble emphasizes that he was not opposed to power-sharing:

I was opposed to Sunningdale. It seemed to me that the government's proposals were unworkable, and, worse than that, I felt they were destabilizing the constitutional position of Northern Ireland. So, I had no hesitation in supporting the huge anti-Sunningdale petition which got 360,000 signatures which set up the success in the first election in '74 when we won 11 out of 12 seats.

He recalls that what became the Ulster Workers' Council (UWC) strike that, with crucial loyalist paramilitary support, brought down power-sharing and killed Sunningdale, was an idea that began to emerge as a result of Craig arguing that the success of Vanguard, the DUP, and the UUP anti Faulkner candidates in the Assembly election was not enough. Craig circulated a letter:

> not just to the Vanguard, but amongst unionists generally in October '73, saying that people were going around just talking as if we had been successful. Vanguard got seven seats, and DUP got eight and the unpledged unionists had a further ten. Bill said that our campaigns in the Assembly election failed because our opponents were on the way to agreement on the administration within the terms of the Sunningdale Agreement, and we've got to take account of that situation and decide what we're going to do, you know, not just to oppose that, but to prevent that taking effect...he said, 'We need to design a strategy, programme to that purpose.' The letter did not mention an all-out strike, but the idea was going around.[31]

The option of a general strike was not new: in 1972 there had been a limited shut down by the Loyalist Association of Workers (LAW) as Protestant workers protested at the deteriorating security situation. Craig met with these Loyalist trade union representatives, such as Harry Murray, in Carrickfergus but, Trimble points out, most were unaware that was the point at which the decision was made to form the Ulster Workers' Council, and for it to then organize an all-out strike.

> Now, there had been the Loyalist Association of Workers which had organized some protest action earlier, in '72. Journalists asked who'd been working with the Association and were pretty scathing about them, because they were just shop stewards, and not terribly well-educated shop stewards. The reporters were very sniffy about this and the LAW folk felt quite embarrassed, and so they decided, 'We're going to form a new thing. We want to do it properly, so we're going to have a proper rule book, and all the rest of it'.

Trimble was nominated to help them draft the rule book:

> So, I was delegated to go to them and talk to them about what sort of rule book they wanted, and all the rest. So, I drafted that. But then, Harry Murray, who's the person who organized it, he decided he wanted to bring me round to all his meetings that he was going to at the time. So, I found myself going to lots of meeting with shop stewards who were drawing up their plans about how they were going to organize an all-out strike, and how it would be effective and all the rest of it.
> So, that was an interesting exercise. But, at that time then, when the strike happened, well, the theoretical position that Bill wanted, the workers themselves wanted, as well, was for this to be done by the UWC without involving the political parties. But, it started getting too complicated, and Bill started to go along to the meetings and had to help them to get organized. On the Friday, the first Friday of the strike, I couldn't stand sort of sitting and doing nothing, so I just

went along to their headquarters there, went into the building, and . . . nobody was sitting on the telephone. Nobody was sitting and receiving calls or doing anything. I knew how to work that, it wasn't terribly complicated, so I just sat down there and spent the next couple of hours handling their telephone, with the telephone calls. Getting someone, if they wanted to speak to someone, getting that person, getting them up there, because the phone lines were jammed, they were pretty well jammed, it was difficult. So, I made myself useful over the course of the next week, I then find myself being asked to other things, and to help in terms of the administration. So, it was a fascinating view of what was going on.[32]

The success of the UWC strike and the collapse of the power-sharing Executive meant there would be no Council of Ireland. Sunningdale was dead. In a last-ditch attempt to produce a political accommodation, the new Secretary of State for Northern Ireland, Merlyn Rees, called a Constitutional Convention to decide a way forward. Trimble was elected to it for Vanguard. Bill Craig's political career was effectively ended when he put forward the notion of voluntary coalition, as opposed to the mandatory model of 1973–4, between Unionist parties and the SDLP. Craig had in mind Churchill's government of 1940–5, formed in response to a national emergency. Trimble had already been thinking along these lines independently of Craig and had put it in his election literature:

Well, funnily enough, when things went pear-shaped on that, and I had been elected in South Belfast, one of my critics in South Belfast . . . said he was thinking about maybe criticizing me . . . He said, 'For that reason, I'd gone and got your leaflet,' and, much to his surprise, he had looked at my leaflet and saw that it referred to the possibility of there being a coalition government formed in the normal way. I'd put it in the leaflet, saying . . . 'We don't need to have a statutory structure to create a cross party rule arrangement, that it could happen normally as has happened at times in the past, where people have formed coalitions.' Now . . . when I said that, I was just drawing attention to something that was possible to within the constitutional practice in the UK.[33]

What Trimble did not know—and Craig told him later—was that in 1972 discussions with John Hume and Austin Currie, both senior members of the SDLP, he and another UUP hardliner, John Taylor, 'ended up talking about the idea of having a coalition' although there was no agreement. 'So, that there was a little back story there. The fact that Taylor and Craig were meeting these two was in the public domain, but what has not been in the public domain is that that's what they ended up talking about from wher-ever they started.'[34] In 1976, Craig decided to go public and advocate a voluntary coalition in the Convention. Trimble recalls his reaction when he learned of the plan: 'Bill told me what he was going to do and I wasn't ready for it. I was horrified. I said, "People won't stand for it."'[35] He and

David Burnside (then in Vanguard but a future UUP MLA and MP) tried to persuade Craig not to go through with the policy:

> I remember in the final stages David Burnside trying to persuade Bill not to press the idea but he was determined. After I'd got over my initial shock with what Bill had said to me, and...I thought it through, I thought, this is a good thing. At the time, I was very annoyed that other Unionists didn't fall in behind it. However, in retrospect, I think, the basic problem was with the electorate, that the unionists who represented them were actually accurately reflecting what the state of mind of the electorate was. Because at that stage, the majority of unionists still thought...we were just dealing with a law and order problem, and if the police and the army would just enforce the law, it would stop all these criminal activities, that that was it.
>
> At the same time, amongst nationalists and republicans, they thought they could win through military means. So, once violence had come in and unleashed the sectarian dynamic, then it took a long time for that to work its way through and for the communities to work this out of their system. I think it was not until the late '80s that you were beginning to get a context where agreement was possible. You know, you've got to bear in mind, from the time of the negotiations in the Constitutional Convention, from then until the beginning of the Brooke/Mayhew talks [1991/2], there were no talks between Unionists and Nationalists. There might have been the odd comment, you know, informally in [television] studios, but there was no serious engagement at that time.[36]

The Molyneaux Years 1979–1995

Following the success of the UWC strike, the UUP felt it required a steady hand at the helm. No more ambitious attempts at a political settlement were attempted under the leadership of Harry West nor his successor, the conservative nightwatchman, James Molyneaux. In October 1974, Molyneaux, MP for South Antrim, emerged as leader of the UUP in the House of Commons. An Orangeman who had served in the Royal Air Force during the Second World War, he helped liberate Belsen concentration camp, recalling: 'The sense of shock hit you like a tidal wave. It was the work of the devil.'[37] Politically Molyneaux was closely tied to the Conservatives at Westminster and was heavily influenced by Enoch Powell, the former Tory MP for Wolverhampton—notorious for his 'Rivers of Blood' speech forewarning of racial strife in Britain—who became UUP MP for South Down following the loss of his English seat in 1974. In the absence of a devolved institution and with few local government powers in Northern Ireland, Westminster became the focus point of UUP political activity, so when Harry West failed to secure a seat there, in 1979, the unassuming and cautious Molyneaux became party leader. He was a very different character from the confident Faulkner and the DUP *enfant terrible* Paisley. Reg Empey recalls:

> Well, Jim...was totally different. I mean, in this day and age, you're comparing Jim with current leaders, now, you know, you're a media personality today, but he was as far away from that as you could get. Well, now, Jim was good at the local stuff. Jim would go to open the bun fight at the local choir fundraising dinner, and all that sort of thing. He was good at that, and he had kind of a common touch, he was quiet, reserved, but very steady. So, he was good at steadying things, and he also was one of those people who could sort of contain Paisley. Because, his project, really, he felt that Ian [Paisley] was very emotional and would run off, you know, charge off at various things, and Jim was very solid, very steady, and with his war record, and so on, he was un-attackable, really, by Paisley.
>
> He, therefore, held things together, and did so quite well. The downside of that is, of course, that that means...you don't try and bring about some kind of change, even within the Party, and we'd present him with a situation, then there's a danger to that, that's the downside of what Jim was trying to do. Now, Jim, fundamentally, believed in this place, over here [Westminster]. He didn't really like Stormont, he hated it. He didn't like the concept, and I think his plan, really, was just to have direct rule, but...to change it from direct rule to just normal integration, really, with revised local government structures and no devolution... his philosophy was, keep her steady, keep her linked into the centre, and don't go in for any adventures. That was his policy, and it worked for him, and it worked for the Party.[38]

What Molyneaux had to balance was the new division within the UUP (there were no power-sharers to be seen or heard any more). Integrationists believed Northern Ireland should be governed as the rest of the UK then was—there were no devolved parliaments or assemblies in Scotland and Wales—so that the region would witness assimilation into the British state rather than being cast adrift to float into the Republic's orbit. In contrast many within the Party remained staunch devolutionists who were convinced the return of a Northern Ireland parliament or assembly would provide a bulwark against Westminster's apparent lack of commitment to the Union. Molyneaux, under Powell's influence, was firmly in the former corner.

In the aftermath of the Republican hunger strike of 1981, in which ten prisoners starved themselves to death to attain 'political status', Margaret Thatcher's Conservative Government created a new Northern Ireland Assembly that would require the agreement of 70 per cent of elected members before powers would be devolved—known as 'rolling devolution'. While the UUP emerged once more as the largest party in the elections to the Assembly, the institution itself was, in ways, stillborn—perhaps struggling for political life in an incubator might be more appropriate—as the SDLP refused to take their seats thereby vetoing the 'cross-community' requirement for rolling devolution to occur.[39]

This demonstrated the essential problem in the governance of Northern Ireland: the refusal of the nationalist minority to be governed without power-sharing, although at the time the UUP put the SDLP's motives down to its desire for a united Ireland and a fear of the rising electoral fortunes of Sinn Féin[40] as a competitor in the wake of the hunger strike.

In terms of what passed for a political vision for Northern Ireland, some clear water was put between the UUP and the DUP, which remained wedded to a return to a majority-rule Parliament,[41] in the UUP's *The Way Forward* proposals in 1984. For Molyneaux, the key paragraph read:

> The time is now ripe for both communities in Northern Ireland to realise that, essentially, their problems will have to be solved in Northern Ireland by their political representatives and that any future prospect for them and their children is best provided for within the Northern Ireland context. This will require a mutual recognition of each other's hopes and fears. Only rights can be guaranteed, not aspirations.[42]

The next phrase in the document, the UUP leader concluded, was 'probably the most telling for an Ulster Unionist leader to use': it was the responsibility of the majority to persuade the minority that the Province was also theirs.[43] But this was not to be done by power-sharing: *The Way Forward* emphatically ruled this out, on the basis that:

> The majority will not accept the power sharing principle which they believe would be utilised as a platform for unification, while the minority representatives are, in any event, presently not interested in power sharing but solely in the withdrawal of the British guarantee of the constitutional position and the creation of a framework for All Ireland institutions.[44]

In an environment of direct rule, it was a plea for the return of devolved powers to local democratic bodies and an attempt to bridge the difference between integrationists and devolutionists within the Party by making the Northern Ireland Assembly an administrative body unable to legislate. Devolved administrative power would be divided between appropriate Committees of the Assembly, whose function would be to examine in detail and advise on the ultimate decisions to be taken by the entire Assembly. There would be no Cabinet, although a General Purposes Committee might serve a coordinating function among the parties. Minority participation would be encouraged by the absence of a Cabinet government with its concomitant requirement of a dependable constant majority. Minority rights would be secured by a Bill of Rights. Finally there would be no institutional Irish dimension although the UUP did not object to an 'Irish dimension' in the form of state recognition of the legitimacy of the fostering of distinctively Irish cultural activities in Northern Ireland nor to state funding of such activities.[45]

It was, as Molyneaux summed it up, a demand for 'equal British rights for all British citizens'.[46] That, however, was the problem: there was no appeal to the Irishness of even constitutional nationalists nor much encouragement to think through long-term strategies. And this went right to the top. As Empey recalls:

> The Troubles, the destruction and the [declining] economy...all of those things required a different approach from unionism, but Jim didn't sort of try to have any sort of big project, he just kept her steady, and safe, where he came out successful for quite a long time. But, he wasn't interested, he hated these summits and talks... I think, he got that wrong. I mean, he had too much faith in Parliament...However, some of us who were keener on devolution, and involved in local government and stuff, which was really the only show in town in those days...we saw it from a slightly different perspective. In that, the way I would've tried, and others...we'd have suggested this. Then, he [Molyneaux] was very good, you see, at handling you, because, [Molyneaux would say] 'Okay, well, we'll set up a wee group here, and you and Bloggs and Smithers, go away and draw up a wee paper.' So, he'd occupy you, you see, he had a good technique. You know, keep 'em busy and that keeps them away from causing any trouble. Then a report would come out, and you discussed it, and disappear...So, he was a master at that, he really was excellent. He was good at managing people in that way, he kept us all occupied.[47]

Molyneaux's leadership was summed up, by his biographer, as 'The Long View'.[48] Despite the grumblings over the lack of accountability and criticisms concerning the effectiveness of the counter-terrorist strategies of the security forces, the bottom line was that an immediate political threat to Northern Ireland's constitutional position within the Union had receded since Sunningdale. Direct rule allowed unionists to rest on the constitutional guarantee that there would be no change in that status without the consent of the people of Northern Ireland. Even when Thatcher and Taoiseach Charles Haughey initiated an Anglo-Irish rapprochement in 1980, Molyneaux retained his faith in the British premier's overt unionism. Empey remembers realizing how 'it was the old story...people just didn't trust London...Jim kept telling us, "Look, these guys will be okay".'[49] This faith was reinforced by Thatcher's robust rejection of any of the options outlined, by the constitutional Nationalist parties in Ireland, in their New Ireland Forum report of 1984 calling for a unitary Irish state; joint British-Irish authority over Northern Ireland; or a federal/confederal Ireland.[50] As Danny Kennedy explains, in this context it was easy to be drawn to the Molyneaux strategy:

> full integration at the time seemed attractive. Molyneaux, as our leader, was selling that quite a bit...the difficulty was, you see, the SDLP...I mean, it's ironic, but they were seen as being very green and unreasonable. So, maybe, the better option,

the safer option for the Union was going to be integration of some form. But, '85 changed all that.[51]

November 1985 did indeed move the UUP from its false sense of security. On the 15th of that month, at Hillsborough Castle, Thatcher signed the Anglo Irish Agreement (AIA) granting the Irish Government the right to be consulted on certain matters in Northern Ireland. The shock among rank-and-file UUP members was a key factor undermining Molyneaux's credibility according to Kennedy:

> Well, Harold McCusker was our local MP, and he gave voice to it very, very well, and reflected grass roots unionism...that we had, literally, been betrayed by our own government, and particularly, our own Prime Minister. All through it...I mean, I had just been elected earlier in May of '85 to the Council, and we were being told on a political level, 'Nothing to worry about.' In fact, Northern Ireland played England in a World Cup qualifier, and we drew 0-0 at Wembley...and the following day, us...the Young Unionist movement, went to Westminster, because we were still in London. There were telephone calls to'ing and fro'ing, and there was a lot of speculation that something was going to emerge on the Friday at Hillsborough. Even on that Thursday, we were being told, 'This won't happen. There's nothing to worry about here,' you know, 'This is only speculation. This is a nest of vipers that Jim had encountered with Enoch [Powell].' You know what I mean? 'Everything was fine.' It emerged that everything wasn't fine, and I think, that let us down quite a bit. Yet, you know, although he was a good leader, and a fine man, and all of that, and a good parliamentarian...so, he [Molyneaux] didn't get the road. You know what I mean? Any other leader might have expected to have been replaced, or whatever. But, I think, there was a crisis for Unionism, rather than just simply the Ulster Unionist Party. I think, they found themselves outmanoeuvred, particularly, by Hume. It was, 'What was the response to be?' Ditching Molyneaux and Paisley wasn't going to solve it.[52]

Molyneaux was caught unawares regarding the breadth and details of the deal. It was a substantial, but not terminal, blow to his leadership. According to Empey:

> When you had the Troubles going on and people being killed...people felt that if we had some of our own hands on the tiller, at least we could, maybe, carve out a better form of government. But, Molyneaux's line was, 'Look, stick with these guys [The Conservative Government] here, they'll be all right on the night.' What was perfectly clear was they were working away behind the scenes, and we said to Jim there, 'This is what they're doing,' and he didn't seem to fully grasp that. When it came to the Anglo-Irish Agreement that was pretty well, for most of us, the rank, it was last straw, because Jim had been saying, 'You know, this type of thing can't happen'...Then, all of a sudden, Thatcher comes out with it, and there's a thing at Hillsborough, and our MPs were fed a copy through the [castle railings] by a journalist. Now, [Norman] Tebbit [a senior Conservative Cabinet Minister] was

supposed to be the person who liaised with Jim on some of this stuff, and there would be some in the Conservative Party who would say that Jim knew more than we were aware of. I don't know whether there's any truth in that or not. But, one thing was clear, the Irish Government couldn't understand, they assumed that London would've been keeping us in the frame, the same as they were keeping the SDLP in the frame. Right? That was not the case. So, I think, they were a bit shocked at our reaction, because they assumed we knew a lot of this. I don't know if they knew at the top, but the rank and file certainly didn't know about it.[53]

Molyneaux was forced to admit that his hope of building peace, stability, and reconciliation, within the bounds of Northern Ireland, by incremental confidence-building measures had been 'snuffed out' by the Anglo-Irish Agreement. There was a second casualty of the AIA: stability, because this depended on consent of the governed but there was none from Unionists.[54] A claim by the British Government that the Irish territorial claim was superseded by a new declaration in the Agreement was shown to be false when a legal action taken in Dublin, by the UUP's Christopher and Michael McGimpsey, saw the Irish Supreme Court hold that, notwithstanding the Anglo-Irish Agreement, the relevant part of the Irish Constitution, Articles 2 and 3, constituted a 'claim of legal right' and that ministers in the Irish Government were under a 'constitutional imperative' to give effect to this claim. In a show of Unionist solidarity and resistance to the Agreement, Molyneaux was drawn into a pact with Paisley—what many UUP supporters would have previously regarded as an unholy alliance. But the *entente cordiale* between the UUP and the DUP was crucial in preventing wider Unionist-Loyalist anger metamorphosing into large-scale violence. Nevertheless killings did increase and Molyneaux protested, privately, to Thatcher that the Anglo-Irish Agreement was the cause of this, writing: 'on humanitarian grounds I beg you to review and re-cast the Government's whole political and security strategy and indicate how much longer, to use your own words at the [AIA] signing ceremony, you are "prepared to tolerate a situation of continuing violence."'[55] The Prime Minister's reply was dismissive, describing the UUP leader's claim as 'misleading' in attributing the violence in Northern Ireland to the Anglo-Irish Agreement and pointing out its preceding longevity.[56]

With the illusion of a 'special relationship' between the UUP and the Thatcher Government in tatters, unionists were faced with an impasse: how to remove an Agreement that, unlike 1973–4, did not require their participation. Molyneaux did not exaggerate when he told the House of Commons: 'I have to say honestly and truthfully that in 40 years in public life I have never known what I can only describe as a universal cold fury, which some of us have thus far managed to contain.'[57] But how to channel that anger? Civil unrest risked escalation to widespread violence and making Northern Ireland ungovernable—exactly what the IRA wanted. Political action remained the only rational choice for the Molyneaux-Paisley alliance if this was to be avoided. But one attempt, under the 'Ulster Says No' banner, backfired spectacularly when all fifteen unionist MPs resigned their seats in protest at the Agreement, triggering by-elections. Most of the constituencies were uncontested by nationalist candidates and unionists put up dummy candidates called 'Peter Barry' in four constituencies—after the name of the Irish Foreign Minister—but the UUP's Jim Nicholson lost his Newry and Armagh seat to Seamus Mallon of the SDLP. Empey was scornful of the policy:

> Of course, you've got to remember, the leadership was all over here [London], apart from those who were still left in local government. There was nothing in between. So, whenever they came up with the bright idea of doing the resignations—remember that? They did the resignations and fought the by-elections, and people changed their name to Peter Barry, and all that stuff. I wrote to him [Molyneaux] suggesting that he leave Nicholson in place as night watchman, because it's a dodgy seat, and so on. He wrote back, and he said, 'Well, in a war, sometimes there are sacrifices that have to be made' and this sort of stuff. So, that was his way of kind of reacting to things, kept everybody occupied, kept them all doing something.[58]

In an attempt to generate some new strategic thinking within Unionism (or possibly to give the illusion of such a move) Molyneaux and Paisley commissioned a Task Force to look at options. It was composed of Harold McCusker, the UUP MP for Upper Bann; Peter Robinson, the MP for East Belfast and Deputy Leader of the DUP; and Frank Millar, the Chief Executive of the UUP. It reported to the two unionist leaders in June 1987 and recommended that, if the Anglo-Irish Agreement could not be negotiated away, the unionist leadership would have 'no alternative but to seek an entirely new base for Northern Ireland *outside* the present constitutional context'.[59] Article 1 of the Anglo-Irish Agreement purported to recognize and safeguard the right of the people of Northern Ireland to self-determination, concerning itself only with a decision by the majority of the people of Northern Ireland either to remain within the United Kingdom or alternatively to join the Irish Republic. However, it seemed to the Task Force 'inescapable that the same Article could be invoked to give effect to a majority decision in favour of some other alternative'. While the Task Force Report did not spell out what an 'alternative constitutional arrangement'[60] might mean, it was clear that the inference was independence from Britain or Ireland. This was political dynamite, so Molyneaux (and Paisley) took the option of sidelining the report, something which, for Danny Kennedy, constituted a strategic error:

> In the end, they went for the report of McCusker, Robinson and Frank Millar, the Task Force thing. But, when they got far enough distance away from the crisis, Molyneaux and Paisley ignored it, and dumped it. I think, those were fundamental

mistakes, and, I think, that warrants serious criticism. But, for those of us who were loyal troops, you were loyal . . . the one thing about, generally, the Ulster Unionist Party, until, I suppose, '98, the Ulster Unionist Party was tremendously loyal, tremendously loyal to all of its leaders, or tried to be. Tried to give people enough room, even O'Neill, in the early days. Chichester-Clark didn't last very long. Faulkner, I suppose, you know . . . you see, Faulkner did what Trimble did. Faulkner had a hardline reputation out of office. In office, that changes, and then people say, 'Oh, well, where's this man going? What is his position here?' Then, you had Harry West for a wee while, and then Molyneaux stayed at the ship, but he didn't lead you anywhere.[61]

By 1990 it was clear that no matter how much huff and puff Unionists put into their 'Ulster Says No' campaign, there was little they could do to blow the Agreement house down. Only negotiations could possibly do this. Under Peter Brooke, and Sir Patrick Mayhew his successor as Secretary of State for Northern Ireland, the UUP and the DUP were forced to engage with John Hume's SDLP and the Irish Government if they wanted rid of the Agreement. The talks covered the 'totality of relationships' and comprised three elements: Strand One (the internal government of Northern Ireland); Strand Two (North–South relations between Northern Ireland and Ireland); and Strand Three (East–West relations between the United Kingdom and Ireland). Empey is convinced the talks came close to success but foundered on the rock of Dublin's refusal to commit to a change in Articles 2 and 3 of the Irish Constitution: the 'difference between "could and would"'. Albert Reynolds was the Taoiseach, having succeeded Charles Haughey who had, by now, been brought down by one scandal too many. Empey lamented Haughey's absence:

> Charlie was a showman, and he could've put on a show, you could've actually, maybe, done a deal with Charlie. Albert was a somewhat different character . . . Had Charlie been there, I think, Charlie would've done the deal. I got that feeling, he was a showman, he could've done this, he could've carried it. But, I don't think Albert felt he was strong enough.[62]

Attempts at agreement on changing Articles 2 and 3 were further hampered by the opposition of the Irish Foreign Minister, Pádraig Flynn, with Empey regarding him as a Fianna Fáil traditionalist:

> When we got down to Dublin, it all boiled down to this paragraph on Articles 2 and 3. The draft contained a line which, if I recall correctly, 'The Irish government could amend Articles 2 and 3.' I'm paraphrasing. We said, 'That's no use, we want the thing to be changed to, The Irish government would, in the circumstances of an overall deal, amend Articles 2 and 3.' So, at lunchtime, Pádraig Flynn took himself off, and he then went to Albert and we got hammered, and that was it.[63]

There were no substantial Strand Two negotiations and a potential North–South body because, according to Empey, 'we had no interest in those, if we hadn't solved the Articles 2 and 3 issue. So, nobody was paying a huge amount of attention to that, because if you hadn't got the basics sorted, it didn't matter.' In fact, in Strand One there remained a vast gulf between the UUP and DUP, on the one hand, and the SDLP on the other regarding the internal governance of Northern Ireland. Empey, who was in charge of the UUP's Strand One team, is also certain that the negotiators were making progress here:

> the problem, really, was that after you'd had a session, the next day, the secretary would produce the minutes, so John Hume—who never appeared at them [the meetings]—but the [SDLP] boys would've been phoning him ... overnight, and we practically had to redo the whole minutes every day, because John didn't like this, or John didn't like that. We never believed John was serious about an internal deal.[64]

Under Hume's influence, and based on his experiences in Brussels as an MEP, the SDLP sought an ambitious model for the governance of Northern Ireland: an assembly overseen by three commissioners appointed by the UK and Irish Governments and the European Community. It was greeted with horror by the unionist parties; the UUP and DUP were at the opposite end of the spectrum, offering only a general purposes type committee to coordinate the business of other departmental committees in an assembly. The UUP were unprepared to offer a 1973-type power-sharing executive for, as Empey recalls:

> Molyneaux was fanatical about trying to keep it at committee stage, a committee type operation. He didn't want an embryonic government, as such ... he really wanted local government and Westminster, full stop. But, under pressure from many of us, we wanted some kind of re-creation of Stormont, and that rolled over into the '96–'98 negotiation, because that was our initial position. It had changed towards the end, but that was the initial position. But, if we'd had that 'would' in Dublin, we would've had a deal then. I have absolutely no doubt about that.
>
> So, it's hard to believe that you come through all of that, and bear in mind, the violence was still raging, the Troubles were still on, and the difference between 'could and would'. I recall it very vividly, and Flynn was obviously one of the old Fianna Fáil grandees from the west of Ireland, and all the rest of it, and Albert [Reynolds] only, literally, into office. ..., and probably, Flynn wouldn't have been in favour of it anyway. But, that's how close it came, and I think, we could've got that deal in '92.[65]

The Brooke-Mayhew talks were not, however, the only show in town: unbeknown to the UUP, the Thatcher Government had opened a secret line of communication to the IRA and a number of exchanges had occurred. John Hume and Gerry Adams had also been in talks and this formed the background to their 'Hume-Adams' proposals to end the IRA campaign. The momentum generated by this was seized on by London and Dublin to eventually find expression in the Downing Street Declaration (DSD) of December 1993, signed by Prime Minister John Major and Taoiseach Reynolds, in which the British reiterated the consent principle but also stated it had no selfish strategic or economic interest in Northern Ireland.[66] The purpose of the Declaration was to undermine the republican claim for continuing their campaign while at the same time reassuring unionists there would be no sell-out. Once more, concerns were felt about Molyneaux's leadership as even senior members of the UUP were kept in the dark about what was going on in the lead-up to the Declaration. Empey was again frustrated:

> Well, you see, my view is that we never got it [the information on negotiations], it never kind of filtered through to our level...So, I can't tell you what he [Molyneaux] was told, and what he wasn't told. I just don't know. But, that was the problem all along, you're confronted with these things out of leftfield without any prior warning, or knowledge. In retrospect, the level of distrust with Dublin or, with London, at that stage, was so high after what had happened in '85, that unless you had it from the horse's mouth, you just...and even then, you would find it hard to believe.
>
> But, I do recall going into Major's room in the Commons one time...and John talked a good game, and he seemed to be sincere enough...But, I just don't know what Jim was told...Well, I suppose, like everything else, part of it [the Declaration] was designed to give us reassurance, I guess, on the position on the constitution...but we'd had all of that before. I mean, they [the UK and Irish Governments] put out an argument that the Anglo-Irish Agreement did the same thing, but if you hadn't solved the problem of the territorial claim, nothing else really mattered in terms of the constitution...That's why all of these things ring hollow to some extent...and unless, and until, that big issue had been dealt with, the principle of consent and the removal of...the territorial claim, that opened up the Strand Two issues...[67]

In fact, Molyneaux had been consulted on the DSD, although the exact level of input he had remains unknown. Major had decided to 'take Jim into our confidence, listen to his views, and keep him briefed' following a difficult Anglo-Irish negotiation in Dublin in September 1993. The Prime Minister regarded Molyneaux as a 'wise man, canny and experienced'; Major also knew that if the final Declaration was to have any chance of success then there had to be some unionist input to make it acceptable to the majority community.[68] British–Irish negotiations then intensified in the aftermath of the 1994 IRA ceasefire leading, in 1995, to London and Dublin publishing their Frameworks Documents as a model for discussion in all-party talks. Empey recollects that Molyneaux 'gave us reason to believe that he was surprised by it'. This seems to be about the content of the Frameworks

Documents as, from an early stage, Empey and other senior UUP members became made aware that there was going to be some form of UK–Irish joint document. Empey emphasizes a meeting he, Jim Nicholson (the UUP's European Parliament member (MEP)), and Jeffrey Donaldson (a protégé of Molyneaux who would go on to succeed him as MP for Lagan Valley) had with Michael Ancram, the Minister of State at the Northern Ireland Office, as a key moment. They came away disconcerted:

> We thought Michael was just telling us lies, and we became so concerned that we actually left the meeting early . . . we came back to Jim, and we said, 'Look, Jim, there's going to be a document here.' Well, he says, 'Document, what document? I was speaking to John Major, and there will be no document or any of that.' We said, 'There's going to be a document, and this is what it's going to be, and they're telling you porkies.'
>
> So, he did appear to be surprised by that, and we certainly picked it up very quickly, and we were very clear that that's what was going to happen. So, he took people at face value. I mean, he liked Major and they got on, but the system at that time . . . I mean, Paddy . . . Mayhew—he denied that he'd been talking to the Provos behind the scenes, and it was perfectly clear they were talking behind the scenes. So, he had gone on TV and actually lied. So, we were in pretty bad form about that, we just said to him [Molyneaux], 'Look, there's a document.'[69]

There was indeed a document and, as with the DSD, Molyneaux knew there was one but chose not to take up Major's offer to find out what was in it, giving him plausible deniability. Molyneaux had based his whole strategy on cultivating personal and honourable relationships with successive Prime Ministers. On 20 December 1994, John Major met with an upset Molyneaux who, despite requests to the Northern Ireland Office, had not been shown the draft Frameworks Documents discussed with the Irish and had been merely briefed in general terms. In a further meeting, with Major on 24 January 1995, Molyneaux, refused an offer to see the Frameworks text, raising objections to what he believed were its key provisions following leaks on the Irish side, including from the former Taoiseach, Albert Reynolds, who gave the impression that the proposals would lead to an imposition of joint UK-Ireland authority over Northern Ireland.[70]

Just prior to the publication of the Frameworks Documents, Molyneaux came to see David Trimble (who had joined the UUP in 1978 and gone on to become MP for Upper Bann) to say he had a 'feeling that things at Belfast had gone wrong, and that people had gone too far'. At the same time, Trimble was receiving telephone calls from Reg Empey, in Northern Ireland, also saying that he had got the feeling that things were going badly wrong at the Belfast end, and blaming the UK Government. There had been discussions— no more than that—with the Northern Ireland Office, but now 'Reg was worried that Jim was going to pile the blame onto the people in Belfast who were at the discussions, and saying that he wasn't part of it, and all the rest of it.'[71] The following morning was the day of publication for the Frameworks Documents. Trimble was in early to the Houses of Parliament, before Molyneaux, as 'Jim didn't come in early…he waited until he could get off-peak fares [on the London Underground] coming in.' A copy of the Frameworks Documents had been delivered to Molyneaux. Trimble recalls:

> the Government sent a large envelope, private and confidential, to Jim's office. I remember, you know, we heard rumours about it and I got in early. We wanted to know what was going on. I asked Jim's secretary, 'When's Jim's coming in?' 'Oh, he'll not be in until 11.30am, or a quarter to'. Well we would have to comment publicly on this. Eventually, I just decided, 'Look', and I lifted up the envelope and we were then in a position to comment on the Frameworks paper.
>
> There was a factor in the background that made me particularly anxious. It looked as if a gap was opening up between the leadership in London and the team in Belfast that was talking to our government and the Irish. Molyneaux came to me at one stage and said that he had a feeling things in Belfast had gone wrong and that our people had gone too far.[72]

The Framework Documents proved the death knell to Molyneaux's leadership. In addition to the loss of confidence in him among colleagues, the aftermath included a poor parliamentary by-election result, the UUP outpolled by the UK Unionist Robert McCartney in the North Down seat previously held by the Popular Unionist James Kilfedder. Although it contained proposals (in a separate British segment) for a new Northern Ireland Assembly the joint British–Irish paper contained a scheme for a North–South body with consultative, harmonizing and—crucially—executive powers. It was a return to the Council of Ireland. Molyneaux's quiet, calm, conservative approach to coaxing successive British governments to take account of unionist concerns was in tatters. In a subsequent leadership challenge, at the ruling Ulster Unionist Council, a young Unionist, Lee Reynolds, won 15 per cent of the vote. Molyneaux won by a large margin but decided to stand down as a matter of honour. Empey offers this assessment of Molyneaux's leadership:

> He had good personal relationships with all of us, really. Jim had no enemies, as such. I mean, you take any of the leading lights over here [Westminster] at the moment, we all know they've got people in an opposite camp who hate their guts, and all. That was not the case with him. It was very hard to get up and find anybody who would take him on, because everybody liked him, and they felt he was a good, solid man, and a good unionist, and all that.
>
> But equally, one would have to say, strategically—while it might have kept the Party together—strategically, I think there was a decade there when unionism didn't get its head around the changing tectonic plates of what was happening

in Ireland, and elsewhere. So, I suppose, you could argue that that was...by the time the stalking horse appeared, and while the stalking horse was defeated, I think, he got 15 per cent of the vote, and that was really enough to start the thing going, because a lot of people could see, 'Look, we're just treading water here, we're not at the game. We're not getting anywhere, and we can't trust London at all. They just are not reliable.'[73]

Molyneaux had tried to stay close to the government of the day, after the UUP's position under the Conservative whip had been ended by Heath after the February 1974 election. The UUP leader's caution allowed the *Guardian* to conclude upon his departure that 'he was never a leader who would put forward a new strategy for Northern Ireland for the simple reason that he had none beyond making the best of a bad job',[74] whilst the new thinking now required following paramilitary ceasefires led to Molyneaux being described as a 'victim of the peace'.[75] Yet as Westminster leader of his party, Molyneaux at least moved the UUP from a one-time label (from the Labour leader Michael Foot) of 'parliamentary B Specials' to a grouping with which Labour or Conservative governments could at least attempt to do business.[76]

David Trimble Becomes UUP Leader

The person who emerged as the leader to replace Molyneaux was, to the surprise of many, David Trimble. He was conscious that the Molyneaux leadership was coming to an end, 'because things were going wrong, and he'd been there a long time...that it was just a matter of time'. His successor, it was assumed, would have to come from the Westminster Parliamentary Party. Trimble's feeling was that John Taylor, MP for Strangford, 'would go for it'.[77] He shared an office with Taylor: 'We got on and still do get on well.'[78]

At the outset of the contest Trimble was ambiguous, at best, about taking part. His thinking was that if there was going to be a leadership contest and Taylor won 'he will have to have to look for somebody to act as his right-hand man. I thought, this could be nice for me, I could be close to the action without the burden of leadership. But when it became apparent that Trimble had indicated he was ruling himself out he began to be approached by UUP members who urged him to run. According to Trimble:

> in the newsagents I bumped into a leading member of the Lagan Valley Association...He was very annoyed with me for ruling myself out. He said, 'We were depending on you.' I got that from a couple of other people, as well and realized I had demeaned myself in their eyes. So, I then started changing my position.[79]

A group who had been urging Trimble to stand then formed a small team to canvass UUC delegates. They found there was considerable support for a

Trimble candidature and he began to realize 'I had to be careful about whether to go in for this, because if I go for it, I'll get it. That was partly on the responses, at early stage, were coming from the telephone canvassers.'[80]

Despite Trimble's personal confidence he could win, he did not start out as favourite to succeed Molyneaux. That mantle, or burden, was carried by John Taylor who had a reputation as a hardliner. Taylor had been nearly killed, in 1972, during an assassination attempt by the Official IRA which saw him riddled with bullets. Trimble, on the other hand, had been somewhat closeted in Queen's University and had only been MP for Upper Bann since 1990; what he did have, in common with Taylor, was a reputation as a hardliner, built upon a propensity to go red-faced and storm out of television interviews, alongside the television image of him walking through Portadown, hand in raised hand with Paisley, as a controversial Orange Order march was forced through a mainly Catholic area in his constituency by the police.

The candidates for the leadership were all drawn from the Parliamentary Party: Trimble, Taylor, Willie Ross, Ken Maginnis, and the Reverend Martin Smyth. Danny Kennedy, one of the delegates, found it

> astonishing that Taylor was beaten, actually. Taylor was the clear favourite that night and had gone in with the expectation of everybody at the time, but he just didn't perform on the night. He waved his glasses about, he rambled a bit...He made a dreadful speech.

Kennedy supported Taylor

> to the very end, actually...people round me were saying, 'Oh, you know, you haven't picked the winner, it's Trimble, get on board here.' But, I just thought, at the time, that Taylor had more experience, and was slightly more solid. Trimble made a very good speech. Ken Maginnis, in content, had a very good speech, but he was viewed as too liberal, and he had no Orange connection to fall back on...So, David emerged as the victor.[81]

Kennedy reflected that, following the result, the old guard of Ross and Smyth, 'those two in particular, couldn't get over that, couldn't stomach it'. Molyneaux was 'cute enough about it, and sort of didn't say anything publicly, but there was a sense that the establishment, at the very top, weren't delighted that, you know, they had a new Young Pretender'.[82] Reg Empey says that Taylor blew it:

> I was a party officer at the time, and I was on duty that night...collecting the ballots, and all that. Taylor was the winner coming into the building, there was no doubt, but his speech to the delegates, I'd never heard him speak worse. It was, put the glasses on and the glasses off, and he wasn't fluent, he didn't seem to have anything written down that he was going to deliver. It was the worst performance I've ever seen from him...Taylor won on the first count, I remember that. But,

whenever the eliminations started, I watched a group of people at the front that were from up around Foyle and all around there, and I said to myself, 'This is not going to work.' I think, David was the last to speak, and it wasn't an inspiring speech, it was very steady, academic, it was a wee bit of a lecture, really—typical David—fine, a good solid performance.

As the candidates with the least votes were eliminated one at a time, I think, it was Smyth and Ross who went first, the only one who survived was Ken. So, it was Ken, Taylor and Trimble . . . Surprisingly, we expected a lot of Ken's votes would go to Taylor, but they split and Trimble got a fair slice of them. Largely because of his performance, which was not brilliant, it was solid and it was steady, whilst Taylor's had been so hesitant, and so out of character that, I think, it shocked a lot of people. So, I think, Taylor lost it on the night; that would be my reading of it.[83]

The new leader was a firm devolutionist. His reading of the situation, prior to the Anglo-Irish Agreement, was that unionists were more concerned with preventing nationalists exercising power over them than they were with exercising power themselves; so, while a return to Stormont was desirable in theory, it was not then considered worth the compromise entailed in an accommodation with nationalists. The 1985 Agreement changed all that. With a 'form of Dublin rule', direct rule from London 'no longer seemed so benign or tolerable and the desire to restore a measure of local control over local decisions became stronger' even if this meant it could only be achieved at the price of a compromise with northern nationalism.[84] The Anglo-Irish Agreement, then, was the game changer: for unionists, like Trimble, if they ever wanted to regain some control over their destiny then 'not an inch' and 'what we have we hold' was no longer credible as a position.

Trimble's election came in the aftermath of the Provisional IRA ceasefire in 1994. The IRA's political wing, Sinn Féin, had been barred from the successor to the Brooke-Mayhew talks as the IRA refused to state whether their 'cessation of military operations' was permanent. As an alternative the Conservative Government came up with the proposal that republicans could demonstrate commitment to exclusively peaceful and democratic means by decommissioning its arsenal of weapons. In the first press conference after he became leader, Trimble was asked for his position on decommissioning:

I said, Well, decommissioning is a part of a bigger issue, and the bigger issue is, are they [the Republican Movement] going to be committed to peace through democratic means? We're just using decommissioning, as it has been brought forward by the government, as being the litmus test of whether we agree. Because, if you're committed to peace through democratic means, then you've no need for a private army, and if you've got a private army, you won't be committed to peace. But then, the obvious thing is, you're going to have to wind up the private army and disband and decommission, and all the rest of it.

Crucially Trimble pointed out that a commitment to peaceful and democratic means

> could be evidenced in other ways, not just decommissioning, but it could be done, it could be done by republicans saying, 'We are now absolutely committed to peace through democratic means, and we're going to wind up the paramilitary whatnot, and the illegal activities and so on and so forth to do that.' Or, they could say, 'Well, we've demonstrated our commitment to peace and democracy by ending punishment beatings.' I mentioned a number of options like that.[85]

Soon afterwards Trimble had his first meeting, as leader, with John Major. The Prime Minister was 'very cross' with him, complaining that Trimble was undermining the Government's position on decommissioning. A more flexible approach was taken by the Leader of the Opposition, Tony Blair. When they gathered for the November 1995 Remembrance Sunday ceremony at the Cenotaph, the Labour leader asked to talk to Trimble:

> Over to me comes Blair and [Paddy] Ashdown [Leader of the Liberal Democrats], and they want to have a word with me. They said, do I think that Major is firmly committed to decommissioning as a concept? Because, they [Blair and Ashdown] say, if he is, we're prepared to support him, but we don't want to support him on this and then find he's changed his position, and we're all left high and dry. So, they asked me, what do I think of that? . . . I said that this is what Major said to me . . . So, it looks to me that he's committed to it.
> Blair said, at the time, that he didn't really think that decommissioning was the right thing to focus on . . . He said, 'The issue that you should use is the consent issue, and that they'd [the Republican Movement] got to sign up to the consent issue.'[86]

The problem Trimble had with this approach was whether Gerry Adams, the President of Sinn Féin, could be pinned down with an appropriate form of words on consent. At this early stage there was plenty of evidence for the Sinn Féin leader interpreting the consent formula in a way unacceptable to unionists and while Trimble did not interpret this as a deliberate strategy to

> make our situation worse . . . there was an element of that in there . . . they'd make progress, and at the same time, try to do as much they could to divide and disrupt the Unionists. So, there was an element of that, but, I think, another element was, they hadn't told their foot soldiers where they were going.[87]

Sinn Féin, particularly in their dealings with the British and Irish Governments, played on the danger that there might be a split in the republican movement. The key point, however, was that Trimble had a less than hardline commitment to decommissioning in principle: there were other ways in which he was prepared to measure a Republican commitment to democratic and peaceful means.

The UUP's outline of a political agreement had been approved by the UUC Executive Committee in November 1995. It envisaged modest structures of governance based upon a committee system overseeing a ninety-member Assembly, with participation only from constitutional parties. The UUP knew that the Framework Documents could be diluted. Major was aware that documents which Trimble dismissed in his 1996 party conference address as 'a halfway house between the Union and a united Ireland'[88] were unsellable. The UUP critique of the Frameworks Documents was that they saw 'power transferred to a joint body dominated by the Dublin government'.[89] Major thus opted for elections to a Northern Ireland Forum in 1996, a move supported by the UUP as part of a process of, 'in the absence of prior decommissioning, establishing democratic bona fides',[90] although the IRA ceasefire fractured soon afterwards. Following Major's 1997 general election catastrophe of 1997, the new Labour Prime Minister, Tony Blair, was not reliant upon unionist votes, meaning the UUP had to concede ground on the inclusivity of the deal and attendant conflict management measures, neither of which the party hitherto had been upfront about. In March 1997, the UUP insisted that they 'will not allow themselves to be drawn into a position which provides for the arrival at the table of Sinn Féin. There is no evidence, or even a commitment that they are intending to pursue their political objectives by exclusively political means. Quite the reverse.'[91] Yet the IRA's July 1997 renewal of its ceasefire meant that Sinn Féin would indeed be at the table and the UUP decided to remain. Trimble told his party conference in October that year that 'our hearts led one way and our heads the other. It is the hallmark of this Party that it does not take the easy option ... The crucial reason for Unionists staying in these Talks is that nothing can come out of them without our consent.'[92]

Trimble, retrospectively, saw the change in British and Irish personnel by the time of the second IRA cessation as crucial. In common with several other Northern Ireland political parties, the New Labour Government was sympathetic to the incorporation, into domestic law, of the European Convention for the Protection of Human Rights and Fundamental Freedoms whereas the Conservative Government had been opposed. Trimble believed that the legal protection of human rights was an 'indispensable part of any agreement'. Furthermore, while the Tories were prepared to make an exception for Northern Ireland devolution, they were opposed to the idea for the rest of the UK. New Labour were not and one of Trimble's pet projects was the concept of a Council of the British Isles,[93] an idea dating back to Vanguard. In the 1970s it appeared a fanciful notion; but by the late 1990s it was a realistic prospect. Trimble wanted any North–South dimension of an agreement to have symmetry with the East–West component. With the second IRA ceasefire and the change of governments in London and Dublin, the decision to admit

Sinn Féin to talks in the absence of decommissioning had left Trimble a choice: to stay or walk out, exiting with the DUP. He chose to stay. His decision proved seismic for his party and his country.

Notes

1. Interview with Jo-Anne Dobson, 29 Jan. 2016.
2. Interview with Reg Empey, 30 June 2016.
3. Interview with David Trimble, 30 June 2016.
4. Interview with Reg Empey, 30 June 2016.
5. Interview with David Trimble, 30 June 2016.
6. John Hewitt, The Coasters, http://johnhewittsociety.org/the-coasters-1969.
7. Interview with Mike Nesbitt, 16 Dec. 2016.
8. Interview with Mike Nesbitt, 16 Dec. 2016.
9. Interview with Reg Empey, 30 June 2016.
10. Interview with Ross Hussey, 27 Jan. 2016.
11. Interview with Ross Hussey, 27 Jan. 2016.
12. Interview with Reg Empey, 30 June 2016.
13. Interview with David Trimble, 30 June 2016.
14. *Daily Telegraph*, William Craig (obituary) 27 Apr. 2011.
15. Interview with Reg Empey, 30 June 2016.
16. Interview with David Trimble, 30 June 2016.
17. Interview with Jim Rodgers, 20 May 2016.
18. Interview with Jim Rodgers, 20 May 2016.
19. Interview with Danny Kennedy, 28 Jan. 2016.
20. Interview with Danny Kennedy, 28 Jan. 2016.
21. J. Tonge, M. Braniff, T. Hennessey, J. W. McAuley, and S. A. Whiting, *The Democratic Unionist Party: From Protest to Power*, Oxford: Oxford University Press, 2014).
22. Interview with Ross Hussey, 27 Jan. 2016.
23. T. Hennessey, *Northern Ireland: The Origins of the Troubles*, Dublin: Gill & Macmillan, 2005; T. Hennessey, *The Evolution of the Troubles 1970–72*, Dublin: Irish Academic Press, 2007; T. Hennessey, *The First Northern Ireland Peace Process: Power-Sharing, Sunningdale and the IRA Ceasefires 1972–76*, London: Palgrave Macmillan, 2014.
24. Interview with Danny Kennedy, 28 Jan. 2016.
25. Hennessey, *First Northern Ireland Peace Process*.
26. HM Government, *Sunningdale Communique*, London: HMSO, 1973.
27. Interview with Danny Kennedy, 28 Jan. 2016.
28. Interview with David Trimble, 30 June 2016.
29. Interview with Reg Empey, 30 June 2016.
30. Interview with Reg Empey, 30 June 2016.
31. Interview with David Trimble, 30 June 2016.

32. Interview with David Trimble, 30 June 2016.
33. Interview with David Trimble, 30 June 2016.
34. Interview with David Trimble, 30 June 2016.
35. Interview with David Trimble, 30 June 2016.
36. Interview with David Trimble, 30 June 2016.
37. *News Letter*, 10 Mar. 2015.
38. Interview with Reg Empey, 30 June 2016.
39. C. O'Leary, S. Elliott, and R. Wilford, *The Northern Ireland Assembly 1982–1986: A Constitutional Experiment*, London: Hurst, 1988.
40. Ulster Unionist Party, *Devolution and the Northern Ireland Assembly: The Way Forward*, Belfast: UUP, 1984.
41. Democratic Unionist Party, *'Ulster: The Future Assured': Proposals by the Ulster Democratic Unionist Party*, Belfast: Northern Ireland Assembly Group, Belfast; DUP, 1984.
42. UUP, *The Way Forward*, 1.
43. Hansard, House of Commons, 26 Nov. 1985, vol. 87.
44. UUP, *The Way Forward*, 2.
45. UUP, *The Way Forward*, 2.
46. Hansard, House of Commons, 26 Nov. 1985, vol. 87.
47. Interview with Reg Empey, 30 June 2016.
48. James Molyneaux, *The Long View*, Belfast: Greystone, 1989.
49. Interview with Reg Empey, 30 June 2016.
50. Government of Ireland, *New Ireland Forum Report*, Dublin: The Stationery Office, 1984, 19–21.
51. Interview with Danny Kennedy, 28 Jan. 2016.
52. Interview with Danny Kennedy, 28 Jan. 2016.
53. Interview with Reg Empey, 30 June 2016.
54. Hansard, House of Commons, 26 Nov. 1985, vol. 87.
55. PRONI CENT 3/82A Molyneaux to Thatcher, 24 Mar. 1987.
56. PRONI CENT 3/82A Thatcher to Molyneaux, 28 Mar. 1987.
57. Hansard, House of Commons, 26 Nov. 1985, vol. 87.
58. Interview with Reg Empey, 30 June 2016.
59. Unionist Task Force, *An End to Drift*, Belfast: Unionist Task Force, 1987, 1.
60. Unionist Task Force, *An End to Drift*, 2.
61. Interview with Danny Kennedy, 28 Jan. 2016.
62. Interview with Reg Empey, 30 June 2016.
63. Interview with Reg Empey, 30 June 2016.
64. Interview with Reg Empey, 30 June 2016.
65. Interview with Reg Empey, 30 June 2016.
66. Interview with Reg Empey, 30 June 2016.
67. Interview with Reg Empey, 30 June 2016.
68. John Major, *The Autobiography*, London: Harper Collins, 1999, 450.
69. Interview with Reg Empey, 30 June 2016.
70. Major, *Autobiography*, 466.
71. Interview with David Trimble, 30 June 2016.

72. Interview with David Trimble, 30 June 2016.

73. Interview with Reg Empey, 30 June 2016.

74. *Guardian*, 29 Aug. 1995, 12. 'Retired and undefeated. But James Molyneaux always lacked new ideas'.

75. David Sharrock, *Guardian*, 29 Aug. 1995, 11. 'So farewell then Jim, victim of the peace'.

76. P. Dixon, ' "The Usual English Double Talk": The British Political Parties and the Ulster Unionists 1974–94', *Irish Political Studies*, 9 (1994), 25–40.

77. Interview with David Trimble, 30 June 2016.

78. Interview with David Trimble, 30 June 2016.

79. Interview with David Trimble, 30 June 2016.

80. Interview with David Trimble, 30 June 2016.

81. Interview with Danny Kennedy, 28 Jan. 2016.

82. Interview with Danny Kennedy, 28 Jan. 2016.

83. Interview with Reg Empey, 30 June 2016.

84. D. Trimble, 'The Belfast Agreement', *Fordham International Law Journal*, 22.4 (1998), 1144–5.

85. Interview with David Trimble, 30 June 2016.

86. Interview with David Trimble, 30 June 2016.

87. Interview with David Trimble, 30 June 2016.

88. David Trimble, Speech to the Ulster Unionist Party annual conference, Galgorm Manor Hotel, 19 Oct. 1996.

89. Ulster Unionist Party, *Response to 'Frameworks for the Future'*, Belfast: UUP, 1995.

90. Ulster Unionist Party, *The Democratic Imperative: Proposals for an Elected Body for Northern Ireland*, Belfast: UUP, 1996.

91. Ulster Unionist Party, *Pathways to Peace within the Union*, Belfast: UUP, 1997, 1.

92. David Trimble, Speech to the Ulster Unionist Party annual conference, Slieve Donard Hotel Newcastle, 25 Oct. 1997.

93. Trimble, 'The Belfast Agreement', 1145–9.

2

Country Before Party

The Long Good Friday

The decision by David Trimble and the UUP to remain in talks designed to put the principles of the 1993 Downing Street Declaration into effect saw them attacked by the DUP. Ian Paisley led his party from the negotiations upon Sinn Féin's arrival. This left the UUP dependent on the parties associated with loyalist paramilitaries for any accord—the Ulster Democratic Party (UDP) and the Progressive Unionist Party (PUP)—as the talks were predicated on 'sufficient consensus'. Because the Northern Ireland parties in the negotiations had been through an elective process to partake, this meant that a majority of unionist participants and a majority of nationalist participants had to *separately* reach agreement. The UUP needed the UDP and PUP for a majority of unionist votes whereas the SDLP had a majority of nationalist votes and Sinn Féin could not veto any deal supported by John Hume's party.

The accession of Trimble to the UUP leadership marked the triumph of former Vanguard members in shaping the direction of the UUP: joining him in his talks team, as his number two, was Reg Empey and another former Vanguard member, the late Professor Anthony Alcock, from the University of Ulster. Trimble was a different sort of leader to his UUP predecessors or competing unionist contemporaries: not only did he populate his talks team with those of a legal and academic background but he had thought through his strategic constitutional objectives on the basis of what was and was not a threat to Northern Ireland's place within the Union. His starting point was that the Anglo-Irish Agreement had fundamentally altered the political landscape to the detriment of unionism. While the British Government asserted the Irish Government had a consultative role in the Anglo Irish Intergovernmental Conference set up by the Agreement, for him this lacked credibility and was undermined by statements from Irish politicians that the Agreement went beyond a consultative role in the day-to-day running of Northern Ireland. Trimble pointed out that at no point did the Agreement say that the Republic's role was limited to consultation.

Trimble's Ambitions

In terms of what he wanted from the negotiations, Trimble was again different to preceding unionist leaders in that he rejected a reductionist insular architecture limited merely to Northern Ireland and, at a stretch, to the island of Ireland. He saw the 'totality of relationships'—the phrase first employed during the birth of Anglo-Irish cooperation in 1980—in East–West terms rather than just a North–South one, referencing the Vanguard *Community of the British Isles* publication from 1972[1] as an influence. This did not mean Trimble was oblivious to the 'Irish dimension'. He pointed to two schemes which involved an element of joint Belfast–Dublin authority. These were the Great Northern Railways Board, wound up in 1958, and the Foyle Fisheries Commission, which was established in 1952—the latter by parallel legislation in both jurisdictions. Trimble believed unionists wanted to know what the ultimate object of any North–South relationship was to be and they wanted to be sure that the relationship would not be prejudicial to the continued existence of Northern Ireland.[2] This made the North–South body in the Frameworks Documents unacceptable for it was a doppelgänger of the Council of Ireland from Sunningdale—a body with *executive* power independent of any governmental body in the Republic or Northern Ireland and therefore with the potential to become an embryonic all-Ireland government.[3]

The second fundamental principle on which Trimble operated was that unionists could not enter into any North–South relationship with a state that maintained a claim to sovereignty over Northern Ireland as was the case in Articles 2 and 3. As Trimble pointed out, in the 1973 Sunningdale Agreement the British Government identified Northern Ireland as part of the United Kingdom while the Irish Government did not. The status of Northern Ireland was mentioned in the Anglo-Irish Agreement but did not identify what that status actually was. As Trimble explained, in the constitutional law of the Republic of Ireland, Northern Ireland 'is part of the Republic and . . . it is clear that the Republic's government is constitutionally incapable of recognising the status of Northern Ireland as part of the UK'.[4] The 1985 Agreement did not, therefore, reinforce the constitutional guarantee that Northern Ireland would remain part of the United Kingdom for as a long as a majority wished it to remain so, since, in the Republic's law, Northern Ireland was not part of the United Kingdom. While some nationalists focused on the Government of Ireland Act 1920, which contained a declaration that the Westminster Parliament was sovereign over Northern Ireland, Trimble correctly identified the constitutional status of Northern Ireland as deriving from the Acts of Union that stated that the 'said kingdoms of Great Britain and Ireland shall . . . and for ever be united into one kingdom'.[5] Trimble had thus set out his vision almost a decade before and entered multi-party talks with a firm strategy as to what he wanted from the negotiations and this was primarily to secure the constitutional position of Northern Ireland within the Union based on the principle of consent. All other considerations were subordinate.

On 25 March 1998, Senator George Mitchell, the independent chair of the multi-party talks, set 9 April as the deadline for concluding the talks. On 6 April he presented his 'Mitchell Document' to the parties and the entire process went into meltdown. The section on Strand Two envisaged a North–South Ministerial Council (NSMC) that contained a series of Annexes outlining the areas in which the cross-border institution would decide common North–South policies, specific areas where decisions would be taken on action for North–South implementation, and a series of North–South implementation bodies. The Council's authority and functions were to be derived directly from London and Dublin. Effectively, the proposed Northern Ireland Assembly was by-passed. It was not Belfast, but London and Dublin that determined the remit of the Council. There were pages and pages of areas containing proposed North–South cooperation that would be carried out by the NSMC. The UUP's Deputy Leader, John Taylor declared: 'I wouldn't touch this paper with a 40-foot barge pole'.[6]

Tony Blair flew to Belfast to save the talks. The Prime Minister met with Trimble and reassured him he would get the Irish Government to retract their demands[7] and effectively said he 'would negotiate for him'.[8] The British were 'terrified' Trimble would walk out of the talks without further ado.[9] Strand Two had been negotiated between the British and Irish Governments and Dublin had insisted on the offending annexes on North–South bodies; Blair had agreed the text of the draft agreement himself.[10] The key was persuading the Taoiseach, Bertie Ahern, to overturn the advice of his senior advisers. Ahern's concern was he was already going to propose to the Irish people that they amend their constitution and remove the territorial claim to the North. If he did so and got nothing in return 'he would look like an idiot'. He had no confidence that the unionists would agree to the creation of the North–South bodies at all unless they accepted them in advance and they were enshrined in Westminster legislation rather than left to the goodwill of the Assembly.[11] As Ahern put it, the unionists wanted the consent principle enshrined, an Assembly, the Irish constitutional claim on the North gone, 'and they want to give fuck all in return'.[12]

The Taoiseach, who had to return to Dublin for his mother's funeral before journeying back to the North again, detailed Paddy Teahon, one of his senior aides and Dermot Gallagher, from the Irish Department of Foreign Affairs, to negotiate any changes; in turn Jonathan Powell, Blair's Chief of Staff, worked with Reg Empey. At a tripartite meeting with Ahern upon his return, the British, and the UUP witnessed a seminal moment: Ahern indicated his government would agree to radical changes to Strand Two.[13] In return Trimble offered Blair a proposal accepting six North–South implementation bodies and giving a list of sample areas of cooperation between Northern Ireland and the Republic to be laid out in an annexe[14] to reassure the Irish the NMSC would have a real role: it would not have any functions upfront but it would be for the Northern Ireland Assembly to agree at least six matters for future cooperation and implementation. Thus it would be the Northern Ireland Assembly deciding North–South cooperation rather than the UK and Irish Governments or the Council. When Blair put this to the Irish they accepted. The British thought 'we had had agreed text'. Then 'things began to unravel'.[15]

The problem was the republicans: Gerry Adams and Martin McGuinness (Sinn Féin's chief negotiators) complained 'all the big concessions' had gone to the unionists who were the perceived winners while republicans were seen as the losers, with McGuinness warning the IRA could return to violence.[16] The Irish then came back with a proposal for 120 implementation bodies which the British surmised was to keep Sinn Féin in the talks.[17] Blair 'completely flipped' when he saw them: he shouted at all of the British officials and 'was mildly impolite to the Irish'. He told Ahern there was absolutely no chance of selling the new draft to the UUP: the Irish had to negotiate on the basis of the UUP terms. Ahern agreed.[18] Blair's comment was 'an expletive uttered thrice'.[19]

The broad agreement in Strand Two was the catalyst for movement in Strand One. Here, the main players were the SDLP and UUP. Previously the UUP had been dismissive of a return to 1973-style power-sharing, calling it 'dishonest to require unionists to enter into power-sharing with other parties whose intention it is to abolish, even in the long term, the framework within which that power is shared'.[20] Now, having secured most of its aims in the talks, the UUP was faced with conceding to the SDLP if it was to secure a return of Stormont. When Seamus Mallon, the SDLP deputy leader, outlined his party's key demands, Trimble just remarked 'yes, yes, yes, yes, yes, yes'.[21] Stormont would return but it would be in the form of an inclusive power-sharing executive—which would include Sinn Féin.

As far as Trimble was concerned he had achieved *all* his strategic objectives. The Good Friday Agreement (as it became known, although the UUP always preferred 'Belfast Agreement') dealt with constitutional issues unambiguously, avoiding a repetition of the mistake made in the Sunningdale Agreement and the Anglo-Irish Agreement, providing for the repeal in their entirety of the territorial claim in Articles 2 and 3: a new Article 2 recognized the right of persons on the island of Ireland to be part of the Irish nation if they so wished.

A new Article 3 set out the aspiration of a united Ireland but recognized that this could be 'brought about only by peaceful means with the consent of a majority of the people, democratically expressed, in both jurisdictions'. 'The first paragraph of the Agreement recognized that 'it is for the people of Northern Ireland alone, without any outside interference, to determine the destiny of Northern Ireland'. The NSMC would, unlike the 1973 proposed Council of Ireland, have no supra-national characteristics and drew its authority from the Northern Ireland Assembly and Dáil Éireann. Furthermore, the NSMC was balanced by the creation of a British–Irish Council (BIC) consisting of the British and Irish Governments and the regional administrations within the British Isles.

So for Trimble, and the pro-Agreement elements in the UUP, the Union had been secured by the recognition of the consent principle; the end of the Irish territorial claim; the explicit declaration of British sovereignty over Northern Ireland; no change to the Act of Union; the recognition by the Irish government of Northern Ireland's membership of the UK; the return of an Assembly; the ending of the democratic deficit; and a symmetrical relationship between the NSMC and the BIC.[22] But these successes were not what split the UUP and the wider unionist community.

Around midday on the Good Friday the parties to the talks had received the new text of the agreement and 'all hell broke loose'. Trimble informed Jonathan Powell that his party was in general revolt.[23] Alongside prisoner releases and a commission to look at the future of the Royal Ulster Constabulary (RUC) the agreement did not link decommissioning with Sinn Féin serving in the Assembly's power-sharing executive. Decommissioning now became the major issue. To prevent the UUP collapsing the talks, Blair came up with the idea of a letter[24]—one, as Blair recalled, that suggested that, 'if people did go back to violence and there were insufficient ways of getting rid of people in those circumstances from the democratic process once they had shown that they were not prepared to abide by the democratic process, then we would review the rules for that'.[25] Blair also rang the President of the United States, Bill Clinton, and asked him to talk to Trimble. The UUP leader recalled:

> I told the President I was aware of what Blair was planning to do and if that solution was delivered, 'then we've got an agreement', but if it was to be delivered he needed the Irish Government and the SDLP 'to give us space for it to happen'.[26]

Trimble and his deputy John Taylor were prepared to accept the letter and, therefore the Agreement. But a key member of the UUP team, Jeffrey Donaldson, was not satisfied—the letter was not part of the final Agreement but a separate document which no one else had signed up to as part of the deal. Donaldson's unease could not be assuaged, as he felt that the discussions were going nowhere, that we were not going to get the kind of safeguards and the changes to the text of the Agreement . . . I informed the leader that I was returning to my constituency. It wasn't a walk out, in the sense that the negotiations had been concluded anyway. I just felt that the terms of this Agreement were unacceptable. I was devastated.[27]

Empey backed Trimble; he recalls the intense focus in the final hours of negotiation as the talks entered Good Friday, the decisive moments when a decision had to be made:

I do recall with that last night, it was an all-nighter, and we had this ghastly room in . . . Castle Buildings where negotiations took place, which had no daylight. It had just artificial light all the time. I remember the heating was controlled from a building in the High Street—there was some computer system that they controlled. So, of course, naturally enough, it went off at a certain sensible time, and of course, everybody was still there. Because everybody was still there, had been there all night, there was no food, and people were getting angry, tired. Trimble had been sent home for a few hours to get a rest [at] . . . the Stormont Hotel.

So, that was just how things were. So, yes, we knew there were going to be divisions . . . I mean, [John] Taylor had a whole list of things that he was unhappy about. Whenever the [party] officers took the . . . decision [to support Trimble] . . . where, by that stage, there must've been 50 or 60 people in there. I do recall this— and in fairness to David, it was leadership, I suppose—I think he had to get up on a chair or on a table, and he said that Mitchell had sent a message down to him . . . he needed to know, was he for, or against? David said, 'I intend to go up to see him . . . And I'm going to tell him, I'm agreeing to this, and those who wish to come with me, you'll be very welcome to do so . . . ' And that's how it was done, and, of course, we'd had the Donaldson walk-out, and all that stuff. So, yes, we knew it was going to be difficult, yeah . . . it's the bigger question. Were there issues that we unhappy about? Yes . . . It was just the view that we didn't see circumstances where the ducks on the constitutional side were going to come into alignment again. Where are we going to get a coincidence of developments? Because, don't forget, we had seen that it was Bertie [Ahern] who fixed the North–South stuff, and, you know, Taoisigh come and go, so if he wasn't there, would we get somebody better? We're looking round the room at the other elements who were likely to replace him, and we didn't see that we were going to get anybody better.

We had Blair, who was gung-ho for a deal, and again, we just felt that the whole apparatus—having had two years of this, don't forget—there just wasn't anything left in the tank that would keep the thing going. So, yes, we could've held out, and that would be true at any point in time, but when any negotiation comes to a certain point, you've got to balance the thing up. For us, the constitutional issues had to be right. Otherwise, what was the whole 20/30 years for? We felt that the stars had aligned on those issues. But, inevitably, in any agreement, there's stuff that's not right.[28]

At the time there were, and continue to be, calls for a voluntary coalition—on the model originally advocated by Craig and Trimble back in the 1970s—thereby excluding Sinn Féin. But, in 1998, it was not an option as far as Trimble was concerned:

> the inclusive Executive was created because it was the only way we could get an agreement. We weren't going to get an agreement out of the coalition because the SDLP couldn't do that, or didn't want to do that. The SDLP didn't want to be in a position of excluding Sinn Féin, and I understand their position on that ... It would've been nice if we could've done it on a voluntary basis, rather than on the compulsory coalition. Although, the compulsory coalition as has now been demonstrated, isn't actually compulsory, you can, maybe, decide not to take office, which has happened. I did say from time to time, that the compulsory coalition was done in order to get sufficient agreement to have an agreement, and that in time, it would become redundant, and it will change. But, it will only change when people are ready for the change.[29]

The UUP, in this view, had cracked the big constitutional and governance questions and locked nationalists into a partitioned Northern Irish executive and assembly. As Empey put it 'if Sinn Féin were tied into the Agreement, they were tied into the constitutional framework. So, they were, effectively, gridlocked within the UK.' The other factor determining the UUP acceptance of the deal was that SDLP was the dominant nationalist party. So, if Sinn Féin were tied into the constitutional framework then 'they were making far more significant compromises than we were. Because, on our fundamental constitutional positions, things were correct constitutionally, right along the line.'[30]

But this was not enough for many UUP members: Sinn Féin in government without prior IRA decommissioning equated to terrorists in the executive while retaining a private army. Furthermore, the sight of paramilitary prisoners released within two years of the Agreement was a bitter pill for many to swallow. Danny Kennedy complained:

> Nobody was conditioned for '98. Nobody really knew. No unionist leader had been brave enough to set out the terms of what a deal should be, what it would mean in terms of dealing not only with nationalists but also republicans and violent republicans. Nobody had set the scene at all. We had, unfortunately, been fed on a diet of 'No Surrender'—there would be no deal.[31]

With a referendum on both sides of the border to approve or reject the Agreement, a majority of UUP MPs, including Jeffrey Donaldson, joined with the DUP in opposing the Agreement; James Molyneaux also came out against the Agreement as did a future UUP leader, Tom Elliott, who, while 'very strongly' in support of the UUP going into the multi-party talks was a 'soft "no"'. 'I didn't go out to campaign against it, but it was clearly known within the Party that I was opposed to it, the reasons mainly being were that

I felt we could've done something a little better, especially around the release of prisoners and decommissioning.' He believed there should have been a direct correlation between the release of prisoners and decommissioning:

> Prisoners shouldn't have got out without decommissioning. That was my main aspect to it. I had a few other minor issues, but I knew that broadly in the terms of an agreement, you're not going to get everything you want. But that was the main crux for me, I felt that we were letting people out of prison without any guarantees.[32]

Elliott's subsequent experience as UUP leader confirmed his contemporary criticism of 1998: 'deadlines come and go...what I always learn is, when there's a deadline, it's never stuck to'.[33] This reflected the numerous deadlines set by the UK and Irish Governments at subsequent talks: they were set as immovable and nearly always ignored by the participants whereas, in 1998, Mitchell's declaration that he was returning to the United States if a deal was not struck by Good Friday added real focus and drama to the talks. Elliott recalled being at UUP Party Executive meetings on Maundy Thursday, before the Agreement, and then on the Saturday morning, afterwards: his plea to Trimble on the Thursday evening was

> 'Don't do anything hasty, you know, you don't have to sign up now. If it's not right, don't do it'. He had to judge, in fairness to him, at that stage, had he got enough to sell it to people? I think he was getting there. Look, they weren't going to pull the plug. Mitchell would have went (sic) home for Easter and came back. But that's how life is, that's how talks are.

Elliott acknowledges:

> it wouldn't have taken much to get the likes of me over the line...I felt David Trimble took Northern Ireland, not just the Ulster Unionist Party, but took Northern Ireland to a stage that no other leader would have. So, I had a huge amount of recognition for him, and I had a huge amount of respect for him for doing that.[34]

Trimble's response is that leaving the talks without agreement would put him and the UUP at a disadvantage; at this time the ground rules were that there had to be 'sufficient consensus' for there to be a deal. Effectively this meant an agreement between the UUP and the SDLP. Trimble took the decision that the time to agree was now:

> because we'd got as far as we could at that stage, and if we didn't agree, then the story would be that it has failed, there has not been an agreement, and there has not been an agreement because the Ulster Unionists would not agree to these proposals coming from the Government. I considered that that, actually, would be very bad from our point of view. I'd formed the view quite some time previously that republicans must have known in '97, when they went into the talks, that they

were going into talks where they did not have a veto. I had a veto. The Government had a veto. The SDLP had a veto, but Sinn Féin and the DUP had not, because of the sufficient consensus rule.

The Mitchell principles [committing all parties to pursuing change through democratic and peaceful means] were perfectly crafted as to only be operative if there was an agreement.... The Mitchell principles did not ask the republicans to sign up to these principles of peaceful and democratic means, but just to accept an agreement...and not to try to change it except by peaceful and democratic means. So, the Mitchell principles were not going to bite unless there was an agreement.

So, we'd be in a situation where there's no agreement, we have lost the opportunity to get the republicans buying into the Mitchell principles and we'd be blamed for all that, and we're opening the door to what Sinn Féin wants to do, which is to have a situation where they and the SDLP, and the British Government, and the Irish Government, and the other parties, are all blaming Unionists for the failures. Then they could run the line of saying, 'The problem is Unionism'. And they can go back to the Anglo-Irish Agreement mode of saying, 'Governments have to take things ahead, and...override the unionist veto'.[35]

Losing the Peace

It had also come as an 'unpleasant surprise' when, at midday on Good Friday, Trimble saw the final draft of the Agreement outlining prisoner releases. Subsequently Trimble understood that this was inserted by the two Governments in the small hours of Friday morning, when Sinn Féin, disappointed with the other parts of the Agreement threatened to walk out. In response to UUP concerns, the British Government showed them a draft of the release scheme including a number of safeguards. Trimble noted that these were some consolation and concluded, in the knowledge that this was something that governments were always likely to do, that he could not justify treating this as a reason to collapse the deal. This reflected two aspects of Trimble's response to the prisoner issue. The first was that he took a strategic and logical view of the releases, concluding that he had achieved his main aims and he could not throw away his gains over something that was beyond his control. The second aspect of his logical approach meant he underestimated the immense emotional impact the early prisoner releases would have on the unionist community, who saw those convicted of politically motivated killings or bombings as simply terrorists. Trimble had reflected upon previous emergencies:

Now, normally, in those, there had been internment and at, and sometimes before, the end of the violence, all the internees were released. Admittedly there hadn't been many people convicted of offences but in the '56 border campaign [the IRA campaign of 1956–62] there were a handful of people who had been convicted through the courts on that occasion. They were all quietly released within 18 months.

We knew prisoner release was coming when we got the draft, all we did was to look at what the nature of the scheme proposed, and what I was looking at was to see that there was a power of recall, when people were released on licence...

It [prisoner releases] only became a mistake when [Mo] Mowlam [the Secretary of State for Northern Ireland] went and released a whole lot of people, for them to go down to [a Sinn Féin ard-fheis] in Dublin...and then for them to be paraded around and appearing on the news on a Sunday, when it was the only news story. And it was replayed again and again, and again with the result that by the next morning, most unionists were up in arms about the issue. So, her handling of the issue made it a problem.[36]

But for others it was simply the best that could be achieved in the circumstances and it was necessary to end the killing. Danny Kennedy voted yes in the referendum, but remained emotional over the prisoner release aspect of the deal:

Principally, because of my experience in South Armagh, I had seen what had happened in my community in South Armagh, the impact of the Troubles. It was really difficult, really difficult. I'm sorry...we lost very lovely people, and Kingsmill [where ten Protestants were shot down by the IRA in 1976], and all of that. I knew in my heart that we had been promised justice, but we'll never get justice. So, the best way was some kind of political settlement. That was very hurtful, because it would've been prisoners out of jail, it would've [meant] widespread reform of the RUC...and that was very, very tough. But, we had to draw an end...we had to stop the funerals, because the impact on my community in South Armagh was devastating.

So, that was difficult, and it was difficult to sell that in part to people in the community, but, you know, I took a view, and I remember going home that night and saying to my wife, 'I'm going to support this, whatever it costs, because, I think, it is, ultimately, the right thing to do.' I think, there was a period where it could've been, perhaps, sold better, or explained better. There was huge damage, I mean, Paisley and [Peter] Robinson [deputy leader of the DUP], for cynical, political reasons, I think, they understood what needed to be done, but they weren't prepared to do it themselves, and saw political opportunism. I've no regrets about it. I think, it could've been sold better, and I think, in some ways, we could've firmed up our position on certain things. There's no doubt about that. But, was it the right thing to do? Ultimately, yes.[37]

Roy Beggs, whose father was one of the UUP MPs to oppose the Agreement, voted No, although 'I actually was prepared to accept much of the compromises that were in it. But...frankly, if the prisoners and guns were linked, I could've bought into it. So, I'm not a purist, but I recognized that the issue of the guns was not definitive in the terms of the Agreement'. In retrospect, however, Beggs concluded that, despite his misgivings, his Party leader had been right in accepting the Agreement:

> I remember, later on, having an interesting chat with David Trimble, and I says, 'Why on earth did you do the deal, when, you know, clearly, it wasn't just nailed?' He said, 'Well, that was all that was on offer'. Looking back, was it the right thing to do? Yeah, it was. Was I reasonable in voting against it? Yeah, it was a reason to vote against it, because it wasn't nailed. But, what I look at today is, I and many others, don't have to regularly look under our cars for bombs, that's what it was like. In the course of my time, in the early 2000s, I came under two police threats, one from extreme loyalists, one from the [dissident] Real IRA, where, you know, there were indiscretions with the police on personal security. You know, that tension for politicians has largely left. It is a better place out there for my kids. I don't worry if my kids are going to Belfast that there's a bomb going to go off at this minute in time.[38]

Although the referendum was won, with Northern Ireland voting Yes by 71 per cent to 29 per cent rejecting the Agreement, only just over half of Protestants voted in favour (see Chapter 3). These divisions were played out in the Ulster Unionist Council (UUC), the ruling body where Trimble was challenged in a succession of votes, particularly on his decision to jump first and enter a power-sharing executive with Sinn Féin before IRA decommissioning had occurred. Decommissioning became the straightjacket that enveloped the Trimble leadership. He was tied to securing it as proof the IRA's war was over even if he, and others, did not regard it as final proof of the end of the Troubles. Empey argued that, 'decommissioning in the modern day and age is meaningless' given arms can be procured relatively easily, 'whereas the constitutional things have longevity'. He pointed out that for all Paisley's 'bluster' in attacking the UUP on the issue, killings subsequently attributed to members of the IRA showed 'They're still using the stuff—supposedly decommissioned weapons'.[39]

The Agreement committed all parties to use their influence to achieve paramilitary decommissioning. Sinn Féin, however, claimed it was entitled to participate in government on the basis of their electoral mandate. Unionists insisted that the political and military leaderships of the republican movement were, if not identical, at least overlapping. As critics had pointed out, the Blair letter was not part of the Agreement and, after six months had passed, there was still no executive formed, as the Sinn Féin leadership of Adams and McGuinness denied they were members of the IRA Army Council. For Trimble the key element in the Agreement was the conditions it imposed on those holding office, who were required to use only democratic, non-violent means, with non-compliers excluded or removed from office under these provisions.

The claim, by anti-Agreement unionists, that republicans were not committed to peaceful and democratic means, or to the Agreement itself, appeared to be borne out a mere twenty days after the Agreement. The IRA issued a statement declaring that the accord 'falls short of presenting a solid basis for a lasting settlement...Let us make it clear that there will be no decommissioning by the IRA'.[40] The impasse between the UUP and Sinn Féin continued as successive British–Irish deadlines came and went. There was finally some movement with the appointment of Peter Mandelson as Secretary of State for Northern Ireland. His proposal to Adams and McGuinness was that there should be 'visible moves' to IRA decommission or he would initiate the 'nuclear option' of restoring direct rule from London. Mandelson's plan was to get the UUP to recognize republicans' right to pursue a united Ireland by peaceful means and allow Sinn Féin into an inclusive executive. In return Sinn Féin would declare opposition to violence and endorse a political process committing the IRA to decommissioning.[41] This would require a leap of faith by Trimble and the UUP, to build trust. George Mitchell was persuaded to again to return to Northern Ireland and chair a review of the Agreement involving the Ulster Unionists and Sinn Féin. As a result, Trimble was prepared to enter an inclusive executive 'on the basis that decommissioning would follow within a matter of weeks'. This belief was not a result of any overt promises made by the Sinn Féin leadership to Trimble that IRA decommissioning would result:

No, they didn't tell us that. Those took place on the basis of...it was Empey and myself, and Adams and McGuinness, and George Mitchell in between. Adams and McGuinness were taking the line of, 'We're Sinn Féin'...I eventually stopped that line by saying to them, 'Well, look, on this basis, there's no point me speaking to you. I would like you to tell me who it's down to, or I'll have to go and find out who I should be speaking to in the IRA in order to get the decision on this matter.' A long pause, and then, Martin McGuinness says, 'You are speaking to the right people'.

So, while they kept saying to us, 'We can't guarantee, no, we can't commit to'...and all the rest of it, I repeatedly went through to Martin, saying, 'You're saying that there is no hope of getting decommissioning until an Executive has been formed and I'm saying to you, that if an Executive is formed without decommissioning then within a very short period of time, I'll be out of office and the whole thing will have collapsed.'

I got down to the point of saying, 'You know, within a month or two, this is what will happen. Now, knowing that this is what is going to happen, do you still want me to go ahead with it?' I got them to repeat it and say, 'Oh, yes, we want you to go ahead with it'. And I'm saying, 'And you realize then that if you're asking me to go ahead with it against this background, then that's on the basis that decommissioning will happen, and that there will be consequences if it doesn't.'

Now, I remember at one stage Mandelson saying to me that they were playing a very good hand in these negotiations. I said, 'What do you mean?' He said, 'Well, they've no idea which way you're going to go'. I replied that 'I don't really know much about which way I'm going to go—I keep changing my mind whether to do it or not.'

The final meeting we had, which was in Belfast, it was only on that meeting when the penny dropped to Adams and McGuinness that I was going to do it, and they immediately started saying to George, as much as to anybody else, 'Now, look, we can't guarantee, we just can't guarantee...' Mitchell turned round on them, and he said, 'Now look, Gerry, I want it firmly understood the 31st January is the final cut-off date.'[42]

After the UUP and Sinn Féin made their public pronouncements the IRA agreed to nominate a representative to enter discussions with General John de Chastelain, head of the Independent International Commission on Decommissioning (IICD).[43] The UUP MLAs, however, still wanted a clear-cut commitment to decommissioning and Mandelson agreed to meet them and promised to 'stand by you', taking the blame if the process collapsed.[44] The tensions within the UUP were such that members like Roy Beggs, now an MLA, were close to leaving the party, although the prospect of joining the DUP was a step too far: 'What made me stay? Well, I didn't like what I saw with them. I recognized that unionism had to be more moderate than they [the DUP] were, if we wished to maintain the United Kingdom.'[45]

The other factor that made Beggs stay was the critical Assembly vote in 1999 before Trimble went into the Executive with Sinn Féin. His inclination was to vote against participation and 'I think, in my mind...I was probably on the pathway to potentially leaving' the UUP. Despite pressure from the party Whip in the Assembly ('turned the screws'), Beggs continued to stand firm. What finally swayed him to side with Trimble was bumping into one of the leader's advisers, David Kerr, who made a last-minute plea and stressed that the issue had boiled down to not 'letting Sinn Féin off the hook'. It was the turning point for Beggs:

I certainly felt a great weight upon me, that my actions might let Sinn Féin off the hook, to enable them to walk away from the process, and blame big bad Unionism... well, that was the start of my rethinking. Then, I had a chat with a few close friends, and I had a chat with my dad [an anti-Agreement MP]. My dad said, 'Ultimately, you have to decide for yourself.'...which I thought was a wise choice for a parent to decide, rather than push me in one direction, or the other.

Ultimately, I decided to not place myself outside the Ulster Unionist Assembly group, which ultimately would have happened and I could well have the lost the vote for them. But, it was for those reasons that I'd come around to thinking that I didn't want Sinn Féin to be off the hook and blame unionism for the collapse of the Assembly.[46]

Attempting to reassure party members in advance of yet another UUC meeting, Trimble warned: 'No guns—no government means just that.... If there is no decommissioning there will be no government.'[47] It was enough as the UUC backed the Mitchell deal by 480 votes to 349. On 2 December 1999 direct rule ended and the Belfast Agreement came into force: at midnight powers were devolved to the Assembly; later that morning, at a treaty signing ceremony in Dublin, the British–Irish Agreement replaced the Anglo-Irish Agreement and saw the NSMC and the BIC come into existence, while the new Articles 2 and 3 of the Irish Constitution replaced the old ones. In the afternoon an inclusive Executive (minus the DUP who refused to attend) met, composed of the UUP, SDLP, and Sinn Féin. Later that evening the IRA announced it would appoint a representative to meet the Independent International Commission on Decommissioning. But there was no IRA decommissioning, not even a gesture. On 11 February 2000, Mandelson suspended the Executive and restored direct rule. The IRA, in response, withdrew from talks with the IICD. Prior to agreeing to the deal, Trimble had secured an undertaking from Mitchell that if:

> Adams and McGuinness didn't deliver, that he would point the finger at them—which he didn't. I have a pretty clear idea although nobody said to me why he didn't, and I didn't ask him but I was fairly certain that it would've been Clinton who would have asked him not to do it. Because, we know from Mandelson's memoirs, that on the afternoon, on the evening of the day in which Blair suspended the Agreement, which he was doing in response to a promise to me, that Clinton phoned him up and begged Blair to rescind the suspension and reinstate it. So, if Clinton was saying that to Blair, and that Clinton then knew that George was going to blame Adams and McGuinness for the breakdown you can see what would have happened. I think what George did, to be fair to him, was go to Seamus Mallon [the SDLP Deputy Leader and Deputy First Minister], and Seamus...worked into an interview that he gave round about this time, that 'I asked George, what was the deal?' And George said the deal was, if the administration is formed in November, decommissioning will occur instantly.' That was fine, but actually, that should have come from George. George should have said, 'That's what the deal is.' Ah! But there we are.[48]

There now began a long and tortuous *danse macabre* with a 'will he, won't he?' combination of whether Trimble would go back into the Executive and a 'will they, won't they?' on the IRA and decommissioning. Trimble's position as UUP leader was eroded but he survived in the post. For Danny Kennedy, this was mainly down to the fact that there was a loyalty factor that Trimble could 'almost fall back on...a fairly high percentage of people who would always support the leader, and say, "Well, he did his best, so we better stick by him."' But then, as the Agreement

> wore on, this stuff about the side deal started to emerge, and other stuff that was coming out, that the Shinners were getting goodies from...and that weakened

him and weakened the position within the Party. If it had been a straight, you know, 'This is the deal, this is our deal. Take it or leave it, and let's go with it' but Trimble was continually undermined, and not supported by British and Irish Governments, particularly British Government. That made his position more difficult.[49]

Police reform was one such blow and Reg Empey thought the 'policing stuff was the most difficult, and it did us the most damage'.[50] For many unionists the RUC, with its title and cap badge of a crowned harp, represented the Britishness of the Northern Ireland state.

While it was obvious that some reform was necessary to make the police, drawn mainly from one community, move to a position of cross-community acceptance, when the Patten Commission reported it saw the RUC become the Police Service of Northern Ireland (PSNI), losing its British-linked title. Moreover 50-50 Catholic to non-Catholic ratio recruiting targets also angered many UUP members. Danny Kennedy explains unionist sentiments:

> That's how that picture of the 302 RUC deaths comes to mean something within the emotional psyche of the broad unionist people. They say, 'Well, what was it all about? What did those deaths mean, then?' You know, 'What are you doing to protect their memory, and to defend their memory, and to say that their sacrifice was worthwhile? Wasn't Gerry Kelly [senior Sinn Féin politician and convicted IRA bomber] in government?'[51]

Trimble recognized the need for policing changes in a less threatening environment but was cognizant of the sensitivities:

> I remember when, shortly after rumours about the Patten report started to circulate, a very senior official in Downing Street asked me what was the problem? I decided to give him one example of a potential problem—'It is being said that the Report will call for the disbandment of RUC Special Branch.' My interlocutor responded, 'Well the intelligent agencies can do so much, but it is RUC Special Branch that we rely on.'
>
> We knew there would have to be major changes, because the police would have to switch from a specialized anti-terrorism role to normal civilian policing. Indeed the RUC themselves engaged in a fundamental review, which provided by far the greater part of the Patten Report. But it was important that the changes be handled sensitively to retain public confidence.
>
> Ken Maginnis and I had a meeting with Patten at an early stage, and I told Patten at length that the symbols were hugely important, and that there would be pressure for changes. I said to him that he might get all the substantive issues right but if he got the symbols wrong then he would foul up the whole process. Curiously, at the press conference on the publication of the Report, Patten quoted this comment without saying that he was quoting me. I think that it was at this occasion that he defended the removal of any element of Britishness from the symbolism on the ground of removing politics from policing. But the Crown and

the Harp, which are the core symbols of the RUC, are national not political and were inherited from the all-Ireland and overwhelmingly Catholic RIC and paralleled by the Irish Guards. Patten overlooked that the Policing Board consists of representatives of political parties.

The change of name added to the hurt caused to the policing family by the failure to acknowledge the service and the sacrifice made on behalf of the whole community.

Interestingly, during the negotiations, at a plenary session, Seamus Mallon raised the idea of calling it The Royal Northern Ireland Constabulary but that suggestion disappeared with the publication of the Report. All that the government could say in defence of this unbalanced report was that it had resisted demands for the abolition and canonization of the police service.

Peter Mandelson became Secretary of State shortly after the report and saw the need to address the problem caused by Patten. That resulted in the award of the George Medal to the service. Another concession we obtained was that the formal, legal title was 'The Police Service of Northern Ireland, incorporating the Royal Ulster Constabulary.[52]

The Patten Report[53] was, according to Trimble, the 'shoddiest official committee report' he had ever seen[54] and was 'riddled with deep flaws' according to the UUP,[55] but the unionist electorate was aware that Trimble and his party was effectively the midwife to the changes to policing which would inevitably follow. While the Patten Report came as a shock to Trimble, it should not have, but unionist involvement in the process was patchy and the Party's intelligence over likely recommendations incomplete.

The impact on many within the UUP was powerful. Russ Hussey recalled:

Patten, I wasn't overly impressed. The Royal Ulster Constabulary had a very proud tradition, a very proud tradition. The number of officers killed reflects their service to this community. I detest those that attempt to muddy the name of the RUC. I would be a fool if I thought they were all golden boys. There were some bad apples. But I know a lot of the RUC officers that were killed, and the circumstances in which they were killed, and I don't think that hurt will ever go away in my lifetime. That's something I'm going to have to live with.

When I was 19 years of age, I saw a colleague who had been murdered, and his father insisted that we go into the wake, a traditional Irish wake. I assumed the coffin would be closed, and it wasn't, and the father insisted we go in. My colleague had a bullet hole in that cheek, in that cheek, and between there and there was a bandage, so the whole top of his head was shot off. I was 19. I'm 57 in February, and that memory has been in my head ever since. So, I'll not tolerate anybody running down the RUC.

I think, people forget that the Police Service of Northern Ireland's full title, is the Police Service of Northern Ireland Incorporating the Royal Ulster Constabulary GC [George Cross]. They had no reason to take away the name, and I think it was a disgrace that they did. They've taken away as many emblems as they could from the uniform, and anyone that knows anything about the history of the RUC uniform would realize that the RUC uniform was more Irish than the Garda Síochána uniform. The uniform was green, the badge was a harp and crown, the button was the harp and crown, and eighteen interwoven shamrocks. The sergeant stripes, interwoven shamrocks. Inspector's pip had a shamrock. Officer's cap had Irish lace, with shamrocks. Chief Constable's cap had shamrocks. All that's gone. All the Irishness has been taken out of the RUC, out of the PSNI uniform for political correctness. Ridiculous.[56]

The Patten Report came the midst of the UUP leadership trying to secure decommissioning and establish an executive. It provided the loud background noise to further attempts to put the power-sharing Humpty Dumpty back together again. After British and Irish pressure on Sinn Féin, another IRA statement was more promising. The IRA indicated that it would resume contact with John de Chastelain's IICD and 'initiate a process that will completely and verifiably put IRA arms beyond use'. As a confidence-building measure, to confirm that its weapons remained secure, the contents of a number of arms dumps would be inspected by agreed third parties who would report that they had done so to the IICD. The dumps would be reinspected regularly to ensure that the weapons had remained unused.[57] Trimble pronounced himself encouraged by the IRA's statement, claiming that it 'appears to break new ground'.[58] However, critics such as Jeffrey Donaldson pointed out that there was nothing in the statement which indicated that it was going to disarm. The problem was that the IRA still retained possession of its weapons and there was no guarantee that all its weapons would be deposited in these bunkers.

Trimble re-entered the power-sharing Executive with Sinn Féin in May 2000 but in October, under pressure from UUP dissidents, had to set conditions on cooperation with republicans in cross-border bodies. Any suggestion the IRA were moving towards a formal declaration their war was over was put in doubt by comments made by Brian Keenan, their Chief of Staff, that there could be a return to violence if the peace process broke down. Trimble then resigned as First Minister in July 2001. By now the atmosphere within the UUP, as Danny Kennedy recalls, was poisonous:

I've got to say, I mean, I was in the Assembly team and was hawkish at the time, because I was mindful of everyone in the constituency and mindful of the people who had stretched themselves enough in some ways, and were saying, 'Well, where's this going to end? I mean, this is just concession after concession here.' Paisley ended up having a field day, they were crawling all over us. You know what I mean? So, I think, it became more and more difficult, and then the special meetings within the Party were being called. I remember going to [a meeting in] Balmoral, to the 'cowshed', it was called, and it was, literally, a cowshed, and it was an awful atmosphere ... It was awful. There were people who were mixing things, and raising things up, and personal attacks being said on people. It was just the most horrible atmosphere for a political party to operate in.[59]

Although, following the displacement of the UUP by the DUP, there would be significant decommissioning by the IRA, it is important to note that this never occurred in conditions radically different to those when Trimble dominated the unionist political scene. Although clergy witnesses confirmed that a large amount of weaponry was eventually put aside, how much of the IRA arsenal was put beyond use remained a mystery. Roy Beggs, therefore, gives Trimble credit for kick-starting the process:

Well, I don't think we would have had decommissioning from the Provisional IRA if he hadn't done it. The biggest hurdle in decommissioning was, of course, to get it started. I think, we all would have preferred much faster, and much more visible decommissioning, but nevertheless, ultimately, what is important, is what is happening out there in the streets. At this moment in time, we have a relatively small Real IRA, the dissident movement, which is still engaged in terrorism, and gangsters. Certainly, I view it as being a much better place than where it was.

Was Trimble right? I think, history has turned out that it was the right decision to make, but equally, it could've turned out wrong. I mean, if decommissioning had not happened, you know, okay, you might have been able to blame Sinn Féin with some regard, but the government PR machine might have just turned round at the same time and blamed unionism. You just don't know how it would've turned out. It was a huge risk, and it was at great cost to the unionist community, to unionist families. I mean, many families had, probably . . . a bit like the Scottish Nationalist debate, there would've been significant disputes within families, within unionism. But, what seems very, very strange is for the DUP, who chased Trimble, abused him, physically as well as verbally, and then they did exactly . . . they are exactly where he was.[60]

For Danny Kennedy the consequences for the UUP in the wider unionist electorate were severe in that Trimble was seen to have gone back on his word:

We fatally, produced a slogan that says, 'No guns—No government'. We got nailed on it, absolutely, nailed on it . . . that was nearly the final straw that broke the camel's back, you know, in that we couldn't achieve 'No guns—No government' . . . it was madness. The slogan became our Achilles heel. We created a rod for others to hit us with, and say, 'Well, where's your "No guns—No government" now?' . . . It's a trait within Unionism that says, 'Well, you've said that, and that's your word, and if you walk away from that, then that's not your word anymore, and we don't trust you as much.'[61]

Trimble's original strategy was to force elections following the initial act of decommissioning, to be re-elected First Minister, and then have

gone to the country saying, 'Look, we've got the Agreement, we've got decommissioning, we're in a position to operate properly, but in order to do that, I need to have a marked majority in the Assembly.'... And there's a chance I could've got it, but when the time came, the Party was still in a state of shock...the Duppers had been really, really nasty...I didn't insist on doing what I had to do.[62]

In hindsight, Trimble believes he should have stuck with his original strategy. Instead he hesitated and the moment was lost. In the ensuing Assembly election in 2003 the DUP emerged as the majority Unionist party in Northern Ireland—the first time the UUP had been displaced from that position since 1921. One old colleague had tried to persuade Trimble to resign before it was too late. He was part of a delegation that

> pleaded with David Trimble about eight weeks before the election—this was the general election—to stand down, because we felt we were going to be annihilated. But he wouldn't listen, and we suffered terribly, as we all know. So, I tried to use my influence, and I was being open and honest with him. I wasn't going behind his back, whereas others were sort of saying, 'We need to convene a special meeting of the Unionist Council to throw this guy out'. I said, 'No, I'll not be part of that, but I want to go and face the man'.[63]

In the 2005 General Election, Trimble lost his seat. He is reflective: 'At the end of day, the electorate are entitled to do what...they're not under any obligation, you know. They do what they do, and there we are.' But he remains consoled by one aspect: 'the DUP are still living in the political world we created, you know'.[64]

Notes

1. Vanguard, *Community of the British Isles*, Belfast: Ulster Vanguard, 1972.
2. D. Trimble, 'Initiatives for Consensus: A Unionist Perspective', in C. Townshend (ed.), *Consensus in Ireland: Approaches and Recessions*, Oxford: Clarendon, 1988, 78–89.
3. Trimble, 'Initiatives for Consensus'.
4. Trimble, 'Initiatives for Consensus'.
5. Trimble, 'Initiatives for Consensus'.
6. T. Hennessey, *The Northern Ireland Peace Process: Ending the Troubles?* Dublin: Gill & Macmillan, 2000, 164.
7. J. Powell, *Great Hatred, Little Room: Making Peace in Northern Ireland*, London: Bodley Head, 2008, 93.
8. A. Campbell and R. Stott (eds), *The Blair Years: Extracts from the Alastair Campbell Diaries*, London: Hutchinson, 2007, 288.
9. Powell, *Great Hatred*, 93.
10. Powell, *Great Hatred*, 91.
11. Powell, *Great Hatred*, 95.
12. Campbell and Stott, *Blair Years*, 290.
13. Powell, *Great Hatred*, 95–6.

14. Powell, *Great Hatred*, 97.

15. Powell, *Great Hatred*, 97–8.

16. Campbell and Stott, *Blair Years*, 291–3.

17. Campbell and Stott, *Blair Years*, 294.

18. Powell, *Great Hatred*, 96.

19. Campbell and Stott, *Blair Years*, 294.

20. Ulster Unionist Party, Press Release at the formal launching of Strand Two of the multi-party negotiations, Belfast: UUP, 1997.

21. E. Mallie and D. McKittrick, *Endgame in Ireland*, London: Hodder & Stoughton, ????, 235.

22. Ulster Unionist Party, *Understanding the Agreement*, Belfast: UUP, 1998.

23. Powell, *Great Hatred*, 103–4.

24. Powell, *Great Hatred*, 105.

25. Mallie and McKittrick, *Endgame in Ireland*, 247.

26. Interview with David Trimble 30 June 2016.

27. Mallie and McKittrick *Endgame in Ireland*, 250–2.

28. Interview with Reg Empey, 30 June 2016.

29. Interview with David Trimble, 30 June 2016.

30. Interview with Reg Empey, 30 June 2016.

31. Interview with Danny Kennedy, 28 Jan. 2016.

32. Interview with Tom Elliott, 13 Apr. 2016.

33. Interview with Tom Elliott, 13 Apr. 2016.

34. Interview with Tom Elliott, 13 Apr. 2016.

35. Interview with David Trimble, 30 June 2016.

36. Interview with David Trimble, 30 June 2016.

37. Interview with Danny Kennedy, 28 Jan. 2016.

38. Interview with Roy Beggs, 28 Jan. 2016.

39. Interview with Reg Empey, 30 June 2016.

40. IRA statement, 30 Apr. 1998.

41. P. Mandelson, *The Third Man: Life at the Heart of New Labour*, London: HarperPress, 2010, 291–2.

42. Interview with David Trimble, 30 June 2016.

43. IRA statement, 17 Nov. 1999.

44. Mandelson, *Third Man*, 292–4.

45. Interview with Roy Beggs, 28 Jan. 2016.

46. Interview with Roy Beggs, 28 Jan. 2016.

47. *Independent*, 26 Nov. 1999.

48. Interview with David Trimble, 30 June 2016.

49. Interview with Danny Kennedy, 28 Jan. 2016.

50. Interview with Reg Empey, 30 June 2016.

51. Interview with Danny Kennedy, 28 Jan. 2016.

52. Interview with David Trimble, 30 June 2016.

53. Independent Commission on Policing for Northern Ireland, *The Report of the Independent Commission on Policing in Northern Ireland (The Patten Report)*, Belfast: UUP, 1999.

54. Ulster Unionist Party Working Party, *A Response to 'A New Beginning: Policing in Northern Ireland': The Report of the Independent Commission on Policing in Northern Ireland (The Patten Report)*, Belfast: UUP, 1999, preface.

55. UUP Working Party, *Response*, 21.

56. Interview with Ross Hussey, 27 Jan. 2016.

57. IRA statement, 6 May 2000.

58. *Irish Times*, 8 May 2000.

59. Interview with Danny Kennedy, 28 Jan. 2016.

60. Interview with Roy Beggs, 28 Jan. 2016.

61. Interview with Danny Kennedy, 28 Jan. 2016.

62. Interview with David Trimble, 30 June 2016.

63. Interview with UUP elected representative 2016.

64. Interview with David Trimble, 30 June 2016.

3

Electoral Politics

The Disorderly Management of Decline?

The first two decades of the twenty-first century yielded electoral misery for the UUP. Early assumptions of a moderate UUP–SDLP unionist–nationalist governing axis to stabilize the Belfast Agreement were swept aside amid repeated electoral reverses for both parties. As Sinn Féin reaped reward from the nationalist electorate for its apparent new moderation, it appeared that unionists preferred belligerence, switching to the avowedly anti-Agreement DUP. Such apparent asymmetry was more complex and even within the unionist bloc this was not a triumph of the extremes. The DUP came to accept virtually all of what the UUP had negotiated. Nonetheless, as UUP elected representatives were regularly rejected, this was a bitter-sweet consolation. Both the DUP and Sinn Féin became successful ethnic tribune parties,[1] viewed as the stouter defenders of their ethnic blocs, whilst moderating their agendas. The electoral price for the UUP and the SDLP was high.

For all the bellicose anti-Agreement rhetoric, the DUP, via the 2006 St Andrews Agreement, enforced only two modifications to the Belfast Agreement. The first was that Sinn Féin was required to support the state's police force. Despite all the bombast which for years had preceded the St Andrews deal, former paramilitary prisoners were not returned to prison, nor policing reforms reversed, under the DUP. Cross-border bodies remained and the DUP First Minister, Ian Paisley did not change any of the constitutional provisions of the 1998 deal, previously denounced as treacherous.

The second change from what was agreed in 1998 was an advancement of the DUP's own position, in that the rules for electing the First and Deputy First Minister were changed. Previously, a cross-community vote was required for the election of both, on a joint ticket. Now the winners in each bloc took all, as post-holders were nominated by the largest party in each bloc, sparing the DUP the embarrassment of nominating a Sinn Féin deputy and Sinn Féin the embarrassment of formally installing the historic enemy of the DUP at the helm. The First Minister would be nominated by the largest party in the largest designation. Given Northern Ireland's demographics, the overwhelming probability was that the winning party in the unionist bloc claimed the First Ministership. The effect was to make elections even more of a sectarian headcount, as the unionist vote was mobilized behind the likeliest largest party in their bloc to prevent any risk of nationalism's largest party, Sinn Féin, providing the First Minister. The effect of the change was to negate the chances of a UUP recovery at the polls. This chapter examines the electoral eclipse of the UUP by its more belligerent rival.

The UUP on the Slide: Elections and Defections

The electoral story of the UUP for the first decade after the Belfast Agreement was one of rapid retreat. Table 3.1 charts the declining fortunes of the UUP from its dominance immediately prior to the Belfast Agreement.

Table 3.1 indicates how the UUP has been removed from its once dominant position within the unionist community, bereft of representation at Westminster, reduced in numbers in the Assembly, and diminished in local government. The UK is set to depart the one institution where UUP representation has held

Table 3.1 UUP versus DUP election performances 1997–2017

Westminster	UUP % vote	UUP seats	DUP % vote	DUP seats
1997	32.7	10	13.6	2
2001	26.8	6	22.5	5
2005	17.8	1	33.7	9
2010	15.2	0	25.0	8
2015	16.0	2	25.7	8
2017	10.3	0	36.0	10
Assembly				
1998	21.3	28	18.5	20
2003	22.7	27	25.7	30
2007	14.9	18	30.1	36
2011	13.2	16	30.0	38
2016	12.6	16	29.2	38
2017	12.9	10	28.1	28
Council				
1997	28.0	185	16.0	91
2001	21.0	154	23.0	131
2005	18.0	115	29.6	182
2011	15.2	99	27.2	175
2014	16.1	88	23.1	130
European				
1999	17.6	1	28.4	1
2004	16.6	1	32.0	1
2009	17.1	1	18.2	1
2014	13.3	1	20.9	1

steady, the European Parliament. The Belfast Agreement may have meant that the Northern Ireland constitutional issue had 'probably been parked comfortably'[2] but it fractured unionism. Only 57 per cent of Protestants backed the deal in the May 1998 referendum, compared to near-unanimity of support (97 per cent) among Catholics.[3] Many within the unmanageable and over-large UUC, effectively the decision-making body within the UUP at the time, did not believe in key aspects of the Agreement and its associated items. Nearly half (45 per cent) viewed it as a step towards a united Ireland. More than half (53 per cent) opposed all-island bodies and fewer than one in five members supported prisoner releases and policing changes.[4] As UUP leader, David Trimble was aware of the electoral risks to his party in supporting the Belfast Agreement but remained confident that the UUP could maintain or even improve its position:

> We could see from the Assembly elections in June '98 the pro-Agreement unionists just had a narrow lead over anti-Agreement unionists. That was consistent with the opinion polls at the time, which had it down at sort of 45–55 [anti-Agreement versus pro-] amongst the Unionist voters. Now, while we started with that limited position, it was perfectly reasonable to expect that we could improve on that situation as we implemented the Agreement. Remember that the Government in the last day of the talks said in their letter to me, that in their view decommissioning should begin in the summer, as soon as the decommissioning schemes are put in place. If that had happened, if decommissioning had started and particularly if decommissioning had been linked to prisoner release, which again was perfectly feasible under the Agreement....our position would've strengthened. Because in the Agreement you've got two, two-year processes. They were not explicitly linked but there was nothing to prevent the government saying, 'we are going to link'. It would have been perfectly viable.[5]

Trimble found it difficult to steer his own party, where he faced a combination of embitterment from individuals over his surprise party leadership success in 1995 and broader opposition to the less palatable aspects of the Belfast Agreement for unionists. He struggled to control his party, let alone force Sinn Féin's hand. Trimble led, but not everyone followed. One of Trimble's successors, Tom Elliott, saw how Trimble was confronted by too many mutineers: 'If you have 45% of our ruling council going one way—and some of them were intent on causing trouble, it makes it very difficult to manage.'[6]

Internal critics could not be converted—even years later. 'I still think to this day, we could've negotiated something much better. I really do', declared one prominent UUP elected representative.[7] A more sympathetic former MLA opined that Trimble:

> leapt out of the plane and said, 'Come on, everybody, follow me', whereas, the other parties, they test the depth first, and as the Shinners would say, 'They

manage their base.'... It was also difficult because he was constantly railing against Sinn Féin, so he was pointing out the difficulties for people, and then having to try and either overcome them, or agree to them, or come up with some sort of compromise.[8]

The former leader rues his inability to restructure his party to facilitate much tighter central steerage, highlighting how internal managerial issues hamstrung broader efforts to sell the advantages of the Belfast Agreement:

> It was impossible, because, after the Agreement, while we were getting support in the party in terms of the Unionist Council, [it] was less than 60 per cent and the party constitution required a two-thirds majority to change it... I had to concentrate on the delegates to the Council and I put a lot of effort into that. What I should have done was put the same amount of effort into persuading the electorate at large and I think that was a mistake, because the electorate at large began to be influenced by the constant barrage of negativity that was coming from the DUP, which I was not actually rebutting as vigorously as I could have done, because my attention was focused on delegates.[9]

Trimble's failure to shore up his party's (and his own) position among the electorate tends to be attributed to a combination of items. There was DUP opportunistic electioneering, denouncing an agreement they were destined to support and pledging to 'smash Sinn Féin' before moving into government. The slipperiness of Tony Blair, ambiguous over the requirement for—and sequencing of—IRA decommissioning in relation to the onset of devolved power-sharing is blamed, as is malevolence from Sinn Féin. As Paul Bew once asserted, the UK government was 'far more sensitive to Gerry Adams's deadlines and reports of IRA activity in England'.[10] As noted in the previous chapter, Trimble did not help matters by agreeing to jump into government with Sinn Féin in autumn 1999 on similar terms to those he categorically rejected in July 1999, when a nationalist-only executive had been formed for a token fifteen minutes.

The lack of clarity on IRA decommissioning could not be overcome by Blair's personal 'guarantees' on the subject. In summer 1999, Blair's *The Way Forward* document, offering republicans seats in governments on the basis that Sinn Féin asked the IRA to put weapons aside, added nothing to what was contained in the Agreement. Sinn Féin offered a literal reading of the Belfast Agreement; Trimble an aspirational interpretation. In July 1999, he lamented that 'Sinn Féin/IRA still appear to retain hopes of bringing their armed movement into the heart of government'.[11] That was what, effectively, the UUP leader had signed up to.

For former UUP MLA Adrian Cochrane-Watson, however, the biggest problem was the Prime Minister: 'We were given pledges by Blair, who, by the way, is the biggest liar in the world and please quote me on that... if he had honoured the pledges he made, perhaps David Trimble would probably still be First Minister.'[12] There were heartfelt divisions within the UUP over whether to back the Agreement, given its painful medicine on policing and prisoner releases and genuine concerns over whether Trimble had achieved the best possible deal.

There was considerable geographical variation in the level of intra-party hostility. Members in Fermanagh and in Strangford, as examples, reported mainly respectful disagreement, rather than acrimony and bitterness, but in some other locations there was internecine strife. Danny Kennedy recalls grim times as the Belfast Agreement:

> not only divided branches, in some cases, it divided families ... it's our version of the Irish Civil War, Fianna Fáil and Fine Gael' ... emotions ran very, very deep, very, very deep. I tried to maintain good relations with everybody through it, and managed, mostly, I think, managed mostly. Jeffrey Donaldson and I had been very close over the years, but we parted on that, and it was never quite the same after that ... The most serious damage wasn't inflicted by either the DUP, or the other parties who were against. The most serious damage was the internal damage ... To think that you can win a vote with little over 50% and expect to keep the Party together, was hopeless.[13]

Trimble's efforts commanded respect as well as dismay within his own ranks. The substance of his achievement and his political selflessness in producing the Belfast Agreement are recognized. Former West Tyrone MLA Ross Hussey asserted:

> David Trimble put his political career, his political life, and this political party on the line. The DUP stood outside chanting, roaring, spitting. I mean, some of the abuse that David Trimble took, if somebody had attacked me the way they attacked him, I'd have broken their jaw, and that would be me being nice. They were absolute animals. But he was prepared to take that risk, and he did what he had to do for peace.[14]

A typical response from UUP members was that, 'history will look more kindly than the electorate on what we did'.[15] The problem for Trimble and the UUP was selling the Belfast Agreement, to sceptics, with polls showing by 2002 only one in three Protestants supported the deal.[16] Political altruism was dangerous and few saw Trimble as its most appropriate salesman.[17] Trimble's leadership deficiencies were highlighted even by supporters of what he was trying to achieve. UUP members in Derry/Londonderry, for example, high-lighted his failure to delegate, offering descriptions such as 'dictator', 'control freak' 'didn't trust people', and 'didn't have a personality'.[18]

The party also looked chaotic, torn apart over the deal with challenges to Trimble a regular feature of the 'Ulster Unionist Council nonsense, where you had 1,000 people or so in a room to try and settle something'.[19] The leadership needed greater central control and a diminution of the power of the virtually autonomous eighteen constituency associations. This internal disorder and indecisiveness contributed significantly to the decision of some of the UUP's most talented figures to defect to the DUP by 2003 and help turn Paisley's outfit, itself hitherto ramshackle and unstructured, but with more top-down order at least, into a dominant force.[20] Those UUP defectors contributed to the sense of unrest, simultaneously exploiting and lamenting those structures but settling in quickly within an overwhelmingly welcoming DUP.[21]

After the departure of a chunk of the party's talent, reforms finally transferred power away from the Ulster Unionist Council to the leader and executive. Belatedly, a coherent structure emerged from a federation of idiosyncratic autonomous constituency associations.

Trimble's successor, Reg Empey, recalls:

I brought in the first structural reforms since the war, I think, and that was a mammoth task, you have no idea. I mean, leading members did everything to stop me. In the Europa Hotel, the first time we'd tried to get the thing through, one was running round pulling people out of the room, because if you went below the 200 threshold, you couldn't continue. So, they blocked the first attempt, but I had a second attempt, and I got it through.

The writ of the leadership is now much greater although this can cause some minor friction, mainly over local candidate selection, with the centre being overly optimistic for several years over how many candidates it was a good idea to run. As one Coleraine local constituency member put it, 'there's always a tension between the local association and what we call headquarters, the central party. The central party is the party who usually has the final say in who runs'.[22] One councillor's chief grumble was how the leader 'wants to select candidates over the heads of the constituency associations'.[23] Complaints over too much central authority are a relatively new departure within the UUP.

Defections during the early 2000s greatly affected the UUP, which struggled to recover from the loss of talent, some of which went on to dominate—and at least partially modernize—the DUP.[24] The most prominent UUP quitters went on to inflict more damage on their erstwhile colleagues. Arlene Foster went on to lead the DUP to electoral drubbings of the UUP and Jeffrey Donaldson played a prominent role at Westminster, not least in helping negotiate the DUP–Conservative Party post-election deal in 2017. 'Jeffrey leaving the UUP did mainstream the DUP in a lot of the unionist community's eyes', was one lament.[25] A UUP councillor commented: 'Arlene [Foster] was always a very articulate, competent individual . . . even my wife said, "Big temptation to vote for Arlene, and vote for the DUP"'.[26] Years later, the defections to the DUP still rankle among some, Ross Hussey uttering some particularly forthright views:

Yeah, well, don't get me going about Jeffrey, because he was a total hypocrite. Because that man was supposed to be a member of a political party, and if you're a member of a party, or any organization, you go with the corporate view. We made decisions at conferences, and at meetings, and before the doors were closed, Jeffrey Donaldson was out speaking to the cameras. He's under a far tighter whip now. He won't open his mouth as quickly for the DUP, because if he did, they would sack him ... So, Jeffrey Donaldson was a total hypocrite, as was Arlene. Both of them got elected on Ulster Unionist tickets, and then, walked away to the DUP, and as far as I'm concerned, the two of them were traitors. As far as I'm concerned, they're the lowest of the low.[27]

According to Danny Kennedy,

Jeffrey [Donaldson] and Arlene [Foster], they were soft noes, because they knew that, in their hearts, there wasn't any alternative, and, ultimately, to achieve devolution, to achieve some kind of settlement, some difficult decision would have to be done, but they weren't capable of supporting it.[28]

Regretting the defections, former MLA Sandra Overend argued that the defectors 'should've stayed the course you know, I don't see any difference in what they moved on to do'.[29] Tom Elliott, elected with Foster as UUP Assembly members for Fermanagh and South Tyrone less than one month before Foster's departure commented:

What did annoy me was, two nights before she left, Arlene and me and constituency officers had a meeting on how we would manage constituency offices and how we would work together. Then two days later, the first thing I'd heard she'd left was on *Evening Extra* [a BBC Radio Ulster programme], that said Arlene and Jeffrey had left.

The loss of four seats at the 2001 Westminster election was a severe blow. The UUP urged voters 'Don't turn back the clock' but the party was necessarily defensive on decommissioning, its manifesto blaming Blair for having failed to deliver his pledge to offer provisions 'preventing such people [paramilitaries] holding office' if they failed to decommission weapons.[30] The DUP's 2001 election message was blunt and unsubtle:

The following were SUPPORTED by the UUP and OPPOSED by the DUP:
Terrorists in government
The RUC destroyed
Murderers released
Executive all-Ireland bodies set up.[31]

The November 2003 Assembly election—a phantom contest to an Assembly that was not to be restored until 2007, yielded further decline with the DUP overtaking the UUP in terms of seats, but at least the UUP's vote share rose marginally. The UUP's 2003 Assembly election manifesto was a thin eight-page booklet, which declared that 'Devolution worked because Ulster Unionists worked', a curious claim to put before the Unionist electorate when the Assembly had not sat for over a year.[32] It contrasted with the pithy assertions of the DUP's offering, such as 'I don't want Gerry Kelly [from Sinn Féin] as Minister for Policing and Justice'.[33] Some of the DUP's criticisms were plain wrong: the description of the North–South Ministerial Council as a 'stand-alone all-Ireland government'[34] was risible nonsense given its absence of executive authority. Nonetheless, other (real) concerns were harming the UUP.

By the 2005 General Election, internal chaos, the collapse of political institutions and the failure of the IRA to complete decommissioning led to disaster, as the party was reduced to one seat and, in a shocking nadir, Trimble was ousted by Upper Bann's electors in favour of the DUP's little-known David Simpson. Hazel Legge recalls: 'I was out canvassing at that election and, in hindsight, we got almost too good a response on the doorsteps. It was like people had said, "Well, there's no point arguing with them, because they're finished really anyway." '[35]

After Trimble's immediate departure as party leader, Reg Empey was elected in June 2005 to the head of a mess. The UUP was in electoral freefall and the DUP was about to steal its political clothes. With the UUP having little idea how to deal with its unionist rival and the UUP–SDLP post-Agreement power-sharing axis having been eclipsed, Empey's best hope was merely to stop the rot. The UUP was also in serious financial trouble, its debt at one point rising to over £1.4 million, with the need to prune staff costs. Mark Cosgrove became party treasurer soon after Empey's leadership accession and moved to manage the crisis:

> I literally applied business fiscal rules to the party's finances. We went from a million pound of debt to 100 grand in a period of austerity. Party will always live within its means. It ain't there to make a profit . . . it's there to provide a political infrastructure. As long as it breaks even over an electoral cycle, that's fine. Members and elected members contribute an awful lot out of their own pockets.[36]

Uncomfortable UCUNF

By 2009, the UUP leadership saw strategic value in forming an alliance with the Conservative Party for the following year's General Election, clumsily titled the Ulster Conservatives and Unionists New Force, UCUNF. The attractions were that the move linked the UUP to UK-wide politics, relaunched the party on a rising Conservative tide as David Cameron rebranded his own organization and potentially made the DUP look more narrow and inward-looking.

The fifty years of Conservative links from the 1920s until the 1970s, propping up Unionist majoritarianism, could hardly be hailed as auspicious but the contemporary political context of local power-sharing was very different. Most UUP members, 67 per cent, feel closest to the Conservative Party, compared to miniscule sympathy for other parties at Westminster. Labour and the Liberal Democrats muster a paltry 2 per cent each, and 19 per cent of UUP members say they do not feel close to any British-wide party. Although desirous of close alignment with British politics, only one-third of UUP members want British-wide parties to extend their reach to Northern Ireland. Nonetheless, the party leader, Reg Empey, wanted to better integrate the UUP within UK politics and UCUNF seemed a way forward.

There had been some encouragement when the UCUNF label was used in the 2009 European election, as the UUP vote share rose marginally, although this owed much to temporary DUP decline after its popular former MEP, Jim Allister, quit to form Traditional Unionist Voice in disgust at the DUP–Sinn Féin pact in the 2006 St Andrews Agreement. The UUP attempted to exploit the DUP's remarkable U-turn in signing up in 2006 to what they had rejected in 1998. Whilst the DUP had moved Sinn Féin's position on policing, there was little else altered by the St Andrews Agreement beyond the DUP and Sinn Féin easing their path to acquisition of the First and Deputy First Minister titles. It was difficult to demur from Empey's assertion that the DUP had 'signed up to the fundamentals, framework and institutions of the Belfast Agreement of 1998', as the UUP leader wondered 'what on earth were the last few years of turmoil and division within Unionism all about?'[37]

The UCUNF alliance was another failure for the UUP. Interviewed on BBC television during the 2010 election campaign by Jeremy Paxman, the Conservative Party leader appeared to indicate that Northern Ireland's public sector was ripe for pruning. The DUP wasted no time in highlighting the risk, using a series of press advertisements outlining Cameron's comments in case anyone had missed the message. The UUP's solitary remaining MP, Sylvia Hermon, opposed the link and stood as an Independent in North Down, trouncing the UCUNF candidate by over 14,000 votes and ending UUP representation at Westminster for the first time in the Party's history. Unionist voters had little interest in the resurrection of an old alliance. The UUP brand seemed either dated or toxic and nationalists were far from keen on any pact more deeply integrating Northern Ireland into the UK.

Having presided over the electoral slide of the first decade following the Belfast Agreement, Trimble encouraged his successor, Reg Empey, in developing the link with the Conservative Party. Indeed, Trimble joined Cameron's party in 2007, a year after taking a peerage. Despite the stark lack of dividends, he continues to defend the idea of a linkage between his former and current parties, arguing that the execution may have been incorrect, but the idea was appropriate:

> The silly UCUNF title was part of the reason [for failure] and Cameron was the man who insisted on that name, on that title. We tried to get something shorter, but Cameron insisted on that. When I went to join the Conservative Party, I said to Cameron, right from the outset, what I wanted to see happening was for national parties to come in, to be functioning in Northern Ireland. What we needed was to change the political culture in Northern Ireland and the only way I could see that happening is by the national parties coming in and then giving people the basic right to move away from a tribal or confessional base, to a socio-economic form of politics. The only way we could get that transformation, from communal politics to economic politics, is through the national parties coming in. Now, it would be the key one to make the changes and get away with it, but the Conservatives by themselves wouldn't do it. But the Conservative thinking was, if the Conservatives come in, that this would then force Labour's hand and we got one seat then that would have been enough to do it . . . If Labour came in, then you'd start changing the nature of politics. In the long run we need to do this, because if we leave politics in Northern Ireland on a communal basis, sooner or later the sectarian thing will turn round and bite us.[38]

Empey believes the alliance was a worthwhile but flawed experiment:

> Well, first of all, the name, it was the Conservatives who insisted on that. I mean, I was against it. I never liked it. The main problem we had was that the local Conservatives were the biggest drag on the whole thing. I had no difficulty over here. I've no difficulty with Cameron, it was all the locals, they were the saboteurs. But, we nearly got away with it. When you look at it, we were one vote short in Fermanagh, and if I'd have managed to persuade another 592 people in South Antrim [the actual margin of defeat was 1,183 votes], we'd have got away with it. So, it was a damn close-run thing.
>
> The irony is that we won the seats back on our own steam . . . The logic of it was that we had a relationship for over 80 years on point, and here we had a modern, rising star [Cameron] who's a leader over here, and so on. Could we take the next step, moving away from the tribal stuff to the more economically focused politics, or more modern politics?[39]

UCUNF had other supporters. Danny Kinahan, ironically elected at the following election when the pact was long-buried, declared:

> I was all for it, but I wanted unionism leading it. I saw it as a way of not just being involved in mainland politics but being part of a union. Where it went wrong was we were trying to fight against Northern Irish Conservatives who look down their noses at anything that's unionist, with an unfair label that we are sectarian. There were also some Conservatives on the other side who really didn't understand Northern Ireland and just wanted the chance of extra seats . . . I went to a meeting

and as I came in the door one of the local Conservatives said: 'We are so looking forward to taking over your party and getting rid of the Ulster Unionists'.[40]

Mark Cosgrove was 'passionate' about UCUNF and despite its 'terrible name' remains unrepentant:

Reg [Empey] came within 600 votes of being in the British Cabinet which I honestly believe from our conversations Cameron would have had him in. To me that would have said a hundred times more about Sinn Féin's failure to bomb and kill us into a united Ireland than a thousand painted red white and blue kerbstones. The problem was the outworking, which was handed down to a very small party on the ground without any experience of politics. Also, not all colleagues would see themselves as centre right. We are a broad church.[41]

However, Sandra Overend was one of many unconvinced by the alliance with Cameron's party:

Well, I remember the negotiations with the Conservatives, and the meetings with party officers and with membership to discuss it, and I really felt that it was pushed too quickly, and there wasn't enough time to negotiate. So, I wasn't content during the negotiations that this was the right thing to do. I didn't think the people would buy it. You know, the name and everything was totally ridiculous. So, I mean, there were particular people within the Party who were pushing that along, and it was like, 'Well, you just have to agree to it now, because, if you don't take it now, we're not going get this opportunity again, and this is where we want to be.' And, yes, I see the advantage of having a UK-wide party and being part of government. So, I could see the benefits. Knocking on the doors, you had to explain every time.[42]

Empey's successor, Tom Elliott, having initially been mildly supportive of the idea, became keen on its burial:

Our relationship with Conservative Headquarters was quite good but our relationship with the Northern Ireland Conservatives was just impossible. They tried to dominate everything. Under my leadership we parted company. I would not succumb to their demands. They were trying to clear the Ulster Unionist Party out.[43]

There is indeed little evidence of warmth from the UUP towards the Northern Ireland Conservatives. Less than one in five UUP members claim any liking for them, although indifference is the most common response. Even had relations on the ground been better it is far from apparent that the alliance would have paid dividends. Untroubled by success, the UUP and local Conservatives parted ways, with the bothersome local Conservatives eventually relaunching as a separate entity, Northern Ireland Conservatives, in June 2012.

The Nesbitt Years: Rebranding and Opposition

Empey stood down as leader in September 2010 and received a life peerage in 2011. His successor, Tom Elliott, was elected with a big mandate, obtaining 68 per cent of the 939 membership votes in defeating Basil McCrea. Elliott could not stop the electoral decline, as the UUP shed a further two seats and 1.7 per cent of its vote share in the 2011 Assembly election compared to the 2007 result. The party also lost 2.8 per cent of its vote in the same year's local government elections, relinquishing sixteen seats. With the UUP's local council seats reduced to ninety-nine, there was little solace to be taken from the DUP's vote share and tally also falling. Elliott quit as leader in March 2012, having held the leadership for a mere eighteen months. Whilst Elliott felt he had enjoyed much backing in rural areas, he also admitted that 'I was really struggling to gain support and respect in the Greater Belfast area, whether elected reps, our associations or the party members'.[44] Danny Kinahan concurs, claiming that some members were unhappy (unfairly) that the 'west was running the party'.[45] Elliott had built upon Empey's restructuring of the party to try and assert leadership authority: 'I started with a level of discipline and people didn't like it'.[46] This involved the removal of a very senior figure from both the party officer and party executive list and the suspension of a number of members.

The election of Mike Nesbitt as party leader in March 2012 was clear-cut, the Strangford MLA defeating the challenger, John McCallister, by 536 votes to 129 of the 1,770 members eligible to vote. McCallister opposed tactical election pacts with the DUP, viewing them as sectarian. He also urged the UUP to quit the Executive, arguing that 'we kid ourselves that voters see us as some sort of plucky internal opposition' to the DUP and Sinn Féin, whereas Nesbitt was at that stage still cautious about abandoning government, fearing diminished relevance.[47] McCallister quit the Party in 2013 to help establish the ill-fated NI21 Party, but resigned within a year and lost his Assembly seat in 2016.

Nesbitt's election appeared a logical choice in terms of restoring UUP electoral fortunes. A personable, popular former broadcaster from a liberal unionist background, Nesbitt enjoyed the advantages of local prominence following his successful regional broadcasting career. Although a political novice, it was thought that he might articulate the UUP's case via the media more plausibly than his predecessors. There may have been small questions over how much he could connect to working-class loyalists—an early offer to spend twenty-four hours with a deprived family 'because I think it's important to get a feel for what it's like'[48]—aroused a minor early controversy, but the UUP's initial electoral priority was to win back the unionist middle class who had abandoned the Party since the Belfast Agreement. Many working-class loyalists had deserted the UUP long before. Nesbitt's credentials as a modernizer were bolstered by the fact he only joined the UUP in 2010 and by his non-membership of the Orange Order. With the Order now claiming only 35,000 members[49] (a figure which nonetheless exceeded the total membership of all Northern Ireland's political parties combined) not belonging was perhaps of greater electoral value in broadening the UUP's appeal. Nesbitt told the UUP delegates in his leadership pitch, 'I don't want to be a super-Prod, I want to be a super unionist'.[50]

Nesbitt inherited problems in terms of his Party's inability to communicate messages, a low level of activism, and the propensity of maverick individuals to go on solo runs. Nesbitt was a firm subscriber to the idea of 'Country First, Party Second, Individual Third', although he acknowledged that not all within his Party were such adherents at the time of his elevation to the leadership, as 'there were individuals who were empowered to say whatever they like'.[51] He claimed that individuals were texting the contents of private party meetings, giving journalists a 'live update'.[52] Nesbitt stressed that, following the failure of UCUNF, there was 'no big idea' capable of transforming party fortunes. He acknowledged the after-effects of the 1998 deal were still present in his early UUP days:

> When I joined, people did not like canvassing, people did not like elections, because you could literally get a kicking on the doorstep in certain areas. I remember campaigning in a housing estate south of Belfast with Daphne Trimble [wife of David] and saying to her 'That was quite positive'. She laughed: 'Quite positive? David and I would come in here and after five minutes the security detail would say "that's it"'. And we only did it so we could say we canvassed. The reception was outright hostility.'[53]

Jim Nicholson was comfortably re-elected to the European Parliament for the UUP in 2014, but his first preference share of votes was down by nearly 4 per cent to 13.3 per cent, a new low for the UUP. That year's local elections offered some hope that a revival was under way, as the UUP's vote share rose by 1.1 per cent and the Party gained a notional eleven seats on redrawn boundaries, as the DUP lost fifteen.

It was the Westminster election of 2015 that yielded a breakthrough for the UUP. A key aim of Nesbitt was achieved as the UUP regained representation in the House of Commons, capturing two seats. Tom Elliott's success in Fermanagh and South Tyrone was aided by a unionist pact, with the DUP standing aside, but his defeat of Sinn Féin was still a notable performance. The accompanying capture of South Antrim by the UUP's Danny Kinahan from the DUP's William McCrea was a major coup. The UUP's vote share rose by only 0.8 per cent and its actual vote increased by 12,000, hardly dramatic and pact-assisted, but this was a fractionally bigger increase than that enjoyed by the DUP, whilst the two nationalist parties' vote percentage fell. The Party gathered for its annual conference later that year in good spirits, seemingly set on the road to recovery, with Nesbitt stating the UUP 'has not been in better shape for many years' and the Party Chairman declaring the election of two UUP MPs as 'transformational'.[54] It seemed a genuine revival. The UUP was also beginning to offer a distinguishing set of ideas: a new system of government and opposition at Stormont; a genuine, agreed Programme for Government in advance of a rush to grab ministerial portfolios via the d'hondt system; explicit acceptance that 'identity must no longer be conflated with sovereignty', and plans to increase inward investment and business start-ups.[55]

The 2016 Assembly elections marked the completion of a full set of contests under Nesbitt. Emboldened by the 2015 Westminster election result, the UUP entered the Stormont contest hopeful of capturing up to four DUP seats but gained none. The DUP's switch of leader from Peter Robinson to Arlene Foster in January that year forestalled any UUP revival. Foster ticked several UUP boxes and her appeal traversed internal unionist boundaries, spanning Church of Ireland moderates and harder line Presbyterians and Free Presbyterians; Orange and non-Orange Protestants; men and women and border and urban unionists. Untypical of the DUP, which prior to her elevation was only 27 per cent female and 28 per cent Church of Ireland, yet sharing its robustness, Foster's appeal seemed potentially broad. As a UUP member of a Coleraine focus group put it:

> when Arlene became Leader, we lost that momentum largely, because we had the momentum against Peter Robinson. But Arlene was a totally different figure, and I don't think we really countered that strongly enough. So, I think the campaign just . . . you know, we had very solid policy papers, a good manifesto, and all the candidates were excellent. I think it was one of the best slate of candidates we've ever had for Assembly, but I just think that the overall messaging was not as clear as the DUP. You know, the DUP, 'We're going to be in government. We want to be First Minister to stop Sinn Féin being First Minister,' and I think that's very difficult to go up against.[56]

UUP 'success' in 2016 therefore amounted to no more than holding the sixteen seats won in 2011, including the three where the UUP victor had subsequently defected from the party. The UUP's vote share fell, albeit by less than 1 per cent and the Party trailed the DUP by a distant 125,000 votes. After the 2016 contest, that left only the forensic brilliance-cum-pantomine villainy of the Traditional Unionist Voice's Jim Allister and the Independent Unionist Clare Sugden operating as unionists beyond the DUP–UUP umbrellas. Running fast to stay on the same spot was an unappealing outcome for a UUP membership hoping to make rapid inroads into the DUP's dominance.

The DUP return of thirty-eight seats matched its 2011 haul, reaffirming the party's seemingly hegemonic position. Of DUP candidates 86 per cent were elected, compared to 62 per cent of those fielded by the UUP. The 2016 contest destroyed any illusions of a rapid UUP recovery towards its pre-Belfast Agreement eminence. The Party Chairman insisted that the UUP now had 'a much stronger MLA team at Stormont that is firing on all cylinders' (half of the team of sixteen were new to the Assembly although six of the eight 'novices' had served as councillors) yet insisted that the leadership would be 'bringing forward proposals for amendments to the candidate selection process and how access to the central candidates list is achieved'.[57] Unless these changes were aimed exclusively at improving the quality of councillors, the proposals suggested continuing leadership concerns over the attributes of some elected representatives.

Whilst there was predictable criticism of the DUP's 'Stop Martin [McGuinness] becoming First Minister' approach, the 2016 outcome indicated continuing mileage in old-style sectarian head-counting. A DUP–Sinn Féin duopoly for almost a decade at Stormont had not eroded the mutual loathing of their support bases. Less than 1 per cent of DUP and UUP transfer votes went to Sinn Féin. DUP to DUP surpluses ran at over 70 per cent, with around 20 per cent going to the UUP. For all the talk of a new Northern Ireland and a mellow campaign lacking in Orange versus Green heat, ethnic bloc voting on traditional lines remained dominant.

Although the UUP's vote share fell less than the other main parties, that was damning with faint praise. The lack of representation in Belfast (just one MLA) was stark. The UUP struggled to explain clearly why voting for a sixteen-seat Assembly party was a better idea than opting for its bigger rival, given the communal head-counting problem. There were also issues of campaign management. DUP vote management remained very good. Only six candidates did not make it to the Assembly, compared to ten from the UUP, even though the UUP fielded far fewer candidates, twenty-six compared to the DUP's forty-four. With careful poster balances and campaigns for their candidates in different parts of each constituency, the spread of first preference votes between each DUP candidate was admirably narrow: the average differential between the vote for each DUP candidate and their nearest running mate in the poll was only 2 per cent, compared to almost 4 per cent for the UUP. The UUP's constituency strategies were less productive and the fielding of three candidates in both South and East Antrim veered on the side of excessive expectation unjustified by previous election outcomes.

There remained considerable difficulties for Nesbitt over how to attack the DUP. The UUP leader could not fight the last political 'war'—the Belfast Agreement—given its outcome for his party, however high the level of disdain towards the DUP for stealing UUP clothes. The UUP had won politically, given how the DUP had ultimately swallowed the Agreement's contents, but had been crushed electorally. During his time as leader, Nesbitt offered the occasional reminder of which party had moved most since 1998:

> The UUP has a credo: country first, party second, individual third... Let's remember where the DUP were during those negotiations [for the Belfast Agreement]. They were on the other side of the crush barriers shouting 'Judas' and 'traitor' and 'Lundy' at the Ulster Unionist Party.[58]

However, Nesbitt saw little mileage in continually rerunning a contest which had so bruised the UUP. As the DUP became increasingly Ulster Unionized, there was little space for the articulation of a distinctive UUP vision.

The UUP's inability to make gains in the 2016 Assembly elections made certain that the Party would enter opposition. The move had been foreshadowed by departure from the Executive in August 2015, the UUP leader stating that it was impossible to work with Sinn Féin whilst the Provisional IRA (PIRA) Army Council remained in business, PIRA members were widely viewed as involved in a revenge killing in Belfast that summer and Nesbitt's political response was informed by the security briefing he received from the Chief Constable of Northern Ireland, George Hamilton.

Quitting the Executive during that summer was popular within the UUP, 73 per cent of members favouring the move and only 11 per cent dissenting. Becoming part of an official opposition at Stormont was even more popular, unanimously endorsed by the Assembly Group and 86 per cent of members supporting the proposal, with a mere 3 per cent disagreeing. In terms of party unity at least, Nesbitt and his leadership team had made the correct calls. There seemed a chance the move might bolster UUP support. Although the public continued to support devolution, disaffection with the Assembly's achievements (or lack of them) had been evident for some time. In 2012, LucidTalk had reported the figure rating the Assembly's performance as good as a mere 8 per cent.[59]

Even if some UUP members may have held reservations over the extent of his enthusiasm for cross-community vote transfers and shared opposition, Nesbitt was ranked highly by many of the party faithful. On a zero (low ranking) to ten (highest) scale one-third gave Nesbitt the highest possible ranking and 79 per cent scored their leader at eight or above, with only 8 per cent of members rating him at five or below. Ultimately, Nesbitt's inability to regrow the UUP's shrunken electoral base can be attributed to many factors, but the idea that his party did not rate him is contradicted by the data.

One of the myths that had developed regarding Northern Ireland's consociational government was that it prohibited the creation of a formal opposition. Whilst there was a requirement for the Executive to be drawn from both communities, this did not rule out an opposition formed from representatives of one or both communities, or from the politically non-aligned. Ironically, it was the opponent Nesbitt defeated in the party leadership contest of 2012, John McCallister, whose bill paved the way for the formal creation of an opposition. McCallister's bill provided for opposition funds and debating time. Following the flatlining of the 2016 election, it made sense for the UUP to at least experiment with opposition, a popular move within the party. According to Reg Empey, when the party took the plunge, the reaction among executive members was, 'Why the hell didn't we do this years ago?'[60]

The UUP's place in government since 2007 had been that of bit-player, marginalized and derided by the DUP and Sinn Féin. Nesbitt argued, 'You had two bigger parties bossing the smaller two parties... we are now unshackled.'[61] The UUP's focus was now upon providing an effective cross-community oppos- ition. Nesbitt indicated how serious he was in straddling the sectarian divide when the SDLP leader, Colum Eastwood, addressed the UUP conference in October 2016. Although Eastwood received a standing ovation from the bulk of the conference attendees, Nesbitt surprised some by going further than his nationalist counterpart in declaring 'vote Mike, get Colum; vote Colum, get Mike'. Three UUP councillors defected to the DUP during the following week. One, Graham Craig, branded the UUP leader a 'hapless amateur... the prop- osition that "vote Mike, get Colum" is any more appealing to unionist voters than "vote Mike, get Mike" has proved to be incredulous'.[62] Another of the October 2016 defectors, Aaron Callan, had previously used his twitter account to compare the DUP leadership to that of North Korea's yet this did not inhibit his willingness to jump ship, such was his dismay at Nesbitt's approach. The UUP had hoped the defector traffic had ceased, even enjoying the return to its ranks from the DUP of Lisburn councillor, Jenny Palmer, amid claims of DUP 'bullying', with Palmer being elected a UUP Assembly member in 2016. It was clear, however, that there remained discontent within UUP ranks. Yet there was also significant enthusiasm for opposition on the lines proposed by Nesbitt. As a Derry focus group member put it: 'I think the SDLP and Ulster Unionists would actually dovetail much better than the Ulster Unionists and the DUP.'[63]

The questions begged were what would the UUP oppose as the fledgling opposition and how could opposition boost the electoral fortunes of the party, given that roles in the Executive had achieved so little? The prominent commentator and former Director of Communications for the Party, Alex Kane, summarized appropriately what was needed:

[Opposition] means more, much more, than complaining about the DUP–Sinn Féin carve-up, because that strategy didn't deliver in 2011 or 2016... It means a careful, costed thought-through deconstruction of the Programme for Govern- ment and a careful-costed thought-through programme alternative to it. It means an end to pacts with the DUP. It means unnerving and wrong-footing the Executive. It means looking like, with the SDLP, a government-in-waiting.[64]

Yet the difficulty lay in how to how to achieve these requirements. A clear Executive Programme for Government was not necessarily sufficiently discernible to oppose. Whilst the 2014 Stormont House and 2015 Fresh Start agreements sketched some outlines, joined-up government was regularly accompanied by DUP–Sinn Féin 'fiefdomry' and expediency, making the UUP's targets difficult to pin down with precision.

It was unclear what policies could be opposed within the Executive, as distinct from objecting to the way it conducted its business. Nesbitt aspired to opposition as a means to achieving better government. The UUP could highlight particularly unsatisfactory episodes and heavily criticized Arlene Foster's previous role as Minister for Enterprise, Trade, and Investment when presiding over the Renewable Heat Incentive scheme, which the audit office reported as widely abused and whose failings would cost hundreds of millions of pounds.

A further difficulty for the UUP lay in the party's legitimate claim that the DUP had stolen its political ideas. If that was the case, why oppose? As one elected representative put it, albeit a councillor not an MLA, 'there's very little difference between our party and the DUP now'.[65] Whilst the vast bulk of the UUP backed moving into opposition, there were a few discordant voices. One councillor regarded going into opposition as needless self-exclusion, diminishing the party:

we were out on the doorsteps talking, and people said to me, 'Are you going to be in the Executive, or are you going to be out of it?' I said, 'As far as I'm concerned, we're going to be in the Executive'. I don't think it's the right decision. I really don't, because, although we now have an opposition, things have changed. To me, it's better being in there. In fact, we have lost people since the Assembly election from the Ulster Unionist Party. I went out of my way to speak to some of these people, and I said to them, 'Look, please don't resign'. It fell on deaf ears. I said, 'Whilst you're in, you can fight. Whenever you're on the outside, you're relying on other people to battle for you'.[66]

A Coleraine member articulated the problem and the possibilities of opposition;

It's very difficult. You need to have very capable MLAs, who are willing to articulate a different view of how government should operate. One of the key aspects that they haven't [got] from the Belfast Agreement is cooperative government. You know, it's them and us government at the moment, and that's the one area we could attack them on, if we have a strong SDLP. You know, when Trimble became First Minister, the relationship in the First and Deputy Minister Office wasn't very good, but if we could articulate and show that, if we have a strong

Ulster Unionist Party, and say, a strong SDLP, then we could create a very cooperative, progressive, future-looking government, you know, that may attract the voters across. That's a very difficult message to sell, because fear is a very potent element within politics here.[67]

Danny Kennedy, one of the few UUP MLAs to have served as a minister, felt increasingly undermined in office by the DUP, drawing the conclusion that for Stormont to work it 'needs a level of power-sharing we haven't seen'. Yet Kennedy was also cautious over opposition:

the idea of jumping up and down for five years and simply complaining about things, is not very attractive. It needs to be properly structured in a way that doesn't leave you simply looking mean spirited and offering sour grapes. Because, an opposition is not simply an opposition. An opposition, to perform its duty, is to be an alternative government, a government in waiting. I think we forget that sometimes. I just have a concern that jumping up and down for five years is not going to do it.[68]

Moreover, whilst the idea of a cross-community government-in-waiting held some appeal, parties in Northern Ireland do not get rich by appeals across the sectarian divide—as Alliance's modest half-century of non-achievement shows. The DUP and Sinn Féin did not look like a joined-up government in waiting prior to elections. They appealed to their respective bases as the parties more likely to achieve a share of the limited spoils for their bloc. The main device used by the DUP was a Petition of Concern in the Assembly, by which thirty MLAs could demand that a decision require parallel (i.e. cross-community) consent. Between 2011 and 2016, of the 115 Petitions of Concern, eighty-six were triggered by the DUP. Given the UUP could not really 'out-tough' the DUP in terms of image, it was perhaps natural for Nesbitt's party to search for votes among a mixture of moderate unionists who still eschewed the DUP but did not necessarily vote, Alliance-leaning floaters, and lower preference transferees from the SDLP. The UUP would struggle to interest non-voters, most of whom do not identify as unionist (or nationalist).

The UUP's move into opposition was predictably derided by the DUP as desperate and enforced by electoral failure not strategy. Whilst a pragmatic Westminster election pact in 2015 had briefly thawed relations, the DUP and UUP leaderships continued to needle each other. Nesbitt complained that 'the DUP's whole being is about trying to destroy other unionist parties' and complained about 'very personal attacks' from the First Minister, Arlene Foster, blaming the 'extraordinary influence' of the special advisers she inherited from her predecessor, Peter Robinson.[69] Foster responded merely by increasing the amount of fire directed at the UUP and its leader, using her 2016 leadership speech to scorn Nesbitt's Opposition alliance with the SDLP's Colum Eastwood as akin to that of the old BBC television comedy characters

'Steptoe and Son', with Nesbitt portrayed as the 'bitter old man' and the pair accused of 'selling junk'. The DUP used the conference to unveil their latest recruits from the UUP, councillors Callan and Craig.

UUP–DUP Divergence: The 2016 EU Referendum

The 2016 UK referendum on EU membership at least offered an opportunity for the UUP to display clear policy difference from the DUP. Riskily, the UUP declared support for the UK remaining in the EU, a position backed by most MLAs (although not by the Party's next leader, Robin Swann) and the over-whelmingly majority of the 100-strong ruling Executive. Once a Eurosceptic party which had advocated quitting the European Economic Community in the 1975 referendum, the UUP's attitude had changed during the following four decades. Whilst always less Eurosceptic than the DUP, whose former leader Ian Paisley had once described the EU as 'the mother of harlots and abominations of the Earth',[70] the UUP stressed the primacy of the nation state and national sovereignty. Under James Molyneaux's leadership, the UUP moved from being anti-Maastricht Treaty to offering support to a beleaguered Conservative government under John Major, to the chagrin of the DUP who accused the UUP of having been bought.

By 2016, the UUP had become persuaded of the economic case for Northern Ireland's place in the UK, given that the region had been a clear net financial beneficiary, via a combination of peace funding and agricultural subsidies.[71] As Northern Ireland voted to remain in the UK by 56 per cent to 44 per cent, the UUP could at least claim to be in tune with public opinion. Yet UUP leadership backing for the Remain case was not matched by its members or supporters. UUP members are more likely to support Brexit (44 per cent) than not (39 per cent) but a sizeable percentage (17 per cent) are unsure. More than half (58 per cent) of UUP voters backed Brexit in the 2016 referendum.[72] Some former senior party figures, perhaps most notably David Trimble, also backed Brexit. There was no evidence of regret among UUP supporters: almost twelve months later, at the 2017 Westminster election, 63 per cent of the UUP's supporters believed it was right to leave the EU. Those UUP voters were evenly divided on whether Brexit would harden the border but were mainly sanguine over the risk of a united Ireland being brought closer, only 20 per cent believing this more likely.[73]

Immediately following the referendum, the UUP leadership accepted the UK-wide referendum verdict, insisting that 'the days of being a "Remainer" or "Brexiteer" are over'.[74] The UUP issued its ten-point plan, essentially for a 'soft' Brexit, allowing 'unfettered access to the EU's Single Market' and safe-guards for the Common Travel Area.[75] The UUP saw itself as 'Euro-realist'. The

Party's immediate post-Brexit referendum annual conference was addressed by a Czech member of the Alliance of Conservatives and Reformists in Europe, which became the third largest group in the European Parliament in 2014. Whilst holding no doubts that the UK-wide referendum result had to be respected, the UUP was cognizant that a hard Brexit would exacerbate existing divisions in Northern Ireland. Mike Nesbitt acknowledged that: 'The Brexit vote had really upset soft Irish nationalists...Unionists would be well served to recognize the disquiet. I have no desire to see the border cease to be invisible.'[76] The UUP's pro-Remain stance appeared to make sense, given its support among the party's upper echelons and the distinctiveness from the DUP it offered. Recognition of the significant EU financial contribution to Northern Ireland, not least in terms of generous agricultural subsidies to some of the UUP's farming support base, seemed a credible position.

Although younger voters are most closely associated with a pro-EU view, student UUP members tended to adopt this position solely on pragmatic grounds, one commenting:

> I worked out in Brussels, I saw first-hand the red tape, the bureaucracy, and the waste of money that goes on. You know, the monthly trip from Brussels to Strasbourg, I still can't quite get head around it...But, then again, with regard to staying in, Northern Ireland, I believe, unlike the UK, on the whole, Northern Ireland gets more financially through peace funding and single farm payments than it gives in. So, I think that's a big issue. Then there's the issue of the border and what happens, and where the border will be.[77]

Despite taking opposing sides during the referendum, there was no post-referendum difference between the UUP and DUP. Both wanted a continuing soft border but not special status for Northern Ireland within the EU, as articulated by former MLA Philip Smith:

> The last thing we want is passport checks at Stranraer, or Cairnryan, or Heathrow. At the end of the day, people need to remember, the bulk of Northern Ireland's trade outside of Northern Ireland is with Great Britain. £9.8 billion comes every year in a subvention. Whilst Europe is important in Northern Ireland because we're net beneficiaries, etc. Britain is key, because without that, we're bust, politically, economically, and socially. So, the link to Britain is our most essential thing. The Republic comes second, obviously, because we do £2 billion trade, or whatever, and because of the porousness of the border now, it is crucially important. We need to do something to secure that. Sinn Féin and the SDLP, obviously, are pushing for a more formalized approach, I mean, they see this as an opportunity to put some clear green water between Northern Ireland and GB. The danger is that it becomes an orange–green thing, rather than looking at the pragmatism of what actually will assist Northern Ireland from an economic and social perspective.[78]

2017: Double Electoral Reverse and a New Leader

Nesbitt's slim chance of convincing sceptics of the value of his electoral approach, based on outreach and cross-community transfers, disappeared in the fevered atmosphere of the snap 2017 Assembly election. Martin McGuinness engaged in one final significant act for Sinn Féin in resigning as Deputy First Minister in January, effectively also resigning Arlene Foster. The dramatic collapse of the institutions followed the furore over the Renewable Heating Incentive (RHI) scheme, under which the DUP-controlled Trade and Enterprise Ministry had offered overgenerous and uncapped subsidies for switchers to greener fuels.

The UUP believed that public anger with Arlene Foster, the departmental minister-cum-DUP leader who had presided over the scheme, would see a substantial shift of unionist votes from the DUP to the UUP. Nesbitt perceived the contest as a referendum on RHI. Regularly criticized for her handling of the crisis, Foster had not, however, misread the mood within unionism. The DUP's vote share fell by a mere 1 per cent and the UUP's vote rose by a paltry 0.3 per cent. Foster had however, misread the mood within nationalism, where a combination of the RHI debacle, Foster's belligerence in calling Sinn Féin 'crocodiles' always coming back for more, failure to make progress on an Irish Language Act or 'legacy issues', Brexit, and sympathy for the ailing McGuinness, allowed Sinn Féin to mobilize its vote, putting on 4 per cent. For the DUP, it was a poor election in terms of seat losses. With the Assembly reduced in size from 108 to 90 members, Foster's party found it impossible to defend their third seat in eight out of nine constituencies and losses elsewhere meant a net reduction of ten seats. Yet the expectant UUP also lost six MLAs as unionism's majority disappeared for the first time in the history of the state. Nesbitt was blamed for having urged UUP voters to straddle the sectarian divide rather than stress unionist unity via lower preference transfers to unionist candidates. Indeed, he made clear he would transfer a personal lower preference vote to the SDLP, to the chagrin of those many unionists whose pro-Union instincts transcended all other sentiments.

Nesbitt resigned immediately, taking full responsibility. He had helped modernize his party and brought in some talent, fast-tracked to MLA candidature, but his overarching projects of advancing his party electorally whilst diminishing the Orange versus Green zero-sum game dominance of Northern Ireland politics could not be judged a success. Echoing laments of other former UUP leaders, Nesbitt regretted how Northern Ireland seemed 'more polarised than ever', his valedictory statement testifying to an aspiration for a non-sectarian Northern Ireland: 'Someday Northern Ireland will vote in a normal democracy; we will vote in a post-sectarian election, but it is now clear it will not happen during the duration of my political life.' Nesbitt had been faithful to his mantra of 'country first, party second, individual third', but to little avail. There had been mixed messages, as criticisms of the DUP and opposition to sectarianism had been tempered at Westminster elections by the necessity of pro-Union pacts fuelling sectarian head-counting.

Nesbitt argued that the biggest single difference between his own party and the DUP was that the UUP's power-sharing was voluntary, not on sufferance. Noble sentiment could not, however, energize the unionist electorate. He had encouraged relatively moderate, 'small u' unionists into the party as a means of its rebranding. Some, such as Doug Beattie, Andy Allen, and Steve Aiken, had, from a unionist perspective, impeccable military credentials—'the military wing of the unionist party' as one jokingly described the group.[79] This background made them potentially awkward for the DUP to combat, as their robustness as unionists and selfless service for their country was nonetheless matched by their social liberalism. Aiken insisted that 'We need to maintain the centre ground, and we need to give the centre ground direction and guidance. If we can give the centre ground direction and guidance, the people of Northern Ireland will see that that is the best way forward.'[80] The difficulty, as the Alliance Party has found over several decades, is that the centre ground remains very narrow. It is not where most voters—as distinct from the electorate as a whole—are often found.

There appeared to be only two possible candidates to replace the departed leader: Doug Beattie, whose aforementioned military service could impress UUP hardliners who might otherwise demur at his liberal instincts such as unequivocal support for same-sex marriage, and Robin Swann, the Chief Whip, whose impeccable Orange credentials could reassure the UUP faithful of a return to more traditionalist offerings. With Beattie declining to stand, Swann became UUP leader without an election in April 2017, the fifth man at the helm in twelve years, during which time very little electoral progress had been evident.

Swann's electoral capacities were soon to be tested. Ten days after his accession, he learnt that he would be obliged to lead his party through a difficult Westminster election, defending the only major tangible successes of recent times, the UUP's two parliamentary seats. Given that one of those was achieved by a pan-unionist pact, in Fermanagh and South Tyrone, it was logical for this to be replicated. Yet the DUP's standing aside could not save Tom Elliott's seat this time as Sinn Féin, to the surprise of few, recaptured the seat. Swann suggested a need for the Electoral Office to examine the number of proxy and postal votes.[81] Beyond Fermanagh and South Tyrone, the 'DUP had already concluded that the UUP was too weak to push for anything'[82] in terms of pacts and was determined to avenge its 2015 loss of South Antrim. Danny Kinahan thus lost his seat to the DUP, despite increasing his vote. This left Swann in the position Nesbitt had inherited, steering a party bereft of Westminster representation, incapable of making Assembly seat gains, devoid of a clear message to take to the Unionist electorate, and seemingly unsellable beyond that electorate.

Although the UUP had fought hard and only lost their two seats narrowly, the 2017 Westminster election highlighted not just the lack of appeal relative to the DUP but also the problem of capturing younger electors eschewing traditional politics. The MLA Robbie Butler recalls speaking at a school:

> Mark Devenport [the BBC Northern Ireland political editor], who hosted it, said, 'Hands up who's interested in voting in the Assembly election?' There were 120 17 and 18 year-olds, and not one hand, not one hand. 'Hands up who's interested in voting on Europe'. Every single hand went up. I'm 44 years of age, and I thought, have I missed something here? Have I missed something? ... I was shocked that the kids weren't interested. They're disconnected. They don't like the politics.[83]

The UUP is not alone in struggling to connect. Only one-third of 18 to 24 year-olds voted in the 2017 Assembly election. However, of that one-third, 32 per cent voted DUP whereas less one in ten of that age group voted UUP. The party's image as an organization in long-term decline was apparent. The 2017 humiliations revived the possibility of fusion with the DUP into a single unionist party. It remained a distant prospect amid the mutual enmity, but there had been several discussions between 2009 and 2012. In December 2009, the Orange Order convened unionist unity talks at Schomberg House, Grand Lodge HQ. In January 2010, the UUP, DUP, and even the Conservatives (given the UCUNF alliance) held talks. Towards the close of Tom Elliott's leadership, but without his authority, senior DUP and UUP figures canvassed the prospect, the DUP representatives reporting to their leader, Peter Robinson. Yet the message from a succession of leaders, Empey, Elliott, Nesbitt, and Swann, did not vary, each insistent there would be no unity on their watch.

Swann used his first party conference speech, in Armagh in October 2017, to offer a reversion to a more traditional unionism. Whilst the leader eschewed such a term, branding his party as radical moderates, the days of flirtations with the SDLP were clearly over, the efforts of his predecessor as leader unmentioned in the leadership address. 'Vote Robin Get Unionism' was the none-too-subliminal message. Not unreasonably, Swann sought to focus upon the inadequacies of the DUP's governance. In his role as Chief Whip he had been effective in encouraging UUP MLAs to be 'proactive in getting the answers to the questions the Executive don't want asked'.[84]

Swann's opening address also attempted to place the UUP on morally higher ground than their opponents, condemning continuing associations of other parties with paramilitary groups. The robustness of his own unionism was apparent. In arguing for a voluntary coalition, Swann offered stances on contentious issues as robust as those articulated by the DUP. His rejection of an Irish Language Act, as the primary example, was well-received by the faithful. Only 5 per cent of UUP members believe that Irish should have equal status to English in Northern Ireland and 93 per cent think that English should be the only official language. The UUP would no longer be seen as 'soft unionists'.

Conclusion

The UUP has continued to struggle since the rapid electoral decline at the expense of the DUP in the immediate post Belfast Agreement years. The debilitating effects of the Agreement have been difficult to stem. Leadership altruism in selling a controversial deal was followed by much pain. A lack of confidence within the UUP over its greatest achievement is evident. By 2017, a wafer-thin majority, 53 per cent of members, said they would again vote yes to the Agreement in another referendum, a figure lower than the 59 per cent who backed the deal in 1998.

For many electors, the image of the UUP is of an organization whose best years are behind it, an ageing outfit struggling for relevance. The UUP has made serious efforts in recent years to rebrand and recruit a younger demographic, not without some success. Seventy-two students signed up in a single day at Queen's University Belfast in Autumn 2016.[85] Yet rebranding and relaunching has also highlighted ongoing problems. The disorderly management of decline between the Good Friday and St Andrews deals was followed by a series of experiments, the kindest adjectives for which were 'brave' and 'unproven'. An alliance with the Conservatives, the promotion of cross-community voting, and the march into opposition all failed to yield electoral reward. The party entered elections in 2017 trying to be cross-community for the Assembly election where it made sense, whilst being unapologetically pan-unionist for a Fermanagh and South Tyrone parliamentary contest. Although unsuccessful in 2017, such mixed messages had worked in 2015 and done no harm at least in 2016.

The rapidity of rise of the DUP and demise of the UUP may, ironically, provide some grounds for optimism, indicating how quickly political fortunes can be reversed. However, there is little indication at present of a 'see-saw' in unionist politics. The divisions over the Belfast Agreement have cooled in fervour but their legacy is evident. There remains a sense of anger among many within the UUP that they were punished for political risk-taking and annoyance that the DUP prospered by condemning, then accepting, those risks. Railing about the perceived unfairness of politics will achieve nothing, however, for the modern UUP. Acceptance of what happened and the articulation of constructive, liberal but constitutionally robust unionism appears the only way forward. The task of taking on the DUP became even harder after the 2017 Westminster election. The UUP's representation was removed at a time when the DUP's had never been more relevant, given the precarious parliamentary arithmetic for the Conservatives. The Party Chairman's reference to 'disappointing outcomes' was the mildest interpretation of UUP election fortunes in 2017.[86]

From the margins, the UUP could only acknowledge the DUP's fortune and skill in demanding largesse for Northern Ireland. As the UUP leader admitted, 'it would be churlish of me not to welcome the money'.[87] DUP hegemony presented a huge challenge. Swann denied that he was moving his party back to the right in response, although it was clear that from hereon he preferred to fish in unionist waters for votes, rather than test other seas.[88] For all the bravery of the Nesbitt era in reaching out across sectarian silos, the chances of the UUP building recovery on seizing a sizeable section of the Catholic electorate are vanishingly low. The UUP's current problem is not enough Protestant unionists voting for it. Catholic nationalist backing would be a miracle cure.

Carving a niche position is difficult given that, as one elected representative put it, 'the DUP has become more like us, and we've stayed pretty much the same'.[89] There is a market for what a former UUP MP described as the UUP's 'middle ground unionism—just right of centre'[90] and Swann appeared to be steering a course in that direction. The UUP's task is to convince the unionist electorate that it can better defend unionist interests than the DUP. The UUP leader insists there cannot be a single unionist party, 'because the unionist people is not a homogenous group that go in one direction ... if we'd one party tomorrow, we'd probably have three on Wednesday'.[91] The UUP has returned to its core unionist base. Whether it can regain its former position as the primary vehicle of unionist voter choice is doubtful.

Notes

1. P. Mitchell, G. Evans, and B. O'Leary, 'Extremist Outbidding in Ethnic Party Systems is Not Inevitable: Tribune Parties in Northern Ireland', *Political Studies*, 57.2 (2009), 397–421.
2. Interview with Adrian Cochrane-Watson, 11 Mar. 2016.
3. B. Hayes and I. McAllister, 'Who Voted for Peace? Public Support for the 1998 Northern Ireland Agreement', *Irish Political Studies*, 16 (2001), 73–94.
4. J. Tonge and J. Evans, 'Party Members and the Belfast Agreement', *Irish Political Studies*, 17.2 (2002), 59–73.

5. Interview with David Trimble, 30 June 2016.
6. Interview with Tom Elliott, 13 Apr. 2016.
7. Interview with UUP councillor and executive member, 20 May 2016.
8. Interview with Philip Smith, 30 Oct. 2016.
9. Interview with David Trimble, 30 June 2016.
10. Paul Bew, 'Trimble Left Spinning in the Wind', *The Times*, 6 July 1999.
11. David Trimble. 'Sinn Féin have Not Yet Proved they are True Democrats', *Guardian*, 15 July 1999.
12. Interview with Adrian Cochrane-Watson, 11 Mar. 2016.
13. Interview with Danny Kennedy, 28 Jan. 2016.
14. Interview with Ross Hussey, 27 Jan. 2016.
15. e.g. interview with Mark Cosgrove, 4 Dec. 2016.
16. J. Tonge, *The New Northern Irish Politics?* Basingstoke: Macmillan, 2005.
17. D. Godson, *Himself Alone: David Trimble and the Ordeal of Unionism*, London: HarperCollins, 2004.
18. Derry focus group, 19 May 2016.
19. Interview with Colin McCusker, 3 Mar. 2016.
20. Interview with Colin McCusker, 3 Mar. 2016.
21. J. Tonge, M. Braniff, T. Hennessey, J. W. McAuley, and S. A. Whiting, *The Democratic Unionist Party: From Protest to Power*, Oxford: Oxford University Press, 2014.
22. Coleraine focus group member, 18 May 2016.
23. Interview with UUP councillor and executive member, 20 May 2016.
24. R. Gomez and J. Tonge, 'New Members as Party Modernisers: The Case of the Democratic Unionist Party in Northern Ireland', *Electoral Studies*, 42 (2016), 65–74.
25. Interview with Mark Cosgrove, 4 Dec. 2016.
26. Interview with UUP councillor and executive member, 20 May 2016.
27. Interview with Ross Hussey, 27 Jan. 2016.
28. Interview with Danny Kennedy, 28 Jan. 2016.
29. Interview with Sandra Overend, 28 Jan. 2016.
30. Tony Blair letter to David Trimble, 10 Apr. 1998, cited in Ulster Unionist Party, *Manifesto 2001*, Belfast: UUP, 2001, 7.
31. Democratic Unionist Party, *Leadership to Put Things Right*, Belfast: DUP, 2001, 2.
32. Ulster Unionist Party, *Manifesto 2003*, Belfast: UUP, 2003, 2–3.
33. Democratic Unionist Party, *Assembly Election Manifesto*, Belfast: DUP, 2003, 10.
34. Democratic Unionist Party, *Towards a New Agreement*, Belfast: DUP, 2003, 19.
35. Interview with Hazel Legge, 10 Mar. 2016.
36. Interview with Mark Cosgrove, 4 Dec. 2016.
37. Ulster Unionist Party, *The St Andrews Agreement: The Real Story*, Belfast: UUP, 2007, 1.
38. Interview with David Trimble, 30 June 2016.
39. Interview with Reg Empey, 30 June 2016.
40. Interview with Danny Kinahan, 13 Apr. 2016.
41. Interview with Mark Cosgrove, 4 Dec. 2016.
42. Interview with Sandra Overend, 28 Jan. 2016.

43. Interview with Tom Elliott, 13 Apr. 2016.

44. Interview with Tom Elliott, 13 Apr. 2016.

45. Interview with Danny Kinahan, 13 Apr. 2016.

46. Interview with Tom Elliott, 13 Apr. 2016.

47. *News Letter*, 2 Apr. 2012, 'Shock at scale of Nesbitt andslide', 6.

48. *Belfast Telegraph*, 3 Apr. 2012, 'It's Day Four at the Top of the UUP', 4.

49. J. McAuley, J. Tonge, and A. Mycock, *Loyal to the Core? Orangeism and Britishness in Northern Ireland*, Dublin: Irish Academic Press, 2011.

50. *News Letter*, 2 Apr. 2012, 'Shock at scale of Nesbitt andslide', 7.

51. Interview with Mike Nesbitt, 16 Dec. 2016.

52. Interview with Mike Nesbitt, 16 Dec. 2016.

53. Interview with Mike Nesbitt, 16 Dec. 2016.

54. Ulster Unionist Party, *Conference 2015*, Belfast: UUP, 2015.

55. Ulster Unionist Party, *Our Vision for You—The Voter*, Belfast: UUP, 2016.

56. Coleraine focus group member, 18 May 2016.

57. R. Empey, 'Report from Lord Empey of Shandon': Belfast: Ulster Unionist Party Conference, 2016, 4.

58. BBC Northern Ireland, *Sunday Politics*, 5 June 2016.

59. *Belfast Telegraph*, 12 June 2012, 4. 'Stormont's Rating is a Greek Tragedy'.

60. Interview with Reg Empey, 30 June 2016.

61. BBC Northern Ireland, *Sunday Politics*, 5 June 2016.

62. Cited in *Belfast Telegraph*, <http://www.belfasttelegraph.co.uk/news/northern-ireland/uup-defector-craig-brands-mike-nesbitt-an-amateur-35168502.html>, 28 Oct. 2016.

63. Derry focus group member, 19 May 2016.

64. Alex Kane, <http://www.belfasttelegraph.co.uk/opinion/news-analysis/what-mike-nesbitt-must-tell-the-ulster-unionist-conference-tomorrow-35148055.html>, *Belfast Telegraph*, 24 Oct. 2016, accessed Jan. 2017.

65. Interview with UUP councillor and executive member, 20 May 2016.

66. Interview with UUP councillor and executive member, 20 May 2016.

67. Coleraine focus group member, 18 May 2016.

68. Interview with Danny Kennedy, 28 Jan. 2016.

69. *Belfast Telegraph*, <http://www.belfasttelegraph.co.uk/news/northern-ireland/arlene-foster-letting-sinn-Féin-off-the-hook-by-focusing-attacks-on-unionist-rivals-claims-uup-leader-mike-nesbitt-35107479.html>, 6 Oct., accessed Feb. 2017.

70. Cited in E. Moloney and A. Pollok, *Paisley*, Dublin: Poolbeg, 1986, 405.

71. J. Tonge, 'The Impact of Withdrawal from the European Union upon Northern Ireland', *Political Quarterly*, 87.3 (2016), 338–42.

72. J. Garry, 'The EU Referendum Vote in Northern Ireland: Implications for our Understanding of Citizens' Political Views and Behaviour': Northern Ireland Assembly Knowledge Exchange Seminar Series, 6, 2016; J. Garry and J. Coakley, 'Brexit: Understanding why people voted as they did in the choice of a lifetime', *News Letter*, 15 Oct. 2016, available at <http://www.newsletter.co.uk/news/brexit-understanding-why-people-voted-as-they-did-in-the-choice-of-a-lifetime-1-7630272>, accessed Feb. 2017.

73. Northern Ireland General Election study 2017.

74. Ulster Unionist Party, *A Vision for Northern Ireland outside the EU*, Belfast: UUP, 2016, 2.

75. UUP, *Vision for Northern Ireland*, 3.

76. Interview with Mike Nesbitt, 16 Dec. 2016.

77. Young Unionists focus group member, 10 Mar. 2016.

78. Interview with Philip Smith, 30 Oct. 2016.

79. Interview with Steve Aiken, 20 May 2017.

80. Interview with Steve Aiken, 20 May 2017.

81. Interview with Robin Swann, 14 Aug. 2017.

82. Alex Kane, 'UUP could soon be in a fight for its very survival if election doesn't go well', *News Letter*, 15 May 2017, 9.

83. Interview with Robbie Butler, 19 Oct. 2016.

84. Ulster Unionist Party, *Conference 2016*, Belfast, UUP, 2016.

85. Ulster Young Unionist Council, *Annual Report 2016*, Belfast, UUP, 2016.

86. Ulster Unionist Party, *Conference 2017*, Belfast, UUP, 2017.

87. Interview with Robin Swann, 14 Aug. 2017.

88. *News Letter*, 19 Oct. 2017, 'Robin Swann. I haven't moved UUP to the right at all', 3.

89. Interview with Jeff Dudgeon, 20 May 2016.

90. Interview with Tom Elliott, 13 Apr. 2016.

91. *News Letter*, 19 Oct. 2017, 'UUP leader rules out any prospect of single unionist party', 2.

4

Who are the UUP Members—and What do they Believe?

Having explored the political trajectory of the UUP, relegated from power to the margins, we now examine the organization's membership. Notwithstanding its political and electoral difficulties in recent decades, the UUP remains a sizeable entity, surprisingly still containing more members, if not activists, than the DUP. Twenty years after the Belfast Agreement that caused so many of those problems, the UUP retained a membership approaching 2,000. But who are those members? Where are they based? And what do they want? This chapter examines the demographic and structural bases of UUP membership. The chapter depicts what motivated members to join the UUP and charts when they joined. We analyse their social and economic backgrounds. National identity, religious, and gendered aspects of that membership are covered in later chapters. The focus in this section is upon providing a comprehensive overview of most other aspects of the UUP membership.

The Demography and Geography of Membership

Perhaps the most striking aspect of UUP membership is the number of long-serving members, people who have spent most of their life in the party. As Table 4.1 shows, the largest grouping, in terms of when members joined, is that of the '1966 and earlier' category.

Given that such a large percentage of members have stuck with the UUP through thick and thin, it can be deduced that the Party commands very considerable brand loyalty. The UUP can be mildly encouraged by an increase in joiners in recent years, a riposte to those who perceived the Party as undergoing a slow death. The appeal of the DUP shrank the UUP's Westminster and council seat shares more than it shrank the overall party size. Clearly the scale and quality of defections was damaging to the UUP, but stocks have

Table 4.1 Period of joining
the Ulster Unionist Party (%)

2012–2016	15.7
2007–2011	10.0
2003–2006	5.9
1998–2002	9.1
1992–1997	9.7
1987–1991	5.3
1982–1986	6.8
1977–1981	5.1
1972–1976	6.1
1967–1971	5.3
1966 or earlier	18.5
Not sure	2.5

at least been partly replenished. Just over one-quarter of the UUP's members have joined since 2007. The leanest years for recruitment were when the UUP, in common with Northern Ireland's other political parties, was powerless under direct rule.

Most UUP members are married (65 per cent). The percentages 'living as married' (2.3 per cent), divorced (1.8 per cent), or separated (1.4 per cent) are all low. Single people account for 14.7 per cent of members, compared to one-quarter of the DUP's membership, and amid the high average age, there is a sizeable percentage (12.6 per cent) of widowed members, more than twice the percentage found in the DUP.[1] Given the high average age, nearly two-thirds of members do not have dependent children. The educational profile of the UUP is very similar to that of the DUP. The largest category is of degree-holders, at 35 per cent, followed by those with no formal qualifications, at 22 per cent. A clear contrast with the DUP lies in the balance between those working full-time and retirees. Of those working, both parties contain a large percentage of self-employed individuals, 28 per cent in the DUP and 33 per cent in the UUP.[2] Trade union membership is held by only 15 per cent of UUP members, although the high level of retirees and high rates of self-employment during working lives partly explain the low figure, as a further 28 per cent used to belong to a trade union. A similar percentage used to belong to the Armed Forces, with 2 per cent currently serving.

The geography of UUP membership provides an interesting contrast with the DUP. Figure 4.1 provides the data for the UUP's geographical distribution and Figure 4.2 those for the DUP.

The UUP does reasonably well in membership percentages in the south and west of Northern Ireland (albeit not in County Londonderry) and maintains a traditional stronghold in Fermanagh. Whilst the defection of Arlene Foster to the DUP in 2003 clearly hurt the UUP, as she took numerous followers, the UUP still has a very sizeable presence in a county which provides only a very

County % of membership

0.6

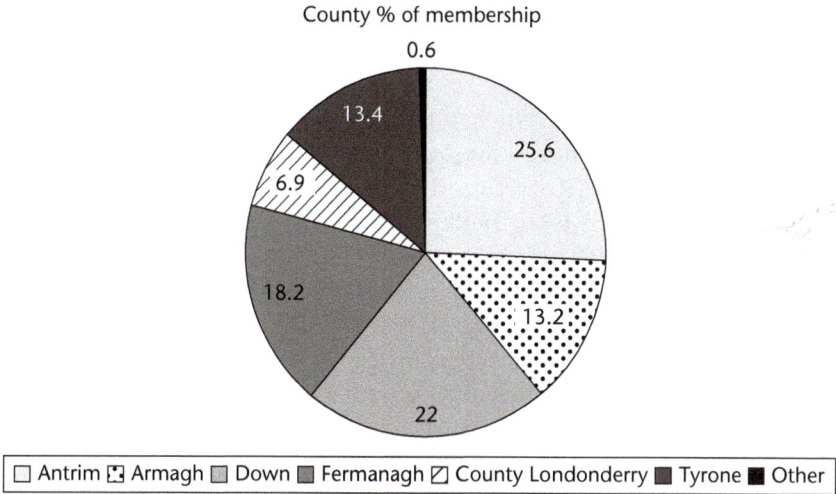

Figure 4.1 Geographical distribution of UUP members by county (%)

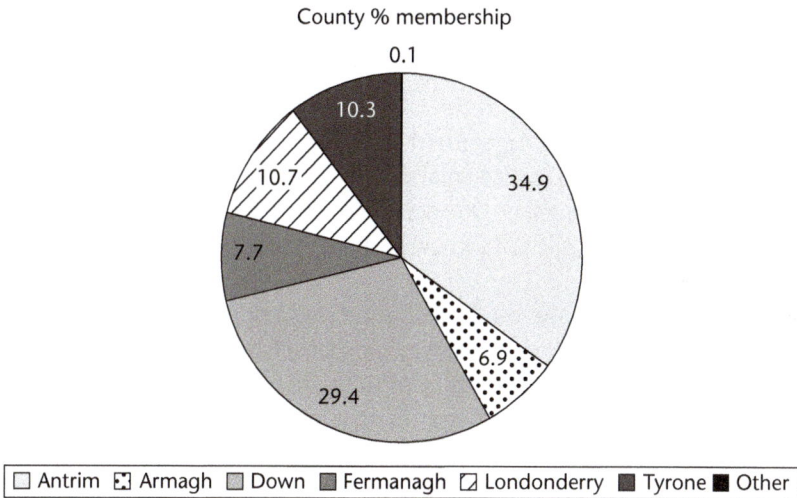

County % membership

0.1

Figure 4.2 Geographical distribution of DUP members by county (2014) (%)

small reservoir of potential members: only 61,805 of Northern Ireland's 1.81 million citizens live there and a majority of those in the county are Catholic. Fermanagh provides nearly one in five UUP members but fewer than one in ten of the DUP's membership.

Predictably, Antrim and Down, as easily the two most populated counties covering almost two-thirds of Northern Ireland's population, provide the largest recruiting grounds for the two main unionist parties. Yet while the

DUP's recruitment pattern faithfully reflects this population proportion, the UUP garners less than half of its membership from these two counties. The UUP needs to recruit east of the Bann and regain strength in Belfast and its suburbs and satellite towns, where it has struggled to attract recruits for years.

Social-class divisions have long been held to be a distinguishing feature between the UUP and DUP. From the 1920s until the early 1970s and the election of middle-class Brian Faulkner, the UUP was led by 'grandees', the landed gentry dominating its highest echelons. A combination of tribal politics, deference, and Orangeism maintained this order until the challenges of the Troubles displaced the upper-class leadership. Despite this change in status, many in the UUP still regarded the DUP as 'below stairs', uncouth and unsubtle fundamentalists engaged in overt sectarian rabble-rousing. These days, UUP leaders are keen to stress their 'ordinariness'. The current incumbent, Robin Swann, began his first address to party conference by emphasizing how he didn't exactly 'fit the mould' as he was raised in a 'housing executive house in Kells', 'the son of a plumber' and a mother who was 'a hospital cleaner'.[3] A former elected representative, ironically one of considerable wealth, described as 'disgraceful' attempts to portray the UUP as 'Big House unionism'.[4] The social milieu of the modern UUP is perhaps better described as more rural than rarefied.

Social-class divisions between the UUP and DUP support bases were considerable prior to the Belfast Agreement[5] but the advance of the DUP into the unionist middle class thereafter made class effects less significant, although they did not entirely vanish.[6] Do social-class differences remain between the party memberships? Table 4.2 indicates the self-ascribed social class of members of the two parties.

As can be seen from Table 4.2, UUP members are more likely to see themselves as middle-class rather than working-class, whereas the converse is true within the DUP. A sizeable minority in both parties do not think along class lines. The percentage claiming working-class status within the UUP is slightly higher than that which would be objectively ascribed according to current occupation, or final job in the case of the large contingent of retirees.

Table 4.2 Self-ascribed social class of UUP and DUP members (%)

	UUP	DUP (2014)
Middle-Class	49.2	36.4
Working-Class	30.0	41.6
No	20.5	18.2
Other	0.3	3.8

Q. Do you ever think of yourself as belonging to a particular class?
DUP figures from Tonge et al., *The DUP: From Protest to Power.*

Approximately 22 per cent of UUP members are manual or blue-collar workers or ex-workers. Average annual household income for a UUP or DUP member is the same, at £30,000 to £34,999. There are differences at the top end, with the 7.1 per cent of UUP members receiving an annual household income exceeding £70,000 nearly double the 3.8 per cent figure within the DUP. Class and income differences do exist, therefore, but they are not large overall and, whatever their historical importance in defining the two parties, socio-economic divisions are not the main modern feature of UUP versus DUP distinctions.

Recruitment of new members requires a strong team of activists, an effective online marketing presence, a good story to tell, and membership incentives. Student members of the UUP clearly enjoyed the camaraderie associated with shared membership on campus, but would other young people joining the UUP enjoy the same social capital and bonding? Recruitment methodology may also need to be further extended. Tellingly, only 4 per cent of members joined online. The majority (63 per cent) joined via the more traditional method of attending a local meeting and signing up. A modern-day UUP meeting is unlikely to be of sufficient visibility for this mechanism to remain viable.

The core recruitment message from the Party understandably remains unchanged—that the UUP is the best organization in which to defend and articulate the case for the Union. Liking the UUP's stance on the Union is the main reason why members joined, 46 per cent offering this reason, with a further 11 per cent joining 'to oppose republicanism'. A sizeable motivation was 'disagreement with other unionist parties', accounting for 15 per cent of members. The percentages joining the UUP because of the organization's economic and social policies, or leader, or for religious reasons, are all in single figures. Whilst the DUP enjoyed a big influx of UUP defectors in the early 2000s amid the post-Belfast Agreement tribulations, forming nearly 20 per cent of the DUP's entire membership, the UUP has received little traffic in its direction from that source. Only 2 per cent of UUP members used to belong in the DUP, only marginally more than have come from the Alliance Party.

Membership Activism

A possible consequence of the unfavourable age profile of the UUP is an apparent lower level of activism compared to the DUP. However, both parties contain plenty of dedicated stalwarts, as Table 4.3 shows, and age does not appear to the decisive element in shaping activism. The percentage of UUP members aged 70 and above who claim to be 'very active' is 16 per cent, only

Table 4.3 Self-reported levels of activism within the UUP and DUP (%)

	UUP	DUP (2014)
Very active	19.2	31.1
Fairly active	40.2	44.1
Not very active	31.8	20.3
Not at all active	8.8	4.6

Q. How active would you describe yourself within the . . . (party title)?
DUP figures from Tonge et al., *The DUP: From Protest to Power*

slightly lower than the overall figure across the Party. The 27 per cent of members aged under 40 reporting a very high level of activism is encouraging for the UUP, but further emphasizes the need to increase youth recruitment.

A lack of dynamism was acknowledged as a source of frustration by many members in open-ended responses to the survey. Common positive open-ended responses indicated that members liked particularly their party's 'broad church', 'sensible unionism', 'principled unionism', 'moderate unionism', 'fair unionism', 'true unionism', 'traditional unionism', and 'the best defence of the union', alongside other attributes such as 'family tradition', plentiful 'opportunities to be involved', 'companionship', and the sharing of time and ideas with 'people of like-minded views'. The main negatives were 'apathy', the 'age profile', the 'need to attract more young people', the need for 'more women', too much 'deadwood', the 'lack of direction or clarity', 'local autonomy eroded', and the need to 'take on the DUP'.

The comments reveal considerable confidence among members that the UUP's brand of unionism was superior to any other form. The members possess a strong belief in the righteousness of their party and its politics. There is much satisfaction with the UUP's promotion of Northern Ireland's place in the UK. On a zero to ten scale, where zero is very poor and ten is excellent, 83 per cent of members scored their party at five or above, with a majority offering a score of eight or more. Despite the frequency of change of leader, the members also rated the party leadership highly, two-thirds offering a score of eight or above. Only 9 per cent of members offered what could be interpreted as a negative view, rating leadership at four or below. A positive message was also offered in terms of organization and communication with members, 77 per cent scoring this at eight or above, although almost one-quarter of members appeared less sanguine, rating this at five or below. Comments from members also highlight the sizeable social capital gathered from belonging to the UUP. Many are appreciative of the benefits of companionship with colleagues of similar political outlook and social milieu.

Table 4.4 UUP members' views on the autonomy of MLAs and leadership control of candidate selection (%)

	Strongly agree	Agree	Neither agree nor disagree	Disagree	Strongly disagree
'Individual MLAs should be able to vote independent of their party's policy positions'	12.0	29.8	16.1	29.7	12.4
'In a modern professional party, the party leadership has to have control of the selection process'	17.9	45.9	13.8	14.7	7.6

Usually a party is most reliant upon members at elections and a sizeable 43 per cent of members say they canvass 'quite a lot' or 'a great deal' during campaigns, commonly via the traditional doorstep method. Indeed, UUP members appear more comfortable with traditional modes of campaigning compared to newer forms via social media. The percentages of members who say they 'rarely or never' use the UUP's twitter or Facebook accounts are 76 per cent and 70 per cent respectively. More than three-quarters of the membership 'rarely or never' use blogs by UUP Assembly members (MLAs) and a majority (54 per cent) are equally rare users of the UUP website. If, as has been claimed, modern campaigning needs to be well-acquainted with social media, there is much work to be done.[7]

The legacy of the Party's less disciplined past is evident in membership attitudes towards the autonomy of MLAs, where there is an equal division between those who support elected representatives taking their own course and those believing in Party discipline. Table 4.4 also highlights some resistance to the imposition of central control over UUP candidate selections. Whilst old habits die hard, it should be noted that more than two-thirds of members appear happy with UUP structures, concurring with the proposition that 'the party's internal decision-making is highly democratic'.

A combination of the ability to have voice and the longevity of membership in many cases may contribute to a considerable sense of loyalty: 88 per cent of members 'strongly agree' or 'agree' (split evenly between the two categories) that they 'have strong feelings of loyalty towards the party'.

A Devolutionist Not an Integrationist Party

Whilst their party is seen historically as far more integrationist than the DUP, particularly when under James Molyneaux's leadership, the UUP members are supportive of devolution and devolved institutions, especially the Northern Ireland Assembly, which has frequently tottered, often on the brink of collapse. Figure 4.3 indicates the very wide margin by which UUP members prefer devolved government to direct rule.

The integrationist myth is also challenged by the views of UUP members on the amount of say that should be afforded to the Westminster government. One-quarter do desire 'a great deal of say' but these are heavily outnumbered by those offering a more restrictive view, with 62 per cent declaring 'some say', 10 per cent 'a little say', and 3 per cent 'no say at all'. Table 4.5 examines attitudes towards the key institutional pillars created under the Belfast Agreement. It shows majority backing for the Assembly and, in a more lukewarm way, the Executive, backing which is not extended to the all-island dimension of the Belfast Agreement, the North–South bodies.

Support for the Assembly is extensive and reflects devolutionist commitment, even though the Assembly was in difficulty during much of the course of the membership survey and, like the Executive, was no longer functioning by the time of this study's conclusion in late 2017. The UUP membership was evenly divided over whether the Executive should be further empowered, to

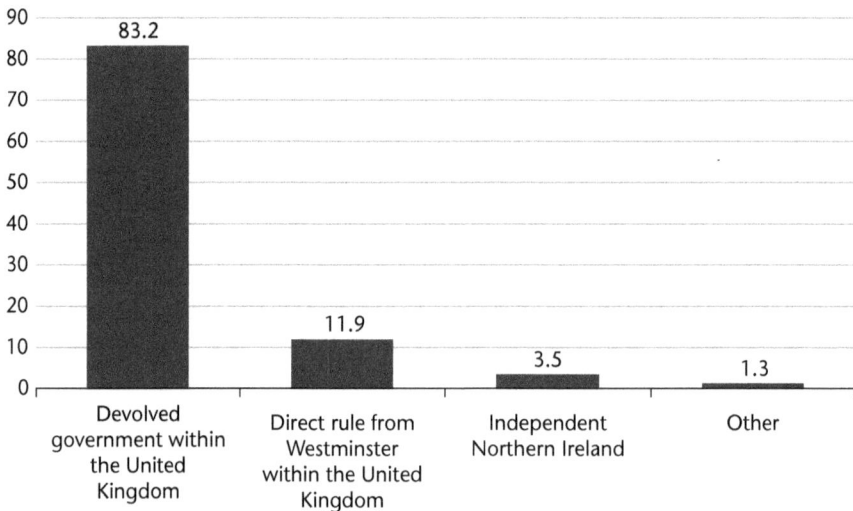

Figure 4.3 UUP members' preferred long-term policy for Northern Ireland (%)

Table 4.5 UUP members' attitudes to the Northern Ireland Assembly and Executive and all-island bodies (%)

	Strongly support	Support	Neither support nor oppose	Oppose	Strongly oppose
Northern Ireland Assembly	21.1	57.5	12.0	5.8	3.6
Northern Ireland Executive	10.1	48.3	18.9	15.5	7.2
North–South/all-island bodies	4.0	27.9	31.2	20.5	16.4

raise taxes. That backing for the Executive is lower than support for the Assembly may also reflect the UUP's decision to quit and form an opposition in 2016, having become marginalized by electors and fellow Executive members by this point. Only one in four members believed that the DUP and nationalist parties had cooperated well in the Assembly, with a majority disagreeing. Asked about whether the UUP and nationalist parties were cooperating well, the most common response (from 41 per cent of members) was to 'neither agree nor disagree' and only 27 per cent thought not. This presumably reflected a reasonable working relationship between the UUP and SDLP, one strongly encouraged under Mike Nesbitt's leadership.

Antipathy towards all-island bodies is far from pervasive, but is a sentiment found among nearly two in every five UUP members. It is a long-standing strain of opinion. Much of the Party found the Council of Ireland dimension of the Sunningdale Agreement in 1973 too much to bear. The all-island dimension of the Belfast Agreement was more modest; a non-executive North–South Ministerial Council and cross-border bodies of modest remit, but clearly still too much for some within the UUP. Opposition to Irish involvement in Northern Irish affairs remains extensive. Asked how much say an Irish Government should have, 67 per cent of UUP members responded, 'none at all', 28 per cent conceded only 'a little say', and only 5 per cent were prepared to go to 'some say'. Only 10 per cent believe that the main Irish parties of Fine Gael and Fianna Fáil should contest elections in Northern Ireland.

To what extent does the UUP membership support the consociational mechanics of Strand One of the Belfast Agreement, of power-sharing between rival ethnic blocs and the existence of mutual vetoes, via the requirement for parallel, cross-community consent for some legislation? Figure 4.4 indicates extensive support (almost two-thirds of the party) for the proposition that power-sharing is the only way forward.

This backing for power-sharing is extended to its mechanics and the operation of mutual vetoes, albeit by a slimmer margin, as 55 per cent of UUP members concur that 'legislation should require the consent of a majority of unionist AND nationalist Assembly members before it can be passed', with 28 per cent disagreeing. The political outcomes of the Belfast Agreement and its revival in 2007, under the slightly modified terms of the 2006 St Andrews Agreement, are lauded by a majority of UUP members as shoring up the Union, as Table 4.6 indicates.

As can be seen in Table 4.6, most members are confident that Northern Ireland's place in the Union has been further cemented by devolved power-sharing. UUP members are confident in the triumph of their unionism. This is supplemented by other survey evidence. Asked how likely is the prospect of a united Ireland, less than 3 per cent of UUP members believed it 'very' and a

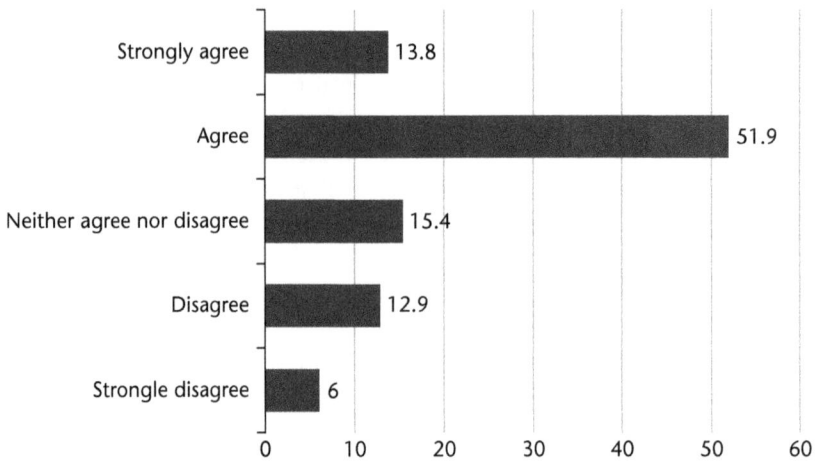

Figure 4.4 'Power-sharing between Unionists and Nationalists is the only way for Northern Ireland to operate' (%)

Table 4.6 UUP members' beliefs on the political consequences of the Belfast Agreement (%)

	Strongly agree	Agree	Neither agree nor disagree	Disagree	Strongly disagree
It has become more likely that Northern Ireland will stay part of the UK	31.4	45.9	14.7	6.0	2.0
It has become more likely that Northern Ireland will eventually join the Irish Republic	2.8	8.5	11.8	44.6	32.3
The experience of power-sharing has meant that nationalists are now more content that Northern Ireland should remain in the UK	9.3	46.3	21.0	15.8	7.6
The experience of power-sharing has meant that one day a majority of unionists will agree to Northern Ireland joining the Republic of Ireland	1.9	2.8	7.7	36.0	51.6

Q. Since power-sharing was restored in 2007, do you think...?

further 7 per cent 'quite', whereas 23 per cent of members saw the prospect as 'quite unlikely' and the bulk, 63 per cent, believed it 'very unlikely'. If not solved, the constitutional threat to Northern Ireland's place in the UK does not appear immediate to the majority of UUP members, even if their unionism is the most important aspect of their politics. Moreover, in the view of most (albeit with a sizeable dissenting majority) the award to nationalists of a stake in the state has made that community more sanguine over remaining in the UK. Whilst this begs the question of what might happen to such acquiescence in the context of a dissolution of power-sharing institutions, these findings nonetheless offer support for the rationale of the altruistic decisions taken by the UUP in 1998, in offering partnership government and recognition of nationalist electoral mandates, to further secure the Union. UUP members appear happier with the state of the Union than Northern Ireland's economic plight within it, being evenly split over whether economic prosperity is increasing in Northern Ireland.

This clear support for devolution and its mechanics does not extend to a conciliatory approach to one of the key issues which has threatened the future of the power-sharing institutions: an Irish Language Act. Whilst far from the only issue destabilizing the institutions, Sinn Féin's demand for such an Act (which the British Government promised to introduce in the 2006 St Andrews Agreement, but did not) and the DUP's rejection of the idea accounted for much of the stalemate regarding a restoration of devolved government throughout 2017. Table 4.7 indicates that a bilingual approach involving recognition of the Irish language is rejected by UUP members, who are more supportive of local support for Ulster-Scots.

In common with his members, the UUP leader, Robin Swann, rejected an Irish Language Act as a 'trojan horse' against unionism[8] and used his first party conference speech in 2017 to confirm that his opposition was as equally robust as anything emanating from the DUP, asserting that such a measure 'would lead to further division' and 'we would know which territory we were in by the road signs'.[9] As Table 4.8 shows, there are overwhelming majorities backing the view that only English should have official recognition and

Table 4.7 UUP members' attitudes to recognition of the English and Irish Languages and Ulster-Scots in Northern Ireland

	Strongly agree	Agree	Neither agree nor disagree	Disagree	Strongly disagree
'Only English should be the official language in Northern Ireland'	63.4	29.4	3.3	2.4	1.5
'English and Irish should have equal status as languages in Northern Ireland'	1.2	3.2	5.8	35.3	54.5
'Provision should be provided for place names in Irish where local communities desire it'	3.2	25.0	18.3	22.3	31.3
'Provision should be provided supporting Ulster Scots where local communities desire it'	8.1	35.1	26.7	16.8	13.3

Table 4.8 Perceptions of the peace process among UUP members (%)

Unionists benefited a lot more than nationalists	2.3
Unionists benefited a little more than nationalists	5.0
Nationalists benefited a lot more than unionists	60.1
Nationalists benefited a little more than unionists	17.1
Unionists and nationalists benefited equally	14.7
Other	0.8

opposing equal status for the Irish language. Opposition is less extensive to Irish place names where locally desired but is still held by the majority of UUP members.

The Peace Process, Security, and Dealing with the Past

Given that the UUP did the hard yards for the 1998 Agreement and suffered consequently, would they do it again? The answer is yes, but only just. 59 per cent of UUP members state that they voted yes to the Belfast Agreement in the referendum: 11 per cent were too young to vote and 6 per cent claim not to remember how they voted! In 1998, 57 per cent of Protestants voted in favour of the deal,[10] so UUP membership backing for the Agreement was a little more extensive than among the wider unionist population and stood in stark contrast to the DUP's members, 68 per cent of whom voted against.[11] If a referendum on the Agreement was held again tomorrow, a narrow majority of UUP members, 53 per cent, would vote in favour, with 42 per cent declaring they would vote against (up 19 per cent from the membership's declared no vote in 1998).

Given that the UUP largely think that the Union is safe, why the modest degree of internal backing for arguably their Party's most significant achievement? Table 4.8 shows how few UUP members perceive unionist gains to be the story of the peace process.

As can be seen in Table 4.8, the percentage of UUP members believing that unionists were the main victors is in single figures and almost four in five members see nationalists as the major beneficiaries, in most perceptions gaining a lot more than unionists. Clearly a defence of the constitutional status quo, viewed as successful by most UUP members, does not translate into a perception that unionists gained from the associated political process. Nationalists, who may be no closer to realizing their ultimate political goal of a united Ireland, are perceived as the key beneficiaries, banking the concessions of a reformed Northern Ireland without giving up on attaining the ultimate prize. On this reading, it is unclear what would constitute unionist 'victory'. Possibly the continued incarceration of IRA prisoners, the outright defeat of republican violence, and the maintenance of the RUC might have been required? Of course, negativity over aspects of the Belfast Agreement ought to be expected, given its electoral consequences for the UUP.

The zero-sum game politics of Northern Ireland is played out in the assessments of the impact of the Agreement, with only one in seven UUP members prepared to concede that there may have been equal mutual benefit for both communities. 85 per cent of those members believe there is prejudice against unionists, with a slight majority of that 85 per cent believing there is 'a lot' of prejudice. Only 8 per cent think likewise in terms of 'a lot' of prejudice against nationalists, although 38 per cent concede that there is 'a little'. That said, there is a broadly positive view of inter-communal relations, in that half of the membership think that relations between Protestants and Catholics have improved over the last decade, with only 7 per cent believing they have worsened.

Also juxtaposed with the UUP's overall confidence in the maintenance of the Union is an apparent nervousness over Northern Ireland's peace. Uncomfortably, not many Party members believe that the Belfast Agreement has brought about a permanent peace. As Table 4.9 shows, only 27 per cent believe that there is a lasting peace in Northern Ireland.

The threat to peace from 'dissident' republicans is clearly taken seriously and the traditional unionist sense of siege under republican threat has not dissipated. Whilst dissident violence has been sporadic, it has not been entirely erased and the peace remains relative. From the year of the Belfast Agreement, 1998, to 31 March 2017, there were 160 deaths, 2,473 shooting incidents, and 1,569 bombing incidents due to the security situation.[12] The bulk of UUP members (68 per cent) believe that dissident republican violence constitutes a 'major threat to peace and security'. A further 30 per cent perceive such violence as a 'minor threat' and only 2 per cent of members view it as 'no threat'.

Sinn Féin has supported the Police Service of Northern Ireland since the party's special ard-fheis on policing in January 2007. As the party of choice for most Catholics, that move could be seen crucial in securing the peace and confirming Sinn Féin's constitutional bona fides. Yet there remains some scepticism over the extent of nationalist change. Whilst many in the UUP (44 per cent) believe that most Catholics support the Police Service of Northern Ireland (PSNI), older suspicions of attitudes to the police within the nationalist community have not dissipated among many others within

Table 4.9 UUP members' beliefs on peace and policing in Northern Ireland (%)

	Strongly agree	Agree	Neither agree nor disagree	Disagree	Strongly disagree
There is a lasting peace in Northern Ireland	5.5	21.7	22.6	34.3	16.0
Policing is benefiting from Sinn Féin's participation on policing boards	4.5	29.5	23.7	30.5	11.9
Most Roman Catholics support the Police Service of Northern Ireland	3.8	41.6	26.1	20.8	7.7
50-50 Roman Catholic and Non-Roman Catholic recruitment by the Police Service of Northern Ireland was a good idea	3.3	20.7	14.3	34.6	27.1

the UUP, with 29 per cent believing that Catholics do not offer such backing and more than one-quarter of members not sure. Opinion is also divided over an important change to policing, with more UUP members disagreeing with the proposition that Sinn Féin's participation on policing boards—a tangible sign of republican acceptance of policing—has been beneficial. Opposition to the PSNI's recruitment via religious quotas is extensive, albeit with nearly one-quarter of the UUP approving. A 50-50 Catholic and non-Catholic policing recruitment policy—equality or sectarianism, depending on perception—was deployed between 2001 and 2011 to redress the gross Catholic under-representation in policing. The Catholic percentage of the Royal Ulster Constabulary at the time of the police's reconstruction as the PSNI was in single figures but rose to 29 per cent in the new force by 2011. Opposition to the use of quotas is found more broadly within the UUP, extending to rejection of schemes of positive discrimination to bolster women's representation.

Part of the UUP's continuing unease over whether the Belfast Agreement can truly be heralded as a triumph may lie in what the deal could not address. Conflict legacy issues continue to be divisive. Dealing with the past is proving as difficult as sorting out the present. A sizeable number of members (38 per cent) consider themselves to have been a victim of the Troubles so it is unsurprising that there is much sensitivity over how best to address the past. The UUP membership's views on what should, or should not, be attempted, appear to be broadly in line with the rest of the unionist population, judging by the evidence from the 2017 Northern Ireland election survey.[13] The views of UUP members are summarized in Table 4.10.

Several of the suggestions eschewed by UUP members are favoured by nationalists. Amnesties are overwhelmingly rejected, seen as a device to absolve republicans, responsible for the bulk of violence, from terrorist crimes. For many UUP members, the 'conflict' was about IRA terrorism, whereas more nationalists are prepared to countenance an amnesty and a truth and reconciliation commission, also rejected by UUP members. Without concomitant

Table 4.10 UUP members' views on dealing with the past

	Yes	No
Amnesties for all those involved in the conflict	10.6	89.4
Truth and Reconciliation Commission	43.4	56.6
All victims should be treated equally	45.1	54.9
Financial compensation	44.6	55.4
Independent historical analysis of the Troubles and the role played by UK/Irish Governments and paramilitaries	55.4	44.6
Investigations into the killings in the Troubles should continue	65.0	35.0
Victims/survivors given information about Troubles-related deaths	85.4	14.6

Q. Which of the following would you like to see to help deal with the past?

amnesties, such a commission is a non-starter anyway and, in any case, few UUP members might see such an exercise as truth-telling. Opposition to financial compensation might surprise, but may be influenced by fear of all victims, including families of dead terrorists, being recipients (as can be seen, the majority view of UUP members is that not all victims are equal) and in any case, the primary motivation behind victims' pursuit of justice is non-financial. Information and investigations are the desires of Party members.

A Right-Wing Party

The UUP is certainly a right-of-centre party, but how far to the right? On a zero to ten scale, where zero is far-left and ten far-right, members place themselves and their party at seven, as shown in Figures 4.5 and 4.6. These scales are far from satisfactory in a Northern Ireland context, as constitutional robustness is often conflated with 'far-rightism'; 12 per cent of UUP members label themselves as 'far-right' (i.e. scoring at the maximum ten) and 10 per cent place their party in a similar category—even though they are not and their party isn't either.

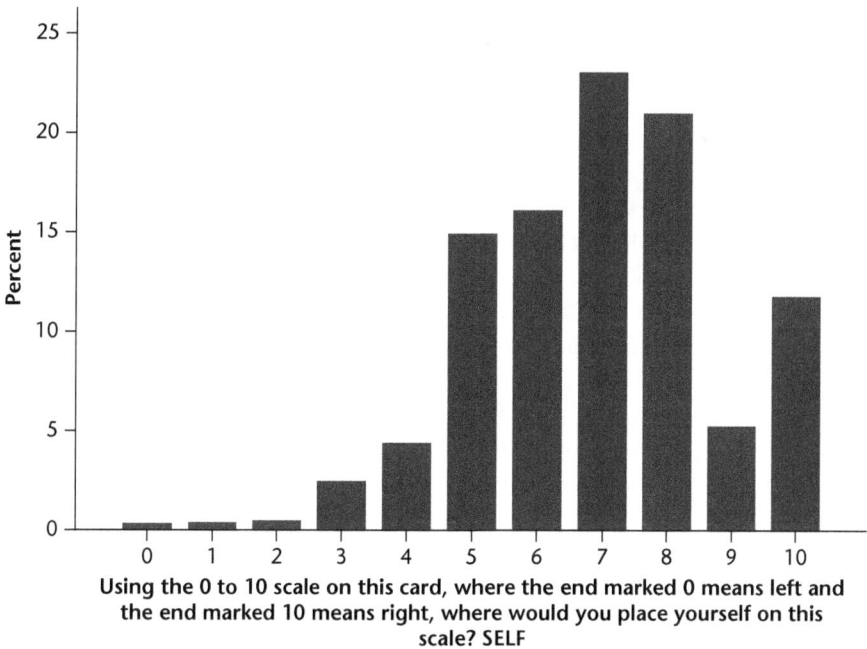

Figure 4.5 Self-placement by UUP members on a left–right scale

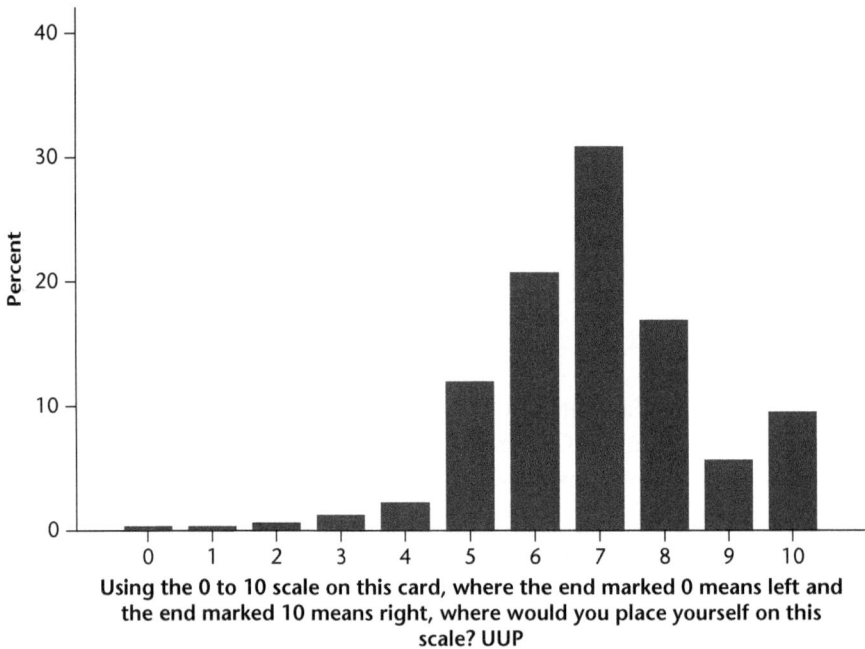

Figure 4.6 UUP members' perceptions of their Party on a left–right scale

The overall findings are to be expected: UUP members place themselves and their party in alignment as substantially right-wing but not extreme. Predictably, the DUP are viewed as extreme by UUP members, placed at nine out of ten on the left–right scale, as Chapter 7 on attitudes to other parties shows. DUP members do not see it this way, as they place their party at seven out of ten on the left–right scale, the same position where UUP members locate their own party, whilst placing themselves at a median score of eight. The DUP membership does see the UUP as a less right-wing party than their own, awarding the UUP a median score of six (and very close to five).[14] Although there is a modest centrist grouping among UUP members, few see themselves as left of centre and even fewer would consider their party as even mildly of the left.

Unsurprisingly given these self and party placements, most UUP members feel closest to the Conservative Party of the Britain-wide parties and there are very few takers for a Corbyn-led Labour Party, as Table 4.11 indicates.

The empathy with the Conservatives is more extensive than that found among DUP members, among whom only 50 per cent declared that they felt closed to the Conservatives (37 per cent said no party),[15] although that study was completed before the Conservative–DUP parliamentary alliance which emerged following the 2017 election. Older UUP members were of course

Table 4.11 To which of the GB political parties do you feel closest? (UUP members) (%)

Conservatives	69.3
None of them	18.5
UKIP	5.3
Labour	2.5
Liberal Democrats	1.9
Other	2.5

politically socialized during the era of harmonious, formalized Conservative–UUP relations, severely weakened by the Heath Government's introduction of direct rule in 1972 and virtually destroyed by Margaret Thatcher's 1985 Anglo-Irish Agreement. Relationships improved to the point where the old alliance was revived, but only briefly, at the 2010 election. UUP members may feel only that the Conservatives represent the least bad option, but nonetheless most opted for them. The percentage inclined to tick the 'none-of-them' box was only half of that found within the DUP.[16] UUP members are quite evenly divided over electoral integration. Asked whether the major British political parties should contest elections in Northern Ireland, 32 per cent support the idea, with 37 per cent opposed and 31 per cent undecided.

Aside from constitutional issues, UUP right-of-centre views may be found in, for example, opposition to the removal of academic selection for schools. Only 21 per cent of members oppose the 11+ examination to determine senior school entrance, with 65 per cent of UUP members supporting the test, which they favour above alternative forms of academic selection and streaming. The members' conservatism (small 'c') is also demonstrated in opposition to change. More than 70 per cent oppose a lowering of the voting age to 16 (the Conservatives and the DUP are the two Westminster parties which also oppose such a move). Party members are also opposed, by almost two to one, to any change in the method of electing MPs to Westminster from First Past the Post to the Single Transferable Vote system used in all other Northern Ireland contests.

Conclusion

Demographic and attitudinal profiling of the UUP membership reveals some strengths and several significant weaknesses. The most obvious asset for the UUP, beyond a reasonably-sized membership still, perhaps extraordinarily, larger than its unionist rival, is a loyal base who have stuck steadfastly with the Party through difficult times and are unlikely to defect given the longevity of membership. Whilst there has been the occasional high-profile quitter in recent years, most defectors have long gone, deserting the party amid the crisis-ridden years of the immediate post-Belfast Agreement era. The current leadership can rely upon the fidelity of the members in a party restructured and better organized than in previous eras. This membership survey reveals that, despite the relentless electoral decline of the UUP since 1998, the party has retained its core membership and continued to attract new members, demonstrating a capacity to motivate and mobilize.

The Party recognizes the need to replenish its membership base and progress has been made as recruitment has risen again in recent times, but the scale of the task requires more than the dedicated efforts of dozens of enthusiastic young volunteers at Northern Ireland's two universities. Among existing members, the Party needs to shrug off the image of a pleasant rural social club—it recruits best where the people are least—notwithstanding the importance of collegiality and comradeship, and project a more dynamic attitude. This requires more vigour from some councillors, who range from the highly talented and impressively diligent (a large majority) to the lacklustre—the poor attendance of the latter at training and information sessions, even when held to coincide with party conference, attracting the frustration of at least one former leader. Change will also require the further adaption of modern campaigning techniques and technologies.

The UUP has a significant achievement to trumpet, a globally acknowledged peace and political deal which upheld its constitutional aims, diminished violence, and was accepted almost wholesale by the DUP, despite that rival's years of false claims of how the UUP had betrayed the unionist birthright. Despite believing that the Belfast Agreement secured the Union and supporting the power-sharing principles of the deal, the UUP's membership remains nervous about the peace, uneasy about dealing with the past, uncertain over its lines of attack upon the DUP, and unsure over its core messages beyond reinforcing a loyal British unionism. Oscillating between different sets of alliances may need to be displaced by a re-emphasis of a core, non-sectarian, progressive but firm unionism. The only alternative is the grim spectre—to a loyal membership—of the merger of two unionist parties, which few within either party truly desire.

Notes

1. DUP figure from J. Tonge, M. Braniff, T. Hennessey, J. W. McAuley,. and S. A. Whiting, *The Democratic Unionist Party: From Protest to Power*: Oxford: Oxford University Press, 2014.
2. Tonge et al., *The DUP*, 4.
3. Robin Swann, Leader's Speech to UUP conference, Armagh City Hotel, 21 Oct. 2017, <https://www.belfasttelegraph.co.uk/news/northern-ireland/uup-leader-robin-swann-2017-conference-speech-full-text-36248477.html>.

4. Interview with UUP former elected representative.

5. G. Evans and M. Duffy, 'Beyond the Sectarian Divide: The Social Bases and Political Consequences of Unionist Party Competition in Northern Ireland', *British Journal of Political Science*, 27.1 (1997), 47–81.

6. J. Evans and J. Tonge, 'Social Class and Party Choice in Northern Ireland's Ethnic Blocs', *West European Politics*, 32.5 (2009), 1012–30.

7. See e.g. K. Dommett, and L. Temple, 'Digital Campaigning: The Rise of Satellite and Facebook Campaigns', in J. Tonge, C. L. Bandeira, and S. Wilks-Heeg (eds), *Britain Votes 2017*, Oxford: Oxford University Press, 2018, ch. 12.

8. *Belfast Telegraph*, 9 July 2017, <https://www.belfasttelegraph.co.uk/news/general-election-2017/irish-language-act-a-sinn-fein-trojan-horse-swann-claims-35910947.html>, accessed Aug. 2017.

9. Swann, Leader's Speech, 21 Oct. 2017.

10. B. Hayes and I. McAllister, 'Who Voted for Peace? Public Support for the 1998 Northern Ireland Agreement', *Irish Political Studies*, 16.1 (2001), 73–93.

11. Tonge et al., *The DUP*.

12. Police Service of Northern Ireland, *Security Situation Statistics*, Belfast: PSNI, 2006–7 and 2017.

13. See J. Tonge, 'The 2017 Northern Ireland General Election Survey', available at <https://discover.ukdataservice.ac.uk/catalogue/?sn=8234&type=data%20catalogue>, accessed Nov. 2017.

14. Tonge et al., *The DUP*.

15. Tonge et al., *The DUP*.

16. Tonge et al., *The DUP*.

5

Safeguarding the Union

UUP Ideology and Discourse

> Ulster people will realize that unless Protestant and Catholics, Unionist
> and Nationalists, can find a way of working together in government for the
> good of the Province, there will be no political stability, no economic
> progress, and no end to violence. The only real alternative to working
> together is to live separately.
>
> (Brian Faulkner, Memoirs of a Statesman[1])

From Northern Ireland's formation in 1921 until direct rule from Westminster
was introduced in 1972, the UUP succeeded in winning every general election
it contested.[2] Throughout that period, the Party was never subject to any
serious electoral challenge, nor was its core ideology essentially contested,
either inside or outside of Stormont. Even allowing for the history of independent unionists, the labour movement, various republican insurgencies
(1942–4 and 1956–62) and the positioning of various nationalist groupings,
an ideological coherence and political hegemony was constructed around the
Union that was seemingly unbreakable, especially when it had the backing of
the state when it was called upon.

It was only following the political and social turmoil precipitated by outbreak of political violence in late 1960s, and the subsequent ending of Northern Ireland's system of devolved government under Stormont, that the UUP's
political hegemony began to disjoint under both internal and external pressure. In recent years, the Party's fortunes have been a tale of remarkable
demise and decline. In November 2003, the UUP lost its position as the
leading unionist party to the DUP. The pattern was confirmed in May 2005,
when in elections to Westminster, the DUP garnered twice the UUP's popular
vote, resulting in the reduction of the UUP representation at Westminster to
just one seat, and was ultimately responsible for the removal of David Trimble
as UUP leader.

This sequence of events led Dean Godson, the author of a comprehensive biography on David Trimble,[3] to describe the state of the UUP as: 'nominally alive but, to all intents and purposes, a goner'. Such an assessment may be deemed by some rather harsh, but to many it gives a clear indication of the Party's decline in fortunes over past decades.

One of the ways in which this downturn is felt by members is through direct comparison with its main unionist rival, the DUP, and is manifest in the oppositional discourses that have become apparent within unionism. The UUP has presented itself as the inheritors of the unionist tradition, representing its true vision, latterly claiming to be the originators of the peace process, and worthy heirs to past generations of unionist leaders. Much of this is now manifest in a public discourse claiming that the party has evolved into a new form of unionism. This has altered, not in its dedication to preserving Northern Ireland's place in the UK, but rather to adopt a civic configuration of unionism, in opposition to a religiously derived, ethnic, or cultural version, favoured by the DUP.

The UUP's articulation of a new unionist imagination for Northern Ireland was embodied in David Trimble's assertion that he wished the Assembly to operate as a 'pluralist parliament for a pluralist people'.[4] This comment was, of course, made with direct reference to another speech, given by Sir James Craig in 1934, in which he said: 'All I boast of is that we are a Protestant Parliament and a Protestant State', but which in popular usage is often misquoted as a: 'Protestant parliament for a Protestant people',[5] a principle which was seen to guide and govern Northern Ireland for the first five decades of its existence.

In the contemporary period, the UUP has struggled to counter the DUP narrative representing the Belfast Agreement primarily through a discourse of losses to unionism position and constant concessions to republicanism. In response, the UUP promoted a discourse which presented themselves as: 'prepared to give up some ground . . . so that the overall siege of this state can be lifted',[6] and representing a sensible and inclusive form of unionism. More importantly, it was also claimed by the UUP that it was their active involvement that forced republicans to sign up to 'democracy and disarmament'.[7] Recognizing this, it was the DUP which had play catch-up in accepting the terms negotiated by the UUP.

The unionist voting public seemed unconvinced, however, by this stance and in consequence the DUP has assumed a position of prominence, indeed dominance, in subsequent years. Voters seemingly prefer the DUP version of history and of unionism, based on moral values and the consistent opposition to all threats, real or perceived, to the constitutional position, to ensure Northern Ireland's future and a Protestant British culture and politics within it.

Under constant pressure from Irish nationalism and republicanism and faced with what sometimes appeared an even fiercer ideological attack from the DUP, the UUP have struggled to define and promote their brand of unionist thinking. As a riposte there has been both consistency and change in the dominant narratives and discourses emerging from the UUP, changes in the message from the leadership and a constant struggle to assert their form of unionism. The views of Howard Thornton are representative in summarizing some of the main contours as follows:

> The UUP have obviously suffered electorally because they took the big risks, as in fact did the SDLP. It was very easy for the DUP to stand on the side-lines heckling in with this, 'No, no, no, no,' and then, to have done the complete U-turn on the strength of the risks that have been taken by our party . . . I don't understand how people can forgive them. You know, for them to have taken no risks, and slam what progress . . . and this is from Sunningdale and from everywhere else . . . every attempt that was made to settle this without all the mass deaths and so on, and so forth. They really have come from our party, and . . . the SDLP. But the extremes just would not allow that to take place . . . Compromise means that you don't win everything you want to win. One has to accept, you can't enter into a negotiation and win everything you want.[8]

This chapter identifies some of the main ideas that have emerged from the UUP in recent years and the discourse used to explain and define these. Discourse, in this sense, acts to both shape common sense beliefs and to reinforce (or sometimes, but much less commonly to transform) existing beliefs and understandings. Consciousness is shaped by discourse, while collective memories and narratives provide the tools to structure perceptions of political and social realities. In understanding discourse in this way, the chapter outlines and provides a framework to understand some of the continuities and changes in UUP thinking as the Party has sought to portray itself as the foremost custodian of unionist interests and belief. Further, it assesses the validity for members of emerging discourses, surrounding a new non-sectarian vision for unionism, and including a partial representation of its history.[9]

The central discourses of the UUP have altered considerably over the past thirty years, away from the desirability of pure majority rule, towards a commitment to create an encompassing and inclusive society in Northern Ireland, and a form of government that reflected this. These ideas have not gone uncontested either within or without the party. Unionist discourses are structured and organized, in that they give privilege and preference to particular moral, political, and social interpretations over others. Such discourses are central to explaining experiences and in giving these meaning in the construction of reality. Moreover, unionists use an accepted range of terminology and hypotheses, the meanings of which are assumed and understood. These are applied to the subjects of the discourse, and unionist discourses (as with all discourses) are underpinned by ideology.

As such discourses play a central role in shaping and privileging particular aspects of unionist culture. Importantly, discourses also represent *actions* as well as symbolic and cultural expressions.[10] As Michael Billig points out:

> ideology operates through the mobilization of discourse. Thus, the processes of ideology, as means of mobilizing meaning, are also means of mobilizing consciousness.[11]

Further, discourses may act as:

> ways of referring to or constructing knowledge about a particular topic of practice . . . which provide ways of talking about, forms of knowledge and conduct associated with a particular topic, social activity or institutional site in society.[12]

Unionist discourses identify and reveal an existential world (that which exists); a moral code (what is seen as good and what is evil); and, most powerfully, and often least obviously, an epistemological order (that which is defined as politically possible and what is impossible regarding change). Here, therefore, we adopt a wide-ranging view that links discourse with ideology, recognizing that discourses are central to our understanding, not just when dealing with representations about identity (see next chapter), but also because they influence social and political practices.[13]

Discourses can enable and facilitate social and political change, but they can also inhibit it, limiting vision, or even the ways in which people contemplate and understand change. In this sense, what are worthy of study are the core elements of UUP discourse, seeking answers as to whether, and in what ways, their narrative has changed, if so, how, and the extent to which this has convinced voters to follow and give legitimacy to their thoughts and actions. How then is the world of unionism best represented, and what are the values and norms represented through identifiable discourses?[14]

It is important to note that UUP party members see themselves as no less unionist, or British, than they once were. Current discourses revolve around debates concerning what the Party stands for, how they can best achieve the unionist vision, and how far members can commit allegiance to these views. Long-standing internal arguments surrounding integrationist and devolutionist (often based on the idea of majority rule) approaches, which peppered unionism in the 1970s and 1980s, appear to have been settled for members, although periodic institutional crises may reopen debate. The UUP adapted to a devolutionary settlement, having been a party often more supportive of direct rule from Westminster during the Troubles than the regional Ulster loyalist DUP with, as the previous chapter indicated, most members regarding devolved government as the best way forward for Northern Ireland.

Another consistent line emanating from the UUP is that they are the rightful legatees of political unionism and it is they who best uphold the tradition of, and remain the direct inheritors of, the spirit of Edward Carson, ensuring the continued constitutional position of Northern Ireland. In the 2017 UUP Assembly election manifesto, for example, this was referenced directly, providing an interpretation of Carson's words to suggest the road forward for contemporary political representatives:

> They must forget faction and section . . . If Ulster does what I ask her to do, and what I hope and believe she will do, in setting up an example and a precedent of good government, fair government, honest government, and a government not for sections or factions, but for all, her example may be followed.[15]

The manifesto continues by providing a rallying call to these values, a 'fair, honest government for all, blind to factions and sections, advancing diversity for what it is, something greater than the sum of the parts'.[16]

The discourses which have become prominent in the UUP seek to convey a set of ideas that are different and create ideological space from its rivals, both outside and inside unionism. But in some cases, this is somewhat difficult. Both the UUP and DUP remain fundamentally unionist and both ultimately seek to ensure and strengthen the link with Britain,[17] but the UUP have found themselves open to accusations of merely offering a less secure form of unionism, or that when trying to compete that they merely represent 'DUP-lite'. In practical terms a key task for the UUP is to differentiate themselves from other forms of unionism (most notably the DUP) while convincing the electorate that they will be no less unfaltering in their core doctrines and attitudes.

This is no easy task for the UUP. As an overarching ideology, the core Ulster unionist discourses are reasonable easy to identify, promoting the maintenance of the link with Great Britain and the continuance of the Union of the four nations, with a 'responsibility to provide an umbrella for all the pro-Union people of Ulster'.[18] In one sense, unionist ideology cannot alter, as its central tenets must always demonstrate steadfastness towards maintaining the link with Great Britain. Yet unionism since the late 1960s has been characterized by its reaction to fragmentation, as debate intensified as to the nature and form that will best ensure the Union.

This has seen the development of conflicting positions regarding the basis for unionist belief, formulated around the extent to which unionism is seen as religiously, culturally, ethnically, rationally, economically, or politically determined. Some of those differences (especially between the UUP and the DUP) are tactical and strategic, or due to the clashing personalities found in everyday politics, but others mark deep-layered ideological differences, which have been exacerbated by electoral completion and the demands of government. The struggle for the ideological heart of unionism and the repositioning of the UUP reveal a far more complex set of ideas and issues than is often apparent.

Core Unionist Arguments

In its classical form, it is possible to identify two main components of Irish unionism,[19] namely, securing Protestantism and its interests on the island; and a belief that the Union would bring benefits and advantages to both Ireland and Britain (and for some time the rest of the Empire). Both these arguments were clearly reflected in origins of Ulster unionism and the political opposition to the Home Rule movement of Parnell in the late 1800s. From its inception, the unionist narrative could be seen as an expression of resistance to the political desires of Irish nationalism, the dangers of an ascendant Catholic nationalism, which it regarded as an illiberal theological and social doctrine, and the great damage unionists believed would be caused to Ireland's economic and social standing should it leave the British Empire.

Irish unionists regarded themselves as part of a greater social and political movement, embracing both Ireland and Britain. This was an ideological position that proved impossible to hold politically, however. Events leading up to and surrounding the Easter Rising, and the subsequent division of Ireland, have been well documented[20] and will not be reviewed here. What is noteworthy is that the circumstances in which the commitment demonstrated by the majority of Irish Protestants to a future for the Island of King and Empire changed dramatically during this period.

The Irish unionist undertaking quickly became the Ulster unionist undertaking, as Northern unionists set about the defence of the six counties in which they had an established majority. The importance of the UUP within this history and its centrality to the politics of Northern Ireland should not be understated. Its structure rested in the Ulster Unionist Council (UUC), formed in 1905, which linked Party, the Orange Order, and Unionist associations in a bond that was to form the foundations for the political structures of Ulster unionism and last for the next century.

Unionism set about a process of 'Othering',[21] solidifying its position institutionally through the UUP and the Orange Order and establishing ideological distance between the two states on the island and within its own boundaries, between those regarded as dependable and those considered untrustworthy; and between those who saw the state as illegitimate and those who were prepared to validate it. But that ideological (and structural) coherence was effectively shattered by events of the mid-1960s and the onset of the Troubles. In recent years, there have been several threads of unionist thought leading to conflicting points on the unionist ideological compass. One analysis of note is the typology used by Porter, who classifies contemporary unionist thinking as gravitating towards the three major poles of cultural unionism, liberal unionism, and civic unionism.[22] Within this, competing

frameworks of political explanations have emerged, which seek to take unionism in differing directions, and ideological change has resulted in a reorientation and reorganization of the UUP.

We can see competing discourses emerge from these positions. On the one
hand, there are those who suggest that Britishness is best understood (and
defended) in its cultural form, a type of identity politics; on the other, there are
those who believe that Britishness is found and expressed best through the
notion of citizenship within a civic model. A useful starting point in seeking to
understand these ideological differences remains Jennifer Todd's distinction
between those who identify as 'British Unionist' (whose primary empathy is
with Britain) and those who regard themselves as 'Ulster Loyalist' (who take the
six counties of Northern Ireland as their principal imagined community).[23]

Cultural Unionism

The advocates of cultural unionism assign pre-eminence to Ulster above
Britain (akin to Todd's Ulster Loyalist tradition) and give much emphasis to
the historical separation of Ulster/Northern Ireland and its cultural distinctiveness.[24] The politics of cultural unionism are most readily seen in the DUP,
especially in its promotion of Protestantism (until very recently at least) and
the Union (today) within the framework of a distinct ethnic identity. This
ideological position gives primacy to the view that Northern Ireland politics is,
and should be, shaped by a Protestant–British ethos, based in common religious and cultural practices, prioritizing the individual's defence of civil and
religious liberties over much else.

Such a set of values is seen as inherently superior to either Irish Catholicism
or nationalism, and hence, there is little dispensation given to such communities, in terms of either recognition of acknowledgement of Irish national
culture, or an 'Irish dimension' within Northern Ireland's politics. Rather, the
DUP has laid stress on policies that have permitted a cultural reading of
unionism to present against Irish cultural identity, such as seen in the resistance to an Irish Language Act, one of the points of discord that caused the
Assembly to collapse in 2017.

The culture that is identified and elevated reveals a strong sense of Britishness, albeit one with elements unique to Northern Ireland and its unionist
people. Cultural unionist identity continues to draw upon a variety of strong
identifiers, the most central of which are: Protestantism; loyalty to the monarchy and Crown; a sense of affinity and belonging with the people in Britain;
a strong perception of shared historical experience and commitment, especially during both World Wars;[25] blood sacrifice for Empire, especially on the

First World War battlefields; and, an overlapping sense of 'British' heritage. This is seen to reinforce the core cultural unionist belief that many Protestants in Northern Ireland remain a distinct cultural community.

Liberal Unionism

Another set of ideas that has emerged may be those classified as liberal unionism, which in Porter's understanding lies close to what Todd describes as the 'Ulster British' tradition. Its main dynamic is secular and it takes its frame of reference as the whole UK. This imagination of unionism involves actively promoting Northern Ireland as just another part of a multi-national, multi-ethnic state, its politics based on equal citizenship, and a non-sectarian form of political engagement. In other words, Northern Ireland should be indistinguishable in its politics and economic position from anywhere else in the UK.

Partition meant the UUP experienced the benefits of an electoral majority that effectively excluded political opponents and created a one-party state[26] in all but name. This situation allowed successive UUP prime ministers to ignore wider socio-economic circumstances in the Province, and especially the imbalances as to power and resources experienced by the Province's Catholic minority. The UUP government relied on this integral unionist majority and maintained its dominance at Stormont by allowing (some would say fostering) paranoia about the constitutional position to develop.[27]

It was this response (or the lack of it) from the UUP that liberal unionist ideology challenged, arguing that, as a counterpoint to nationalism, and if the Union is to be preserved, then its benefits to all must be made more transparent, and unionism must disengage from its sectarian past to present a moderate, non-sectarian liberal face, resisting the pressure to express themselves through cultural unionism.[28] Arthur Aughey, for example, suggests that our understanding of unionism should be based on rational political preference and that: 'unionism has little to do with the idea of the nation and everything to do with the idea of the state'.[29]

Such views have strong appeal to sections of unionism, particularly the middle class, whose sense of Britishness rests in what they recognize as the reality of a civic UK state, rather than any emotional expression, or overt attachment to cultural icons of Britishness, (which have long since ceased to be meaningful to them).[30] At the crux of such views is the desire to project unionism as a rational political choice, one which benefits the vast majority, if not all of Northern Ireland's citizens, through the rights that British citizenship brings.[31]

Civic Unionism

This brings us to civic unionism which forms the core of the transformation of unionism in recent years. At the heart of this notion is the belief that Northern Ireland's state institutions should be seen as a 'common possession of all rather than the exclusive preserve of one group, tribe or tradition'.[32] Northern Ireland is seen as a place where the dominant conflicting political identities of being British and being Irish bump into one another and then transmute into different forms.[33] Northern Ireland, it is argued, must adopt new political and legal practices and develop new socio-economic institutions to encourage the emergence of a more active civil society organized around different principles than those which currently exist. It is only as: 'nationalists as well as unionists are persuaded fully to invest in political life...that an identity based on concerted actions become conceivable'.[34] This goal has remained elusive, but the discourse remains central to core parts of the party, as this member articulates:

> One of the key aspects that they haven't implemented from the Belfast Agreement is cooperative government. You know, it's them and us government at the moment, and that's the one area we could attack them on, if we have a strong SDLP. You know, when Trimble became First Minister, the relationship in the First and Deputy Minister Office wasn't very good, but if we could articulate and show that, if we have a strong Ulster Unionist Party, and say, a strong SDLP, then we could create a very cooperative, progressive, future-looking government, you know, that may attract the voters across. That's a very difficult message to sell, because fear is a very potent element within politics here. So, that's why the fear project worked very well here.[35]

In his writings, Porter recognizes how difficult it may be for unionists to breach the connections and attachments of cultural unionism and how the institutions upon which civic unionists seek to draw are still often perceived as biased towards cultural unionism.[36] The active promotion of cultural and ethnic unionism is deeply embedded, drawing as it does on an established discourse and frames of meaning that appeal to established collective memory and the interpretation of the role of myths, culture, and religion within unionism.

As such these views are entrenched, and they function to oppose and counteract the development of a civic unionism. Nonetheless, to find common ground and develop a new a form of social and political organization, which rises above communal divisions, requires the deeper engagement of unionism in civil society. Porter sums up the issue by saying that if it is to survive unionism must embrace a more flexible form. This must involve giving primacy, not to the Union itself, but rather 'the quality of social and political life' it brings about.[37]

Some of the works of Aughey[38] have proved pivotal in the ideological development of the notion of civic unionism. For him, unionism 'cannot be understood in terms of "national assumptions"' and 'has little to do with the idea of the nation and everything to do with the idea of the state'.[39] From within this perspective the Union is rational in its composition[40] and represents an entirely logical relationship between individuals and the state. Aughey draws on earlier notions concerning an attachment to Britishness, arguing that rather than being marked by some 'peculiar spiritual substance or ethnic identity', it represents an 'acknowledgement by its citizens of the legitimacy of the constitutional relationship'.[41] As Bernard Crick put it:

> 'British' is a political and legal concept best applied to the institutions of the United Kingdom state, to common citizenship and common political arrangements. It is not a cultural term, nor does it correspond to any real sense of the nation.[42]

By separating unionism's strands outlined here (as done elsewhere[43]) we remain mindful of the risks of creating an artificial dichotomy. People's views cannot be boxed into neat categories, and there is never a clear fit between the ideological as it is conceptualized, models produced, and how this is understood by political parties or groups, or the individuals within them. Nonetheless, understanding the binary divide that has emerged between civic and cultural unionism is useful in understanding the nature and direction of contemporary unionism.

While the views are not exclusive, the DUP has a reading of events that is unmistakably imbedded in the loyalist understanding that strongly underpins cultural unionism, whilst the UUP approach has settled towards a form of civic unionist identity. This, of course, is not to deny that there are some secular rational elements within the DUP, or that views of some members of the UUP are still heavily located in cultural roots. These are ideological tendencies, not absolutes. It is possible to see how the differences between the two major parties representing unionism echo in part civic and cultural understandings of what it means to be unionist and how this is reflected in the views of UUP members that follow.

Under Trimble's leadership the UUP gravitated towards a form of civic unionism,[44] or new unionism,[45] with 'the emergence of a significant section of the unionist family looking to make a new deal with Irish nationalism', as there emerged a sense that 'unionists can neither create nor veto developments indefinitely in Northern Ireland' and that to 'govern the place effectively, some serious accommodation is required with at least a section of Irish nationalism, and it has been recognised that, for the interests of unionists, this should happen soon'.[46]

Trimble's discourse drew broadly upon Porter's conceptions and Aughey's visualization for a new form of politics expressed with a different set of political relationships. It was Porter's promotion of civic unionism that provides much of the pluralism model for new unionism. This involved turning away from a traditional unionist discourse to constructing one that is more inclusive and secular and which seeks to embrace both communities within Northern Ireland. In particular, this was to be done creating a sense of political accommodation through overtly recognizing difference.

Central here were strategies that sought to build pluralist institutions to which all political traditions, including both nationalism and unionism, could give allegiance. This was to involve constructing a new symbolism that broke with traditional communal loyalties. The discourse developed at the time within the UUP included claims that they would be: 'pro-active, inclusive, open, pluralist, dynamic, progressive, outward, articulate, intelligent, coherent, professional and confident'.[47]

This reorientation of unionism rested on the developing ideological and political shift we have outlined within sections of the party and a growing realism that power-sharing would be integral to the formation of any devolved government. Hence, the willingness to contemplate entering into some form of at least working relationship with Irish republicanism. This was part of the vision projected by Trimble and his supporters at the time of the Belfast Agreement in moving beyond the commonly expressed notion of simply rejecting the validity of Irish nationalism as illegitimate.[48] This was reflected in a broad discourse that gathered pace across some sections of unionism.

This process expanded the ideological space for the articulation of unionist politics, within which civic visions of life were explored. It was Trimble who was tasked with developing the strategies to make it politically viable and appealing to the wider unionist electorate. His belief that the Union had been 'copper-fastened'[49] and that a settlement, inclusive of republicanism, was a reasonable price to pay for the end of the armed conflict, brought Trimble and his supporters into direct conflict with other fractions of unionism, the anti-Agreement element within his own party and especially the DUP. It was a clash based on interpretations that was to have long-term consequences within unionism.

The dominant populist perspective on Trimble's leadership at the time was that of a hard man of unionism whose views and beliefs had moderated over time,[50] in the same way that Bill Craig had tempered his stance many years before. Trimble himself takes a different perspective, describing the complexity of his transformation in the following terms, asking of himself, was it:

> Trimble who was with Craig in voluntary coalition, indeed some suspect wrongly that I was the author of that idea. Trimble who is regularly chatting to officials at the Northern Ireland Office. Trimble who with Craig and David McNarry produced a policy paper in the late seventies which turns out to be the blueprint for

Jim Prior's 'rolling devolution' plan, which was my idea. They knew where I was that. Trimble who—when Paisley was trying his hand at moderate politics in the Atkins's conference in 1980—where I was actually tracking in that direction and there was a sort of a joint unionist approach. Trimble—who wasn't for going down Molyneaux's integrationist path, which he saw as part of the 'do nothing, lets dig ourselves into our trenches' policy—but was instead going for devolution. And everybody knew, even if I hadn't fully internalized the concept when Bill Craig first mentioned voluntary coalition in 1975 that the need was to do a deal with nationalism. By 1995 the only question was the shape of the deal, if you were going to do one.[51]

The attempts made by David Trimble to reassure those who were sceptical (at best) over the Belfast Agreement, and to establish the acceptability and authenticity of multiple identities, with no profiting of Britishness over Irishness, beyond its numerical superiority, through a parity of esteem, met much unionist opposition. In response, Trimble sought to reform the UUP, including severing formal ties to the Orangeism (even if it was the Order which ultimately broke away first). It marked the final break-up, both ideologically and organizationally, of the old unionist hegemony and ushered in an attempt to demonstrate that the UUP was now a modern, broad-based organization with Northern Ireland's future at its heart. This perspective underpinned Trimble's belief that under his steerage the UUP could bring about an effective and working devolution and an end of the IRA.

The idea of a new inclusive and more broad-minded form of unionism remained a central feature of UUP discourse in subsequent elections. In 2001, for example, the UUP argued strongly that it was their strategy that had forced republicans into making concessions and which was best placed to improve the overall quality of life for all of Northern Ireland's citizens. The UUP set about formulating policy expressing a particular definition of Britishness and it was clear that Trimble, following his new unionist instincts, was willing to recognize nationalist aspirations. He sought to define the UUP in terms of an ideology capable of encompassing all sections of Northern Ireland in a new pluralist concept of society. This was to include a strengthening of inclusive Britishness, resting upon a desire to engage directly in the dealings and business of the British nation.[52]

Trimble, however, failed in his quest to convince enough of wider unionist electorate of his optimistic perspectives, or that the time was right for an accommodation with Irish republicanism. He was continually harried and confronted, largely by the DUP for effecting concessions to republicans, particularly around IRA decommissioning. His position was further undermined by defections from the UUP to the DUP. The period also saw the DUP focus on what they termed the 'pushover unionism' of the UUP and their failure to effectively oppose the Belfast Agreement that in their view had failed the unionist people, not least by rewarding the representatives of terrorism with ministerial office in the Assembly.

With the authority of Trimble and his supporters steadily undermined, the DUP and sections of the UUP expressed open enmity was towards him and the direction in which he sought to take his Party. Moreover, with the Agreement struggling to gain traction, Trimble found it increasingly difficult to offer tangible evidence of the worth of reform. The UUP was unable to convince popular support to make the civic model it promoted the dominant political voice within unionism (meanwhile, within unionism the DUP increasingly came to the fore in electoral terms).

The disillusionment of many unionists with the Belfast Agreement was unambiguous and self-evident.[53] This impression of political forfeiture found direct and meaningful expression at the ballot box and, at the 2003 Assembly election, the DUP overtook its once unionist dominant rival. The UUP discourse at the time strongly projected the view that it had taken most political risks, that it still represented the most acceptable and stable face of unionism, and that it was the UUP that had progressed the peace process, generating a reasonable level of cross-community trust throughout Northern Ireland.[54] According to the former MLA Sandra Overend:

> it started with the Belfast Agreement, in that we did what was best for the people of Northern Ireland, and the Party divided over it, and the Party lost support over it, but it was better for Northern Ireland, and we put Northern Ireland first. We still do. The DUP, they put their party first, and I think that stands. We put ourselves last all the time.[55]

The UUP's slogan, 'doing what's right for Northern Ireland', reverberates throughout the Party. Electoral decline is framed and understood as a by-product of taking bigger historical steps towards securing negotiated agreement in 1998. This sentiment prevails for elected representatives, including MLA Roy Beggs:

> Ulster Unionists are not about getting power for ourselves. We have shown that, in fact, if you look at the Belfast Agreement, we acted not in our own Party's self-interest, not in individual's self-interest, but we acted on community interest, and that is where we are. We want things to be better for the community, which we also strongly believe will be better for the Union in the long term. It's easy to look at short-term things, but we believe that it's important that we have a stable base of Northern Ireland in order to maintain the Union in the long term.[56]

The consequences for the party remain severe, as this member of the Coleraine focus group observed:

> there's a block of voters there who left us . . . and transferred their vote over to the DUP, and they're now comfortable having their vote there. They're still happy

voting for them. You know, the fact that they topped over 200,000 votes for the first time since '07 shows that confidence in the DUP project as it is. It's very hard to counter that at the moment, because you need to make yourself very distinctive and different.[57]

The brand of civic unionism advocated by David Trimble failed to widely penetrate the political consciousness of unionism and resulted in moving the unionist community back into the sphere of 'ethnic' unionism as defined by the DUP.[58] Civic unionism flagged as an ideological and electoral force. Important differences still exist, however, in the ways unionist public discourse is constructed, their relationship with the state and how they conceive their sense of Britishness. Civic unionism caused fissures and splits across unionism and within party ranks, between pro- and anti-Agreement factions. It was a rupture from which the party is still feeling the effects. As one member put it:

> I spoke to all my family members, and there's not one who voted for the Belfast Agreement. That was a huge split within the Ulster Unionist Party at that time, and we've never really recovered from that, it was like a divorce in the family. There were so many members left us over the heads of the Belfast Agreement...you know, we're still trying to get over the aftershocks of that.[59]

Trimble did substantially shift the ideological framework of the UUP outside the framework of the politics of birthright and inheritance, underpinned by the static idea that their future lay ensuring the security of the constitutional link at all costs. Civic unionism did suffer substantial setbacks under Trimble, but the essential notions remained alive. The UUP thus sought to project an image and a discourse that, while holding that Northern Ireland remained British, and 'fully involved in all aspects of life of the United Kingdom',[60] it also sought to ensure a more inclusive and less partisan society. Elements of new unionism still existed and remained the focus for discussion within the Party.

Many of these ideas were taken up by subsequent UUP leaders. All, to a greater or lesser extent, demonstrated a willingness to engage with the principles of civic unionism set down during Trimble's reign. Following Trimble's resignation, his successor as leader, Reg Empey, promised to maintain a 'tolerant and pluralist vision'[61] for unionism. In one of his first public statements he claimed that both the UUP and DUP must recognize that, during the contemporary conflict, some unionist rhetoric had been negative and divisive, and that in some cases this may even have encouraged sectarian violence.[62]

Elsewhere, Empey laid out part of his view of the future for the party:

> The religious background of UUP candidates does not interest me. Their sexual orientation does not concern me, nor their race and I am on record strongly urging more women candidates. I care that all UUP candidates are Unionists. I care that they are committed to a shared future, to delivering national politics to Northern Ireland

and I care that they are talented and capable of winning elections and holding office. I wish to see, and am actively working for, a brand of unionism that encompasses the entire community in Northern Ireland, irrespective of religious background.[63]

Empey wished to establish a UUP at the heart of the Union. The UCUNF alliance with the Conservative Party was established amidst much goading from the DUP, which claimed that the UUP will 'answer to the Tory Party and not to you'.[64] Indeed the UUP's attempt to link with the Conservatives allowed the DUP to again present themselves as a strongly defined ethno-regionalist party who saw their sense of Britishness within the context of being unique to Northern Ireland and which, above all else, ultimately put the affairs of Northern Ireland to the fore.

With the election of Mike Nesbitt as UUP leader in March 2012, civic unionism was given further momentum. Nesbitt was fairly new to politics, having made his name as a local television and radio presenter. He drew heavily on aspects of the civic model when assessing the contemporary state of Northern Irish politics:

What was proposed under the Belfast Agreement set out a vision for a shared future, but what we have seen under the stewardship of the DUP and Sinn Fein following St Andrews has become a shared-out future. In 1998, we did not envis-age a future for Northern Ireland where the Office of the First Minister and deputy First Minister would become a black hole where the child poverty, childcare, racial equality and sexual orientation strategies would disappear because of a failure to agree them. What about the key question, the fix? This isn't just about reforming the institutions—this is also about the relationships. In the opening declaration of the Belfast Agreement, there is a key reference to being dedicated to building mutual trust. This is the critical failure and therefore the core challenge.[65]

Indeed, Nesbitt pushed this line of thinking to its utmost when he proposed that UUP members engaged directly in cross-community voting, arguing that they should not automatically give second preference to the DUP. Arguing that he would be giving his second preference vote to the SDLP, he stated:

I can work with Colum Eastwood [of the SDLP] and he can work with me, not because the law says we have to but because we both know it is the only positive way forward. My unionism is enhanced, not diminished, by embracing diversity. Vote for the candidates you believe will do the right thing by your community, their constituency and this country.[66]

Nesbitt's successor, Robin Swann, whilst moving away from overt cross-community vote transfer ideas, claimed continuity of thought with his imme-diate predecessors, saying that:

Unionism has a lot to offer but it's also making that union attractive to everybody in Northern Ireland, so they know the benefits that are there and it's about promoting a positive unionism, a non-threatening unionism and a unionism that can move forward and be progressive.[67]

He further emphasized some of the underlying tenets of civic unionism in saying:

Ulster Unionists realize that for Northern Ireland to work, it has to be a joint Unionist-Nationalist approach. But it's about working together. It's not about formal relationships at this point in time. I don't think, our society, I don't think Northern Ireland's ready there, as of yet. There's a need for the normalization of politics in Northern Ireland. What happened [the collapse of the institutions in 2017] I think, has set us back 10–15 years, because we're back to 'Them and Us'.[68]

Conclusion

The narratives and discourses projected by the UUP are fundamental to its political being and positioning. These perform several key functions, not least of which are the binding together of the party and its members, often laying down the parameters for understanding the major consequences of political events. These discourses also project the public face of the party in its efforts to secure more expansive support. For the leadership, such discourses are always multifaceted, and in recent years have reflected its attempt to reposition as a centrist party.

Such unionist discourses are, of course, always open to challenge, from both without and within, and the counter understandings offered by the DUP have had success in outflanking and outbidding the UUP, through a discourse immersed in the politics of cultural unionism and evoking a different sense of unionist belonging. Nonetheless, UUP discourses are central in helping some unionists frame an understanding of contemporary events and provide the reasoning and rationalization of the positions taken by the UUP leadership.

The unionism of the UUP places greater emphasis on the civic and political bonds of citizenship and the importance of the British state, rather than the vision of unionism as an ethno-national community. The struggle remains for the UUP leadership to establish a distinct discourse given that some of its membership and the wider unionist electorate have experienced recent an increased sense of political insecurity and ideological fragmentation. The future of the UUP rests on its capacity to win back the confidence of its electorate, while at the same time projecting an inclusive and non-sectarian discourse that is still seen as unionist. That is no easy task for the party.

Notes

1. Brian Faulkner, *Memoirs of a Statesman*, London: Weidenfeld & Nicolson, 1978, 278.
2. See J. Harbinson, *The Ulster Unionist Party*, Belfast: Blackstaff, 1973; D. Hume, *The Ulster Unionist Party 1972–92*, Lurgan: Ulster Society Publications, 1996; G. Walker, *A History of the Ulster Unionist Party*, Manchester: Manchester University Press, 2004.
3. D. Godson, *Himself Alone: David Trimble and the Ordeal of Unionism*, London: Harper Collins, 2004, 923.
4. See D. Trimble, 'Post-Agreement Ireland: North and South', speech given to the Annual Conference of the Irish Association, 20 Nov. 1998.
5. Northern Ireland House of Commons Official Report, 34, col. 1095. Sir James Craig, Unionist Party, then Prime Minister of Northern Ireland, 24 Apr. 1934.
6. H. McDonald, *Trimble*, London: Bloomsbury, 2000, 6.
7. Ulster Unionist Party, *Election Manifesto: A Fair Society*, Belfast: UUP, 2005, 1.
8. Interview with Howard Thornton, 20 May 2016.
9. Dermot Nesbitt locates the origins of this new thinking in 1987 with the *An End to Drift* document published in June 1987. It suggested that unionists should not be ashamed to adapt to 'changing circumstances' and that both the UUP and DUP should discard 'majority rule' as a core principle. Unionist Task Force, *An End to Drift*, Belfast: Unionist Task Force, 1987.
10. J. Potter and M. Wetherell, *Discourse and Social Psychology: Beyond Attitudes and Behaviour*, London: Sage, 1987. See also J. Potter, 'Re-reading Discourse and Social Psychology: Transforming Social Psychology', *British Journal of Social Psychology*, 51(3) (2012), 436–55.
11. M. Billig, *Ideology and Opinions: Studies in Rhetorical Psychology*, London: Sage, 1991, 14.
12. S. Hall, 'Introduction', in S. Hall (ed.), *Representation: Cultural Representations and Signifying Practices*, London: Sage, 1997, 6.
13. Here, we broadly accept Hayward's understanding of the role of socio-political discourse as something that 'may be used to legitimize, accompany, disguise or substitute for change in political values and activity'. See K. Hayward, 'Introduction: Political Discourse and Conflict Resolution', in K. Hayward and C. O'Donnell (eds), *Political Discourse and Conflict Resolution: Debating Peace in Northern Ireland*, London: Routledge, 2012, 1–15.
14. See K. Hayward, 'The Role of Political Discourse in Conflict Transformation: Evidence from Northern Ireland', in K. Hayward and C. O'Donnell (eds), Special Issue on Political Discourse as an Instrument of Conflict and Peace: Lessons from Northern Ireland, *Journal of Peace and Conflict Studies*, 15.1 (2008), 1–20; See also various in K. Hayward and C. O'Donnell (eds), *Political Discourse and Conflict Resolution: Debating Peace in Northern Ireland*, London: Routledge, 2011.
15. Ulster Unionist Party, *Assembly Election Manifesto*, Belfast: UUP, 2017.
16. UUP, *Assembly Election Manifesto*, 2017.

17. Fergal Cochrane observed: 'Unionist ideology contains diverse interest groups with little in common other than a commitment to the link with Britain. While this position remains relatively cohesive during periods of constitutional crisis when they can articulate what they do not want (namely a weakening of the link with Britain), the coherence of the ideology begins to disintegrate when unionists are forced to establish a consensus for political progress.'

18. James Molyneaux, 19 Nov. 1991, cited in F. Cochrane, *Unionist Politics and the Politics of Unionism since the Anglo-Irish Agreement*, Cork: Cork University Press, 1997, 92.

19. J. Ruane and J. Todd, *The Dynamics of Conflict in Northern Ireland: Power, Conflict and Emancipation*, Cambridge: Cambridge University Press, 1996, 88–9.

20. The centenary of 1916 marked a huge outpouring of books on the subject of the Rebellion and its immediate aftermath, of which the following are but a small sample: T. P. Coogan, *1916 The Morning After*, London: Head Zeus, 2015; D. Ferriter, *A Nation Not a Rabble*, London: Profile, 2015; M. T. Foy and B. Barton, *The Easter Rising*, Stroud: History Press, 2015; R. Higgins, *Transforming 1916*, Cork: Tower Books, 2015; C. Townshend, *Easter 1916: The Irish Rebellion*, London: Penguin, 2015.

21. See e.g. material in Hall, *Representation*; S. Hall and P. du Gay (eds), *Questions of Cultural Identity*, London: Sage, 1996.

22. N. Porter, *Rethinking Unionism: An Alternative Vision for Northern Ireland*, Belfast: Blackstaff, 1996.

23. J. Todd, 'Two Traditions in Unionist Political Culture', *Irish Political Studies*, 2.1 (1987), 1–26.

24. B. Graham and Y. Whelan, 'The Legacies of the Dead: Commemorating the Troubles in Northern Ireland', *Environment and Planning D: Society and Space*, 25.3 (2007), 476–95.

25. D. Officer and G. Walker, 'Protestant Ulster: Ethno-History, Memory and Contemporary Prospects', *National Identities*, 2.3 (2000), 293–307.

26. Although he has long faded from the political scene, one of the key supporters of this line of thinking was Robert McCartney, who in political terms was best known as leader of the UK Unionist Party. Over several decades he consistently criticized 'traditional unionism' and in particular the UUP for its failure to develop meaningful and inclusive political policy.

27. Cited in *News Letter*, 7 Mar. 1995.

28. *Irish Times*, 3 May 1996.

29. A. Aughey, *Under Siege: Ulster Unionism and the Anglo-Irish Agreement*, Belfast: Blackstaff, 1989, 18.

30. Hence, e.g. McCartney's advocacy of the Campaign for Equal Citizenship (CEC) in the mid-1980s and its support for the organization of other British political parties in Northern Ireland.

31. J. W. McAuley, 'Divided Loyalists, Divided Loyalties: Conflict and Continuities in Contemporary Unionist Ideology', in C. Gilligan and J. Tonge (eds), *Peace or War? Understanding the Peace Process in Northern Ireland*, Aldershot: Ashgate, 1997, 37–53.

32. Porter, *Rethinking Unionism*, 163.

33. Porter, *Rethinking Unionism*, 183.

34. Porter, *Rethinking Unionism*, 201.
35. Coleraine focus group, 18 May 2016.
36. Porter, *Rethinking Unionism*, 166.
37. Porter, *Rethinking Unionism*, 170.
38. A. Aughey, 'The End of History, The End of the Union', in A. Aughey. D. Burnside, G. Adams, J. Donaldson, and E. Harris (eds), *Selling Unionism Home and Away*, Belfast: Ulster Young Unionist Council, 1995, 1–15; A. Aughey, 'The Idea of the Union', and 'The Constitutional Challenge', both in J. W. Foster (ed.), *The Idea of the Union*, Vancouver: Belcouver Press, 1995, 24–49, 102–22. A. Aughey, 'Unionism', in A. Aughey and D. Morrow (eds), *Northern Ireland Politics*, London: Longman, 1996, 70–96. A. Aughey, 'A State of Exception: The Concept of the Political in Northern Ireland', *Irish Political Studies*, 12 (1997), 1–12.
39. A. Aughey, 'Unionism and Self-Determination', in P. J. Roche and B. Barton (eds), *The Northern Ireland Question: Myth and Reality*, Tonbridge: Wordzworth Publishing, 2013, 36.
40. A. Aughey, *Under Siege: Ulster Unionism and the Anglo-Irish Agreement*, Belfast: Blackstaff, 1989, 1.
41. A. Aughey, 'Britishness: An Explanation and a Defence', in G. Lucy and E. McClure (eds), *Cool Britannia? What Britishness Means to me*, Lurgan: Ulster Society, 1993, 3.
42. B. Crick, *National Identities: The Constitution of the United Kingdom*, Oxford: Blackwell, 1991, 97.
43. See C. McGlynn, J. W. McAuley, and J. Tonge, 'The Party Politics of Post-Devolution Identity in Northern Ireland', *British Journal of Politics and International Relations*, 16.2 (2014), 273–90.
44. Liam O'Dowd lists a wide range of writers including Paul Bew, Brian Barton, Dennis Kennedy, Richard English, and Graham Walker, alongside the politician Robert McCartney, as representative of new unionist voices. See L. O'Dowd, 'New Unionism, British Nationalism and the Prospects for a Negotiated Settlement in Northern Ireland', in D. Miller (ed.), *Rethinking Northern Ireland: Culture, Ideology and Colonialism*, London: Routledge, 1998, 70–93.
45. See J. W. McAuley, *Ulster's Last Stand? Reconstructing Unionism After the Peace Process*, Dublin: Irish Academic Press, 2010.
46. R. English, *Redefining Unionism: An Academic Perspective*, Working Papers in British–Irish Studies, 2, Dublin: Institute for British-Irish Studies, University College Dublin, 2001.
47. *Ulster Review* (1995/6), 15.
48. O'Dowd, 'New Unionism', 78.
49. D. Trimble, *To Raise up a New Northern Ireland: Speeches and Articles by the Rt. Hon, David Trimble MP MLA, 1998–2001*, Belfast: Belfast Press, 2001, 8.
50. BBC News Profile: David Trimble. Available at: <news.bbc.co.uk/1/hi/northern_ireland/765174.stm>, accessed Sept. 2017.
51. F. Millar, *David Trimble: The Price of Peace*, Dublin: Liffey Press, 2004, 44–5.
52. Godson, *Himself Alone*.
53. R. Mac Ginty, 'Unionist Political Attitudes After the Belfast Agreement', *Irish Political Studies*, 19.1 (2004), 87–99.

54. University of Ulster, 'Don't write off UUP and SDLP just yet, conference told', News Release, 22 Sept. 2004.
55. Interview with Sandra Overend, 28 Jan. 2016.
56. Interview with Roy Beggs, 28 Jan. 2016.
57. Interview with Coleraine focus group, 18 May 2016.
58. Millar, *Trimble: Price of Peace*, 217.
59. Interview with Coleraine focus group, 18 May 2016.
60. Ulster Unionist Party, *Securing a British Future for the People of Northern Ireland*, Belfast: UUP.
61. J. Andrews, 'We Can Safeguard the Union', *Belfast Telegraph*, 29 Sept. 2006.
62. *Irish News*, 15 June 2006.
63. Sir Reg Empey, 'I am actively working for a brand of unionism that encompasses the entire community' (2010), available at <http://sluggerotoole.com/index.php/weblog/comments/sir-reg-empey-i-am-actively-working-for-a-brand-of-unionism-that-encompasse>, accessed Aug. 2017.
64. Democratic Unionist Party, *General Election Manifesto—Let's Keep Northern Ireland Moving Forward*, Belfast: DUP, 2010.
65. *News Letter*, 11 Sept. 2014, 5.
66. *Belfast Telegraph*, 13 Feb. 2017, 4.
67. BBC News (2017) 'Robin Swann Set to be Ulster Unionist Party Leader'. Available at: <www.bbc.co.uk/news/uk-northern-ireland-39392985>, accessed July 2017.
68. Interview with Robin Swann, 14 Aug. 2017.

6

Britishness and Northern Irishness

Identity and the UUP

> Unionists can sometimes act defensively. We can be inclined to see
> ourselves as inhabiting an embattled enclave in the islands . . . But there is
> another, more important side to unionism: the belief that all the different
> people of these two islands—England, Welsh, Scottish and from our own
> island too—share far more than divides us; a belief that there is as much
> value in continued and various diversity as there is in mutual conformity; a
> belief that all will gain from being freely associated together within a wider
> union . . . We mean no ill will towards this State when we, who are union-
> ists, say that the Union is in the best interests of all the people, politically,
> culturally, socially and in no small part, economically.
>
> (David Trimble, Speech to the Irish Association[1])

It was not only territorial boundaries that altered with the partition of Ireland;
the social and political framework also changed drastically. For a majority in
the new northern jurisdiction, the term 'Ireland' lost much of its meaning,
as the two states set about constructing and reinforcing ideologies of separate-
ness and division.[2] In so doing, it became another place for many Ulster
unionists. There was a perceptible change in the dominant identity of Northern
Ireland, stressing its 'Britishness' and emphasizing the link with the United
Kingdom, albeit with distinct forms of citizenship and cultural identity.
Northern Ireland had a discrete polity, within which the UUP quickly
assumed representation for many mainstream northern Protestants, fearful
for the existence of the state and concerned about the shape it would adopt.

Crucially, for unionism this involved not only changing existing political
constructs, but also cultural representations through which Ulster unionists
forged their imagined community[3] into a national culture. Politically this was
embodied in the UUP, which alongside the Orange Order and the Royal Ulster
Constabulary, made up the political religious and legal triumvirate of institutions upon which the Northern Ireland state rested. A strong identification

with unionism thus encouraged individuals to further characterize and delineate membership of their group, which in turn offered high levels of support[4] in distinguishing between those deemed loyal to the state and those considered otherwise. As one current member put it: 'I suppose—and I'm not saying I'm right on this—but, they never demonstrated that they were inclusive enough of the full community.'[5]

This collective sense of belonging was especially important to the self-worth and self-concept of unionism.[6] In this context party membership of the UUP played an important role in expressing an individual's sense of security[7] and stability.[8] At the core of this construct was the understanding of Irish nationalism as the 'dangerous other', which was deeply engrained within unionist political culture and identity. Unionism thus sought to reinforce its inclusive sense of identify by openly excluding identifiable others through its major discourses and symbolism, whereby the need for security against external and internal threat is understood and accepted. This sense of unionist identity emphasizes and builds upon a perceived common history, embedded through commemoration and which found expression through notions of collective memory and historical myth.

Unionist historical understanding is often presented as being in direct opposition to nationalist history and identity, which are continually exhibited as threats to the unionist political position. The ideological strands which make up unionist identity are multifaceted[9] (as is nationalist identity) and represents a complex intersection of social, economic, cultural, and political forces. Indeed, the conflict in Northern Ireland rests on an intricate set of exclusive social bonds and interactions resulting in radically different and often conflicting aspirations and identities within in two communities.[10] These competitive and mutually exclusive identities hold great significance politically as members of separate cultural communities reinforce their mutually separate position.

This chapter identifies and outlines senses of identity and belonging within the UUP. It explores continuities and changes within that identity, and how it offers a different understanding of Britishness to that of its main unionist rival, the DUP. Using both survey data and interviews, it also examines the level of exclusiveness of members' British identity, the position of those who identify as Northern Irish within the party, and the ambivalent relationship some have with their sense of Irishness. The political expression of unionist identity takes different shapes and directions.[11] Moreover, the chapter further considers the extent to which Ulster unionism draws on senses of belonging that are fixed, and the extent they are open to processes of negotiation. Finally, the chapter explores the different ways in which members of the UUP draw on a variety of social and political markers to express what they understand as their distinct sense of Britishness.

Britishness and Unionism

For almost all members of the UUP, Britishness is central to their social identity and remains at the core of how they view the world. To talk about social identity in these terms means referring to the understanding of someone in terms of group memberships and, in particular, those groups that are most meaningful in how the individuals define themselves. Sharing Britishness as a social identity does not mean that those who define themselves as such know or interact with every other member who self-designate as members of that category, or that their views are uniform in all things. It does mean, however, that the individual shares characteristics with other members of the same category and, to some degree, events that are relevant to the group as a whole also bear great significance for the individual member. National identity is important in formulating both individual and community identities and tied to the frontiers of beliefs and belonging. Each person can, and does, hold many identities, but not all are equally important in all situations.[12]

In 1968, Richard Rose,[13] in his benchmark survey of Northern Ireland, found that 39 per cent of its population saw their primary identity as British, while some 20 per cent of Protestants gave 'Irish' as their foremost identity. It was only with the outbreak of widespread ethno-sectarian conflict (euphemistically known as the Troubles), that the Protestant sense of belonging altered and British identity was prioritized and given increased validity. Within a decade, the conflict had taken shape, and by the late 1970s over two-thirds of Protestants saw British as the best way to self-classify.[14] Since then the broad trends and patterns in expressions of identity have been clearly identified, with many Protestants expressing a strong rejection of all things Irish.[15] Indeed, the expression of Britishness amongst Protestants strengthened in opinion polls throughout the past three decades, with those identifying as Irish dropping to a mere 3 per cent on average.[16]

As we can see from Figure 6.1, responding to a forced choice 'best identity' question, almost three-quarters of UUP members regard their primary national identity as 'British'. This identification is obviously more widespread than amongst the broader population which contains many nationalist Irish identifiers. In the 2011 census, 40 per cent of Northern Ireland's adult population described their principal national identity as British, while 48 per cent included some sense of British in their national identity.[17] Britishness, of course, finds expression through national symbolism, values, attitudes, cultural values, citizenship, institutions, and achievements.[18] The emphasis put on one or more of these articulations, or the ways in which members draw on these identifiers to construct their major sense of identity, finds expression through the UUP. Such emphases in working-class loyalist communities have led to confrontation and violence. In 2012, the decision of Sinn Féin, the SDLP, and

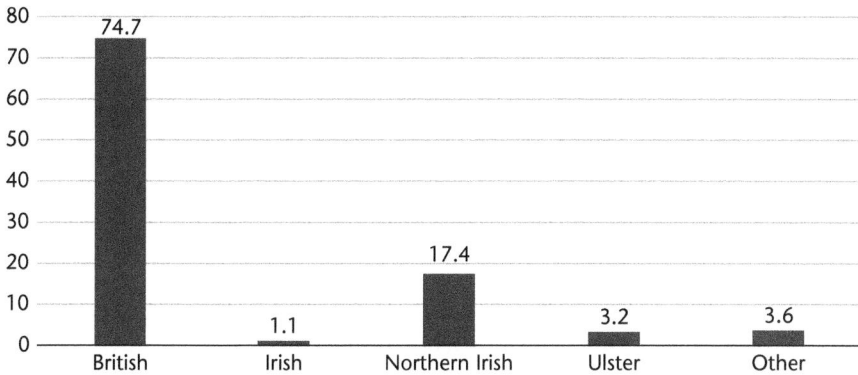

Figure 6.1 Best self-description of national identity among UUP members

Q. *Which of these best describes the way you usually think of yourself?*

Alliance Party on Belfast City Council to remove the Union flag from iconic landmarks in the city, including the City Hall, led to months of loyalist riots. The flag was to be flown only on eighteen designated days of special significance. The UUP membership is split equally, at 45 per cent on either side, between those believing the Union flag should be flown permanently atop public buildings in Northern Ireland and those who prefer the compromise of designated days. Five per cent believe no flags should be flown, 3 per cent believe only a Northern Ireland flag should be displayed, and 2 per cent offered other options.

For some of the UUP members interviewed, the issue of identity was quite straightforwardly stated. As one elected representative stated: 'I'm British. I'm not Northern Irish. I'm British. I'm proud to be British',[19] while a member of the Coleraine focus group put it as follows: 'I would stand up and say, "I'm a unionist, and ... British"',[20] and another simply said: 'Well, I'm British, very much, so yeah'.[21] The views of the former MLA, Jo-Anne Dobson, were fairly representative: 'I just see myself as ... British first, and then I'm from Northern Ireland second.' A UUP member spoke of how they 'still value being British, despite all the failings of what happens in London' and claimed a lack of interest in a united Ireland south of the border. 'Some of the TDs that I've spoken to and ministers, privately, are saying, "We don't want you. We couldn't afford you. We couldn't afford you."'[22]

Which Britishness? Which Union?

Although there is unsurprisingly a strong identification with Britishness among UUP members, there is no common view as to what this sense of belonging meant or what Britishness constitutes. When those interviewed were asked their understanding of Britishness, and what it signifies to them, interviewees provided a number of meanings connected with their social identity. These were located in political, cultural, institutional, and regional references, all of which were used to explain the connection Northern Ireland had to Britain and the relationship of UUP members to Britishness. Hence the following from party members in the Coleraine focus group:

I think it [Britishness] means different things in different regions of the UK, which is what's made Britishness so strong and durable, is that when you to go Scotland and you have a different interpretation of Britishness to here, or to England, or to Wales, you know, that's what's made it so durable and such a powerful identity, that you can be Muslim and British, you can be . . . you know, it's meant that you can be so many different things but still be British.[23]

[Britishness] is a combination of things, it is the history of the place, and that's why I said it means different things in different places, because in Scotland it might mean a completely different thing to here. We might think of the military service here, you know, we're automatically thinking of the army and the police and UDR, and all they did, that was a symbol of Britishness for a long time. Football, for example, is a strong . . . you know, especially when you go into the World Cup or something, you want to see the British teams do well. So, I think it means different things in different places, and it's hard to nail down, and it evolves too. I think it evolves too over time, and it's not like it's set in stone, and it is nailed, and say, 'To be British, these are the three rules, this is what you need to be entered into the British club.' That's why I'm saying, that different regions have different interpretations of it.[24]

Some drew direct comparison between those who expressed Britishness in Northern Ireland and others in Britain. Take the following:

Well, I'd say [people in Britain] are not so intense about their nationality as we are, but they're lax about it in a lot of cases, quite lax about their Britishness. Just like, you get people on mainland Britain who don't care about the Royalty, and they're lax about it, it's there . . . like the Church of England. You know, it's there, and that's . . . it's like a comfort blanket for them, and there are a lot of English people who see Britishness and Englishness as nearly the same.[25]

I think Northern Ireland's more British than most people in England, it costs us more. The fact that we're here and we're British, this is valuable to us. I know, in England, they wouldn't put the same importance to it, but it is to us.[26]

The MLA Roy Beggs defines his sense of Britishness as being part of a wider British nation:

What does it mean? Recognizing the benefits of retaining the component parts of the United Kingdom, you know, it's the fifth biggest economy in the world. Recognizing that even Scotland with its oil, has dangers in going independent with fluctuating oil prices. There is great benefit and opportunities that exist for our people being part of the United Kingdom. I have aunts and uncles in England and Scotland, and cousins there, as well. I have a son now in London, and my daughter's studying in Dundee, and the other son is at Queen's. So, it just seems it's a big part of our wider nation. I follow closely the political world as it affects British politics. I recognize the values that were created when the constitutional monarchy was created, where Parliament was established, and the democratic principles which thereafter were followed, you know, throughout the world. So, I'm just very proud of our history, and feel very fortunate of that the opportunities as a British citizen exist for myself and my kids.[27]

For others, Britishness was tied directly into institutions, such as the monarchy:

Well, it's the State Opening of Parliament today, that's one of the key cornerstones of the British, it's having the Royal Family and the pomp and ceremony that goes with it.[28]

Well, it's being part of the bigger picture of the United Kingdom. It's also the sovereignty of the Queen over the whole of the United Kingdom.[29]

MLA Philip Smith tries to express the choice of identities available to him, and places these within the context of being British on the island of Ireland:

I would say that I'm probably *consider myself British, Ulster, Irish, Northern Irish,* all of them to a dollop there, depending on the situation. I do think at a UK level. I was at university in Birmingham, and I lived in Birmingham for a number of years. I mean, I know it well, and I know London well, and the Home Counties, and I've lived in Sheffield. I *feel British?* I think, to me, it's being part of—I suppose, outside of the USA and China, and, possibly, Russia—one of the largest and most influential countries in the world. A major global economy, still, despite all the cuts made to the military and diplomatic power, you know, we've got some of the trappings of that. Whether it be everything from the monarchy, to Last Night at the Proms, to the BBC, to *Team GB at the Olympics?* You know, so, I cheered for Team GB, not for Team Ireland, despite, obviously, some local people will compete for Ireland, but my heart's not in it. It's in Team *GB.*[30]

For others, the notion of Britishness remained difficult to define in concrete terms. Take this from former MLA Adrian Cochrane-Watson:

I'm trying to think of the right words here. I would be a British . . . but British is too simple a way to describe me. I would be an . . . Ulsterman, who wants to let himself be British. I don't know. I'm not Irish. [and] No. No, I'm not Northern Irish.[31]

Northern Irish Identity and Unionism

The meaning and consequence of a Northern Irish identity has developed over the post-conflict period.[32] It has been argued that a shared Northern Irish identity could encourage and enhance everyday relationships across the community and religious divide in Northern Ireland.[33] Over the subsequent period a growth of a Northern Irish identity has been readily seen, but its significance remains open to much conjecture[34] and remains difficult to assess.[35] This member of the Omagh focus group sought to define it as follows:

> There's a problem with calling yourself Irish, because it's kind of been slightly toxified, you know. I'm certainly Northern Irish. I'm not English, Scottish, or Welsh. There's certainly a distinct identity there.[36]

John Garry and Kevin McNicholl[37] offer three major interpretations of Northern Irishness: as a neutral identity; as a manifestation of the major identities of British unionist and Irish nationalist; and, as a more meaningful distinction for Catholics than for Protestants, who simply project their identity on the superordinate Northern Irish.[38] Fourteen per cent of UUP members identified primarily as Northern Irish. Whilst this is in part a manifestation of British unionism, representing its regional outworking, this identification also seems to represent a cross-community or more 'neutral' form of identity, accompanied by the hope it might be shared across the divide, even if Britishness cannot.

Another understanding by members emphasized expressions of belonging within a particular part of the United Kingdom, as articulated by this member from Coleraine:

> I think Northern Irish is a distinct identity, I think that's part of it. You know, having the Irish...like some of the great statesmen and actors within the stage have been Irish, you know, if you look at the Duke of Wellington, he was an Irishman. So, like, it's very hard to...Irishness does form part of that Britishness and what it has become.[39]

Or this from MLA Robbie Butler:

> For me, I'm proud to be a unionist, but what I want unionism to be is not necessarily representative of a religion, or class of people. I want people to proud to be a unionist because of Northern Ireland, and Northern Ireland's role within the Union. Notwithstanding the fact that, actually, we are our own island, of Ireland too, and that that is pivotal in who we are too. So, I think that Carson got it right, you know, he was an Irishman, but he was a unionist.[40]

Most commonly Northern Irishness is understood and given meaning in unionism by projecting Britishness on the superordinate Northern Irish identity. Again, this was how Robbie Butler put it:

> You know, but, I think that's maybe something that we...I certainly take...you know, I'm British, and I don't expect a nationalist to ever consider themselves British, but I don't think it's too much of them to, maybe, in the future, consider themselves Northern Irish. That's maybe where the future of unionism lies, as well.[41]

The following from members are clear statements of a sense of Northern Irish within a British context:

> We've struggled with the Irish bit [of identity] for years, wrongly. So, you know, people are very proud to say, 'They're Scottish, but they're British. They're Welsh, but they're British. They're English, but they're British,' and we go, 'We're just British, or Irish.' So, there's a wee chink, there's just a little something missing in the identity. I do think it's missing, but I know what I'd like to be...Northern Irish, but with the British identity, and I think that's a major pride, it's a step, it's a massive step to take, in some ways.[42]

This member saw the future of unionism being tied directly to the development of a Northern Irish identity:

> I think that's where the future of unionism lies, in that, you know, if we can push a Northern Irish...the British identity is for unionism...I can't imagine your traditional nationalist ever being incredibly comfortable...maybe in the future, but certainly not in the next twenty years, being comfortable calling themselves British, and all the trappings that go along with that, you know, the Union flag, the monarchy, all the rest. But, I think, certainly in the short term, the Northern Irish identity is something we can all share in. We can all say, we're Northern Irish. If you want, you know, I can say, 'Yes, I'm Northern Irish, but I want to maintain a link with the Union.' Somebody else can say, 'Well, I'm Northern Irish, but I want to join a United Ireland.' But, if we can get to a position where we can all kind of agree, we're Northern Irish, but we want to go in different directions, that's a step forward from where we are at the minute.[43]

As former MLA Sandra Overend explained: 'Well, I mean, I would say that I'm British and I'm Northern Irish. I have no problem saying I'm either.'[44]

Northern Irish identity appears to be more closely allied with Britishness (and Protestants) than it is with Irishness (and Catholics). Moreover, the emblematic Northern Irish identifier is most commonly seen as a Protestant.[45] The views of those surveyed reinforce a construction of identity which extends the view of Northern Irish within Britishness. In Figure 6.2, where, unlike Figure 6.1, hybrid choices are permitted, it is noticeable that 'British and Northern Irish' leads members' chosen identity, albeit marginally over those still identifying exclusively as British. There was also a recognition by some of a certain amount of intergenerational change.[46]

There was also some recognition of the role of the Troubles in the construction of a cultural divide between Irishness and British, and that in a post-conflict society this dichotomy was being reconstructed:

> Northern Irish is distinct...I was born in Lisburn, which part of Northern Ireland, which is on the island of Ireland—I can understand why people struggle with a British identity, and an Irish identity, I can understand why that polarizes you...Because the perception is that you're setting yourself out as strictly, almost

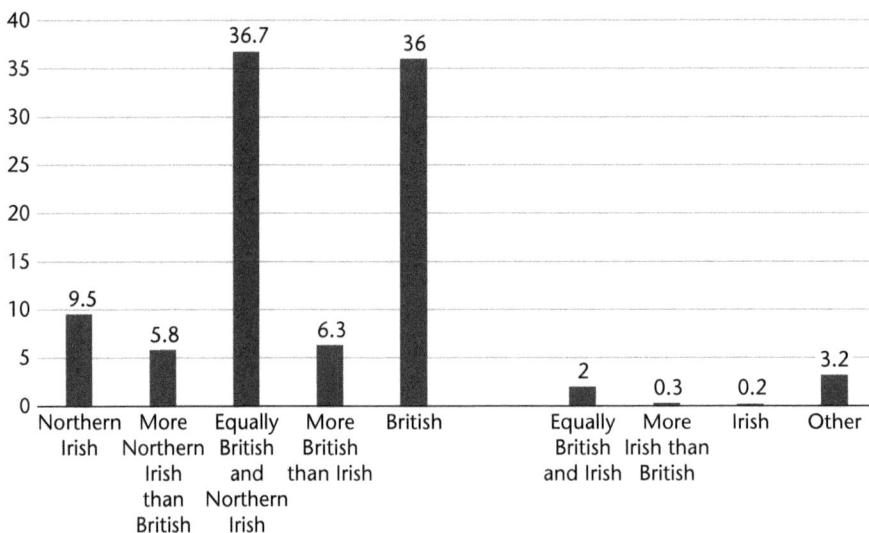

Figure 6.2 UUP members' identity
Q. Which of the following best describes your sense of identity?

exclusively, British...I think the generation who grew up through the Troubles, which is myself, and my family, my age group, my age bracket, that if the solution was to be exclusively British, or exclusively Irish, you miss out about 80 per of the people in this country. It's just a natural part of your being to want to identify with something and be proud of it. I think to try and get try and get everybody to go to one or the other will keep us in a perpetual state of... we move too far, or we had to move too far.[47]

Although, as we make clear later, there is a high degree of Protestant religious allegiance and observance within the UUP, very few of the interviewees foregrounded religion or pointed to the link between religion and politics when asked about their identity. Those who did largely presented it as a private rather than a public affair. Take this from Roy Beggs:

How do I describe my own identity? Well, I was actually doing my Facebook the other day, and I've still got Presbyterian down there, and I actually chose that deliberately. I don't want to be seen as in the Protestant/Catholic side of things. I'm just a Presbyterian, and very, very proud of who I am.

I'm a member of a Protestant faith, but one which tries to be open, which has democratic structures, and thinks that everyone is equal. I think, those are excellent criteria to apply in wider life, as well.[48]

Others focused on the role that religion held for party politics, of which the following views were typical:

I can imagine there being Roman Catholic members of the Ulster Unionist Party, albeit there's very small numbers, but I can't figure, I can't imagine anybody of the Roman Catholic persuasion wanting to be a member of the DUP. Because, I think, that the language and the rhetoric that was over used over the years would've alienated a lot of people. That's what I think, whether I'm right on that, I don't know. That's how I feel, having grown up in Northern Ireland.[49]

Ulster Unionism and Irishness

Although less than 1 per cent of members chose Irish as their primary identity, the number of people who recognized some degree of 'Irishness' in making up their self-identity was noteworthy. Thirty years of political violence 'undoubtedly made Protestants less inclined to see themselves as Irish, and more likely to cling to a British identity'.[50] But while 'Irishness' is denied by many Protestants, particularly those adopting a more cultural interpretation of their identity, many in the UUP adopt a more complex reading. This member for one saw the futility of such an approach, in saying:

> I'm a Tyrone man. I'm an Omagh man. I love Northern Ireland. If I ever go away, you know, I am bloody proud to say that I'm from Northern Ireland. I, obviously, sound different from an English person, and also the Welsh, and the Scottish. You know, it's a...Northern Ireland thing—that people seem to think that your identity is one thing. I am Irish. I am British. I am Northern Irish, and there's dilution of that. To say that you're Irish and British is a dilution of your Britishness, which is nonsense. I mean, if you look back at history, Edward Carson, who is the founder of our Party, and the founder of unionism as a whole, was a really proud Irish unionist.[51]

The broad parameters of this view were once indicated by Reg Empey, when he said:

> Well, I've different identities I suppose. If anybody asked me what my identity is—I'm British. But I'm quite content to be an Irish unionist; no difficulty with that. Some people identify with the locality of Northern Ireland or Ulster, but I see Britishness as being something that applies to these islands...I think there has been a tendency to try and distance oneself from the concept of Irishness but I think that that has been achieved for political reasons and I understand them. But as I say, Irishness is respected on the national flag; it's represented on the Royal Standard. Even when I was Lord Mayor it was represented in every other link on the Lord Mayor's chain.[52]

That many within the UUP have a complex relationship to Irishness is clearly demonstrated by what follows. This relationship is constructed in oppositional terms to the politics of Irishness, but often expressed in quite positive cultural terms. Take this from MLA Doug Beattie, who outlines what represents his sense of identity:

> Oh, I describe myself as an Irishman. I'm a Protestant. I'm happy if somebody refers to me as a Northern Irishman. I'm happy if somebody calls me British. I'm happy if somebody calls me an Ulsterman. But the reality is, I'm an Irishman, and I've been an Irishman all my life. I like that Irish identity that I have. I'm represented by The Sash. I'm represented by 'God Save the Queen'. I'm represented by 12th July. I'm represented by St Patrick's Day, by the shamrock, by a pint of Guinness, by Gaelic games, by cricket. Do you know, I'm as eclectic as I want to be? The important thing about me is this, when you add all of these things together, the important bit is that I believe that Northern Ireland will be more prosperous within the United Kingdom, and that Northern Ireland as a country has got the right to exist. So, all of these other things are just flavours which really feed into that single notion.[53]

Or this from the Party General Secretary, Colin McCusker:

> But, being part of the . . . I suppose, the way I would describe myself, I'm proud to be an Irishman, because I was born on the island of Ireland, but I hold a British passport, which is very, very important to me. I'd like to be able to say I'm British, but again, people think that when I say I'm British, that I'm English.[54]

The former MLA for West Tyrone, Ross Hussey, expressed it this way:

> I always say, 'I'm an Omagh man. I'm a Tyrone man. I'm Northern Irish. I'm an Ulster man, because I live in the province of Ulster. I'm an Irishman, because I live on the island of Ireland, and I'm British by choice.' . . . I don't have a problem being Irish, British, Ulster, Tyrone, Omagh, 'cause I'm all of those things, and we have to be, because that is what we are.[55]

Hussey expanded his perception:

> I think, the Party should project something similar, because we don't have a problem being Irish. I mean, the man that we all live up to, Sir Edward Carson, was a Dublin Irish Unionist. Edward Carson was a thirty-two-county unionist. You know, so, he was a stanch Irish Unionist. We are Irish, we are here in Northern Ireland, and we're as Irish as anybody else. We are the Ulster Unionist Party. You know, so we are, what we are, but we want to maintain the Union with Great Britain, because we believe it is the best possible thing for Northern Ireland . . . I think, the majority of people in Northern Ireland believe that, as well. And the majority of people in Northern Ireland have a similar background to mine, in that we are all British, in that we have all those bloodlines. There's no pure Irish anymore. With people coming and going, and everything else, with the various garrison towns, soldiers coming, marrying, coming back here and living here, we have so many backgrounds, and that's actually going further now when we have a lot of other families coming in from other countries. But, I believe that

Ireland itself, there's no pure Irish. We are all bits and pieces of everything, and that is why, I think, we're all more British than Irish. We all have that connection throughout the four countries.[56]

Former party leader Mike Nesbitt tried to reinforce the cultural aspect of his identity by claiming that 'a lot of unionists, if they won a free weekend to London, or Dublin, would rather go to Dublin'.[57]

Many UUP members were also aware of how Northern Ireland people were regarded outside of their immediate surroundings and acknowledged that beyond the home territory Ulster Protestants readily express a variety of identities, including Irishness. Although this area is under-researched, several writers[58] have provided examples of Protestants who have migrated to England and experienced the rejection by that society of their claims to be British. One UUP member told of his experience:

> But you won't find this discussion [about identity] when you got to England, you're classed as Irish generally, so you are. I mean, you're classed as paddy, aye, you know...No, I mean, you go over there, a paddy that's what you're classed as.[59]

One leading member of the UUP felt forced to adopt to following tactic:

> Whenever we go on our annual holiday to France, the French kids would say, 'Oh, so, you're Irish.' I'd say, 'No, no, I'm British.' 'Oh, so you're English.' 'Oh, no, no, we're not English.' They'd go, then, 'What? Well, are you British?' Then, we just laugh, and say, 'No, I am Irish.'...it was easier and more pleasant to say you were Irish, and you were liked more by the French, if you said you were Irish.[60]

Some writers[61] have, however, made reference to the ways in which unionist constructions of Irishness are very different to the way it is understood by Irish nationalists and republicans. What members of the UUP are signifying, and in many cases, express an affinity with, is very much a cultural form of Irish. It is an attachment with a sense of the topographical and the geographic as opposed to a politicized notion of Irishness, from which they positively uncouple and extricate themselves. There is no sense of Irishness as a national political descriptor, indeed it is often set in directly opposition to a political sense of Britishness outlined previously in this chapter.

Irishness in the broad cultural sense however, is often seen as a core part of that identity, in that many feel that their Irishness is a central part of being British, and that it is this British identity which knits together the people of the United Kingdom. Here, Enniskillen councillor Howard Thornton expresses it in the context of following the Ireland rugby team, but being politically attached to Britain:

If I'm following rugby, I'm Irish. If I'm away on holidays and somebody asks me, I would say, I'm Irish, purely because of accent, and so on. So, I don't have any hang-ups. I'm British, but at times, I mean, I have no problem going down south and standing underneath the tricolour, or, you know, The Soldier's Song, or whatever it might be—no problem. I can't understand why others can't do that here [and stand for the British National Anthem]. Why am I opposed to a united Ireland? First of all, I think, we're better off with Britain. Yeah, you know, I do feel part of Britain.[62]

It is this sense of belonging that dominates politically, which is constructed in opposition to Irishness, which, especially after thirty years of ethnic conflict, has been seen as under the proprietorship of a different community in Northern Ireland. This was expressed by a member in the following terms:

It was 1912, at a unionist conference in Belfast, the sign was 'Ireland forever'.[63] Right, you see in many ways, unionism has sort of forgotten that we are Irish to a certain extent. We have allowed Irish to be seen almost exclusively as nationalist.[64]

It is important to understand the sense of Irishness that is being projected here. As Neil Southern once pointed out, the Irishness that unionists feel comfortable with is the depoliticized form represented by

the regiments of the Irish Guards and the Royal Irish Regiment...the all-Ireland basis for playing rugby, and the religious institutions whose titles include the words *Irish* or *Ireland* such as the Irish Baptist College, the Church of Ireland and the Presbyterian Church in Ireland.[65]

This is very different to adopting Irishness with any political meaning, which is seen to represent something foreign and outlandish, even hostile, to unionism, and to whose political aspirations they are obviously diametrically opposed. The outworking of this position manifested quite clearly in the UUP's opposition to an Irish Language Act, where it was claimed the party had 'no problem with the Irish Language' but were opposed because of its politicization and because 'it was being used to hold Northern Ireland to ransom'.[66]

There are those UUP unionists who gain much of their sense of belonging and identity from the Union itself:

I think the Union has always been very special for me, and it delivers for Northern Ireland. We have always sacrificed a lot for a United Kingdom. I think, when you look at our history of world war, and so on, the Ulsterman has been there in times of need. So, I think, as a United Kingdom...It's something I'm proud of, to be part of. As a wee, small country, I think we fight so much above our weight here. On all the world stage, the voice of the United Kingdom...you know, we're a small country, really, yet we've got the sixth strongest economy in the world, we have. But, on the world stage, we're really up there. I think that's important to me.[67]

Multiple Identities of Unionism

Identity in Northern Ireland goes beyond some simple Protestant/unionist–Catholic/nationalist dichotomy.[68] Waddel and Cairns[69] suggest that most Protestants have multiple identities, the most important in this context are British, Northern Irish, Ulster, Irish, and that these vary according to changed social context.[70] In terms of national identity, some of this thinking has transferred to sections of the Party, which stated recently, it is: 'time to recognise identity is not binary'.[71] This is recognized by some UUP members who seek to express their sense of identity in these terms:

> See, in politics, you want to do your policies in black and white, but identity, for example, is a much more complex issue. Like, you can be British and Irish, you can be all so many different identities. You know, Mike always quotes John Hewitt in the famous poem, where he writes that about, 'I'm European, I'm an Ulsterman, I'm, you know, Irish and British and all that.' I think identity is a very complex thing to address, and trying to get in a binary thing, it is very easy, you know, to say, 'If you can raise the flag, and say, look, I'm the British candidate here...' It's very easy to drum people to support it, where if you say, 'Well, I feel British, but I mostly feel Irish, and I know I partake in this, and I like this...' you know, it makes it more muddied.[72]

Mike Nesbitt used his own biography to make the point:

> So, I consider the binary thing just to be too shallow, that you've got to be British or Irish. My father's side are French Huguenot, and Mum's Ulster Scot. There's a Sinn Féin MLA who came up to me, and he said, 'I heard your speech when you were talking about Henry Joy McCracken, whose parents were traders in Belfast, one Huguenot, one Ulster Scot...'—and that's my family, were traders, Dad Huguenot, Mum Ulster Scot—and he said that his father's side was Ulster Scot and he's actually an Executive Minister, Sinn Féin. So, you know, the idea of the pure Gael, I think applies to a very, very small number of people on this island, and the pure Brit applies to very, very few. So, I think we all are hybrid to some extent, and we're, maybe, beginning to recognize and embrace that, and I think, if you do, it's more honest and it makes things easier.[73]

A similar point is made by Ross Hussey:

> I think that we all, within these islands, have an interconnection. We are related to each other. We know each other. We have family connections. There's very few families that don't have cousins living in England, or in Scotland, or in Wales. We have that connection. There is that interconnection, it's there, it

exists. It won't go away because somebody says, 'I'm Irish, and that's that.' Does that mean, then, you get a chalkboard duster and then wipe out all the bits that don't apply?[74]

Unionism, History, and Memory

Unionist identity and much sense of belonging originates in a specific reading of history. This draws directly on collective memories, formed through shared representations of the past, and agreed, so as to provide clear memory cues for individuals in constructing such identities. These are both learned and adopted, with the transmission, both formally and informally, of ideas and beliefs from one generation to the next, often through a wide variety of everyday interactions. These include commonplace discourses[75] and everyday storytelling which convey a recognizable narrative,[76] reproduced alongside habitual symbolism, commemoration, and memorials.

Together, these provide the tools to interpret experience, thought, and imagination in terms, not just of the past, but also the present and possibilities in the future.[77] In this sense, unionists draw directly on constructed memories, which are crucial in helping them to organize political life, often by referring to seen continuities and the desire to preserve the past. Equally important, however, are the ways this past is altering in order to fit the needs of present.[78] These memories are, of course, still open to interpretation and there is a constant struggle between competing readings of historical events, and their place in legitimating contemporary political concerns.[79]

Some aspects of unionist discourse and ideology become fixed, forming part of the stock of everyday understandings and interpretations of political life, such as the belief that unionism it is the only natural political state for Protestants in Northern Ireland. Other aspects of unionist identity are more fluid and its formation can often be defined and redefined as contingencies demand; framed in one way when core identities are felt to be safe, and reframed in contemporary circumstances. How historical events are remembered carries distinct political consequences, as events of the past are altered to suit present purposes and transmitted across generations by commemoration and memorialization. In recent times, there have been some examples of this by UUP members. Take the following from the 2017 UUP manifesto:

> In our Vision, we will recognise the fundamental importance of your sense of identity.
>
> Our Vision is for all our people. It will not be limited by the old, binary notions that try to dictate you must be labelled Orange or Green, Unionist or Nationalist, Protestant or Catholic. Most people's identity is much more complex than that. If we accept few of us are born with pure ancestral lines, be it Gael or Briton, we

open new possibilities for finding common ground and easing our path to a shared future.[80]

In the search for a united way forward for all our people, we should not forget we have a shared past as our guiding light—a shared past of service and sacrifice, which we remember in this Centenary Year of the Battle of the Somme. The exploits of the 36th Ulster Division and the 16th Irish Division must both be taught.[81]

This is some distance from the traditional unionist reading of these events which sees them as a birth of the nation event and a founding narrative for much that followed. Hence, Mike Nesbitt had this to say:

I could have told you about the Battle of Hastings, and the War of the Roses, unaware of the Battle of Saintfield down the road, because I wasn't taught about it. I'm really glad the government are now sending children to France. I think it was about three or four years ago, I made a call in the run-up to the Centenary of the Somme, 'We should start sending primary school children over to look at the battlefields, because, actually, in terms of sharing, we have a shared past of service and sacrifice.' I have gone for the last number of years, not just to the Somme, so you that have Thiepval [Memorial to the Missing of the Somme] . . . and . . . the Ulster Tower [the monument to the 36th (Ulster) Division is commemorated], but the third event is Guillemont which is the [monument to the]16th Irish Division. I have been there, and I have seen actually guys in Orange sashes, maybe a dozen members of the Orange Order, standing at Guillemont, laying a wreath to the 16th Irish Division, and at the end of it, standing respectfully as the band played, not one, not two, but three anthems, French, British and Irish.[82]

People interpret current experiences in relation to how they understand the past.[83] For many within the UUP this is a much more flexible construct than for other unionists. Howard Thornton gives a good example:

The Commemoration of the Somme . . . Oh, well, my grandfather would have served, you see, with the Fusiliers, the Inniskilling Fusiliers, and was involved with in the First World War. So, yeah, I mean, there was family ties to the British Army at that time. . . . Well, I mean, I suppose, actually, the Troubles. I mean, we have a family history of RIC, RUC. I mean, in many ways, it was the Troubles that actually sort of reinforced and hardened your opinion. But I would always call myself sort of moderate, and not extreme in views, or whatever.[84]

Successive generations of unionists in Northern Ireland hold largely similar worldviews. Forms of both civic and ethnic Britishness remain deeply located across contemporary unionism and an orientation towards the core concepts of each is found across the UUP and the DUP. Social identities are arranged differently and given different emphasis by the UUP and DUP, where the focal point within each differs. Political and cultural orientations are caused, not only by external circumstances, but also by patterns of cultural learning. The sense of identity which finds expression through the civic unionism envisaged by large sections of the UUP draws on notions of an inclusive political community within which all share common civic ideology and culture and have equality before the law.

This seeks to extend Northern Ireland beyond a particular historical or geographical territory, to link it with the rest of the UK. The alternative concept is that of ethnic (or cultural) unionism, which rests heavily on the ideas of common origin and roots and uses tradition and customs to empha-size an exclusive framework. Hence, these unionists express a strong ethnic attachment, constructing the Other and an 'us and them' understanding of the world. Currently, the DUP are more orientated towards an ethnic expres-sion and the UUP towards a civic expression of unionist identity, reflecting how individuals see and define their social identity.

The identity of Ulster Protestants may or may not equate with that of a nation but certainly it bears many similar characteristics, with the member-ship of the political nation state linked directly to identification with national culture. The coupling of culture and state has of course has been a central theme for unionism since the formation of the state, so much so that for many years they had become identical. But for the UUP today:

> Identity must no longer be conflated with sovereignty. The 1998 Agreement stated two distinct facts: First, it is your right to describe your identity as you see it. It is equally valid to be British, Irish, Northern Irish or other. The second fact relates to sovereignty; Northern Ireland is part of the United Kingdom.[85]

Sometimes this argument is presented as the difference between the emo-tional and rational basis for unionism. The construction of Britishness by the UUP in the contemporary period reflects a complex mixture of the histor-ical, social, and political markers. Attempts to categorize this and convey it to the electorate have proved difficult and ultimately unsuccessful. As Alexander Smith observed recently: 'identity and nationalism are rarely questions of the head or heart alone'.[86]

Conclusion

A central focus for this chapter has been the way people construct and recon-struct their identities. The vast majority of UUP members see themselves as British, either exclusively or alongside Northern Irishness, although as we have seen exactly what that means to individuals and how such an identity is constructed must be defined with some precision. While Britishness may act as a superordinate identity, within this category there are important differ-ences in how UUP members construct the term. Important here, are feelings of belonging and connections with the group, and how individuals relate these to the attitudes and behaviours in the social and political order.

The views unionists hold revealing the contradictions between ethnic and civic unionism and the politics and policy are not always well-defined or absolute. Many of the understandings of the Union and unionism given in this chapter display both an emotional attachment to the link between Great Britain and Northern Ireland and a commitment to developing a form of civic politics found elsewhere in the UK. At the core of unionism for many, however, is an emotive and affecting link. The move towards a civic identity by the UUP made sense tactically to establish distance between themselves and the DUP, but does not necessary capture the heart and soul of unionism and has endangered widespread support for the Party. Unionism is not homogeneous or monolithic and we should be aware of the diversity of forms it takes. The UUP influences members' perspectives (and vice versa) to present, what is for them, unionism in its most legitimate form. But that form and the civic approach it promotes is far from universally accepted. Unionism is constructed in a variety of ways by UUP members. This under-standing guides policy, however, this is not done evenly or consistently, nor does it mean that there is a uniform understanding of what the dominant social identity is, or any agreed understanding of what comprises Britishness across the party.

Attempts to express this sense of unionist identity remain fractured and in the contemporary period unionism has rarely found common social or cultural expression. There is a variety of social and cultural elements comprising unionism[87] and those who define themselves as such construct the Union in very different ways.[88] This is compounded by the fact that 'Britishness' is notoriously difficult to define, largely because of its innately 'fuzzy frontiers'.[89] Beyond the UUP there are those who regard unionism primarily as the means to protect the Protestant cultural heritage of Ulster. Within the party, the tendency is to see it as a way to confirm Northern Ireland as simply another political region of the United Kingdom.[90]

The UUP are confident that its understanding of Britishness is located deeply in the broader unionist population and this can be mined in the future. But this is far from certain given recent election results. Add to this increasing multiculturalism and the disparity between the ways Britishness is understood across the United Kingdom and the task of defining and defending the Union becomes even more challenging.

Notes

1. David Trimble, 'Post-Agreement Ireland: North and South', Speech to the Annual Conference of the Irish Association, Glenview Hotel, Co. Wicklow, on Friday, 20 Nov. 1998.
2. B. M. Walker, *A Political History of the Two Irelands: From Partition to Peace*, Houndmills: Palgrave Macmillan, 2012.
3. B. Anderson, *Imagined Communities: Reflections on the Origin and Spread of Nationalism*, London: Verso, 1991. Ulster unionists form a classic example of what Anderson calls an 'imagined community', where they form a group that expresses a common sense of identity, but do not know the majority of their fellow-citizens, do not meet, do not hear from one another; yet they are convinced that they have similar characteristics and belong to an identifiable and unique community.
4. H. Tajfel and J. C. Turner, 'An Integrative Theory of Intergroup Conflict', in W. G. Austin and S. Worchel (eds), *The Social Psychology of Intergroup Relations*, Monterey, CA: Brooks/Cole, 1979, 33–47.
5. Interview with Robbie Butler, 19 Oct. 2016.
6. See A. White, 'Is Contemporary Ulster Unionism in Crisis? Changes In Unionist Identity during the Northern Ireland Peace Process', *Irish Journal of Sociology*, 16.1 (2007), 118–35.
7. O. T. Muldoon, K. Trew, J. Todd, N. Rougier, and K. McLaughlin, 'Religious and National Identity after the Belfast Agreement', *Political Psychology*, 28.1 (2007), 89–103.
8. C. Kinnvall, 'Globalization and Religious Nationalism: Self, Identity, and the Search for Ontological Security', *Political Psychology*, 25.5 (2004), 741–67.
9. R. English, 'The Growth of New Unionism', in J. Coakley (ed.), *Changing Shades of Orange and Green: Redefining the Union and the Nation in Contemporary Ireland*, Dublin: UCD Press, 2002, 95–105.
10. J. Ruane and J. Todd, *The Dynamics of Conflict in Northern Ireland*, Cambridge: Cambridge University Press, 1996.
11. G. Spencer, 'The Decline of Ulster Unionism: The Problem of Identity, Image and Change', *Contemporary Politics*, 12.1 (2006), 45–63; G. Spencer, *The State of Loyalism in Northern Ireland*, Basingstoke: Palgrave Macmillan, 2008.
12. See e.g. M. B. Brewer, 'The Many Faces of Social Identity: Implications for Political Psychology', *Political Psychology*, 22.1 (2002), 115–25.
13. R. Rose, *Governing Without Consensus; An Irish Perspective*, Boston: Beacon Press, 1971.
14. E. Moxon-Browne, *Nation, Class and Creed in Northern Ireland*, Aldershot: Gower, 1983, put the number of Protestants identifying as British at 67 per cent.
15. See e.g. T. Fahey, B. C. Hayes, and R. Sinnott, *Conflict and Consensus: A Study of Values and Attitudes in the Republic of Ireland and Northern Ireland*, Dublin: Institute of Public Administration, 2005.
16. Muldoon et al., 'Religious and National Identity.
17. Northern Ireland 2011 Census, available at: <http://www.nisra.gov.uk/Census/2011_results_detailed_characteristics.html> accessed Oct. 2017.

18. Commission for Racial Equality, *The Decline of Britishness: A Research Study*, London: CRE, 2005.

19. Interview with elected UUP representative 2016.

20. Interview with Coleraine focus group, 18 May 2016.

21. Interview with Coleraine focus group, 18 May 2016.

22. Interview with elected UUP representative 2016.

23. Interview with Coleraine focus group, 18 May 2016.

24. Interview with Coleraine focus group, 18 May 2016.

25. Interview with Coleraine focus group, 18 May 2016.

26. Interview with Coleraine focus group, 18 May 2016.

27. Interview with Roy Beggs, 28 Jan. 2016.

28. Interview with Coleraine focus group. 18 May 2016.

29. Interview with Sandra Overend, 28 Jan. 2016.

30. Interview with Philip Smith, 30 Oct. 2016.

31. Interview with Adrian Cochrane-Watson, Belfast 11 Mar. 2016.

32. Muldoon et al., 'Religious and National Identity'.

33. J. Tonge and R. Gomez, 'Shared Identity and the End of Conflict? How Far Has a Common Sense of "Northern Irishness" Replaced British or Irish Allegiances since the 1998 Belfast Agreement?', *Irish Political Studies*, 30.2 (2015), 276–98.

34. See J. D. Trew, 'Negotiating Identity and Belonging: Migration Narratives of Protestants from Northern Ireland', *Immigrants and Minorities*, 25.1 (2007), 22–48.

35. See e.g. F. O'Toole, 'After Brexit, the Two Tribes Recede—and a Northern Irish Identity Emerges', *Observer*, 12 Mar. 2017; B. White, 'What Nationality do People in Northern Ireland Think they are?', *Belfast Telegraph*, 10 Nov. 2015.

36. Interview with Omagh focus group, 20 May 2016.

37. J. John Garry and K. McNicholl, 'Understanding the "Northern Irish" Identity', Northern Ireland Assembly Knowledge Exchange Seminar Series, Belfast: Northern Ireland Assembly, 2015.

38. See also, S. McKeown, 'Perceptions of a Superordinate Identity in Northern Ireland', *Peace and Conflict: Journal of Peace Psychology*, 20.4 (2014), 505–15.

39. Interview with Coleraine focus group, 18 May 2016.

40. Interview with Robbie Butler, 30 Oct. 2016.

41. Interview with Omagh focus group, 20 May 2016.

42. Interview with Robbie Butler, 30 Oct. 2016.

43. Interview with Omagh focus group, 20 May 2016.

44. Interview with Sandra Overend, 28 Jan. 2016.

45. S. McKeown, *Identity, Segregation and Peace-Building in Northern Ireland: A Social Psychological Perspective*, Basingstoke: Palgrave Macmillan, 2013.

46. For an outline of changes in Northern Irish identity over time, see K. McNicholl, 'The "Northern Irish" Identity is No New Dawn', *The Detail*, 3 Apr. 2017.

47. Interview with Robbie Butler, 30 Oct. 2016.

48. Interview with Roy Beggs, 28 Jan. 2016.

49. Interview with Robbie Butler, 30 Oct. 2016.

50. E. Moxon-Browne, *Nation, Class and Creed in Northern Ireland*, Aldershot: Gower, 1983.

51. Interview with Omagh focus group, 20 May 2016.
52. Reg Empey, cited in F. Cochrane, *Unionist Politics and the Politics of Unionism since the Anglo-Irish Agreement*, Cork: Cork University Press, 1997.
53. Interview with Doug Beattie, 16 Mar. 2016.
54. Interview with Colin McCusker, 3 Mar. 2016.
55. Interview with Ross Hussey, 27 Jan. 2016.
56. Interview with Ross Hussey, 27 Jan. 2016.
57. Interview with Mike Nesbitt, 16 Dec. 2016.
58. See e.g. J. W. McAuley, 'Under a Fading Banner? Some Northern Protestant Experiences of Emigration', in P. O'Sullivan (ed.), *The Irish Worldwide*, vi. *Religion and Identity*, Leicester: Leicester University Press, 1996, 43–69; C. Ní Laoire, 'Discourses of Nation among Migrants from Northern Ireland: Irishness, Britishness and the Spaces In-between', *Scottish Geographical Journal*, 118.3 (2002), 183–99. See also J. D. Trew, *Leaving the North: Migration and Memory, Northern Ireland, 1921–2011*, Liverpool: Liverpool University Press, 2013.
59. Coleraine focus group, 18 May 2016.
60. Interview with Colin McCusker, 3 Mar. 2016.
61. See e.g. Cochrane, *Unionist Politics*; C. Ruppe, 'Devoted to Being British: Young Unionists' Identities after the Belfast Agreement', *Annual of Language and Politics and Politics of Identity*, viii, Prague: Charles University, 2014, 31–45; Neil Southern, 'Britishness, "Ulsterness" and Unionist Identity in Northern Ireland', *Nationalism and Ethnic Politics*, 13.1 (2007), 71–102.
62. Interview with Howard Thornton, 20 May 2016.
63. The actual event being referred to was the Ulster Unionist Convention of 1892. Two banners appeared above the main stage, one reading 'God Save the Queen', the other was in Irish and read 'Erin Go Bragh' (Ireland for Ever).
64. Interview with Omagh focus group 20 May 2016.
65. Southern, 'Britishness, "Ulsterness" and Unionist Identity'.
66. J. Monaghan, 'Ulster Unionists Re-iterate Opposition to Irish language Act in First Meeting with Campaigners', *Irish News*, 11 Aug. 2017.
67. Interview with Adrian Cochrane Watson, 11 Mar. 2016.
68. C. Cassidy and K. Trew, 'Identity Change in Northern Ireland: A Longitudinal Study of Students' Transition to University', *Journal of Social Issues*, 60.3 (1998), 523–40.
69. N. Waddell and E. Cairns, 'Identity Preference in Northern Ireland', *Journal of Political Psychology*, 12.2 (1991), 205–13.
70. R. J. Crisp, M. Hewstone, and E. Cairns, 'Multiple Identities in Northern Ireland: Hierarchical Ordering in the Representation of Group Membership', *British Journal of Social Psychology*, 40.4 (2001), 501–14.
71. Ulster Unionist Party, *General Election Manifesto*, Belfast: UUP, 2017, 13.
72. Interview with Coleraine focus group, 18 May 2016.
73. Interview with Mike Nesbitt, 16 Dec. 2016.
74. Interview with Ross Hussey, 27 Jan. 2016.
75. M. Billig, *Banal Nationalism*, London: Sage, 1995.

76. N. Hunt and S. McHale, 'Memory and Meaning: Individual and Social Aspects of Memory Narratives', *Journal of Loss and Trauma*, 13.1 (2008), 42–58.

77. J. Brockmeier, 'Remembering and Forgetting: Narrative as Cultural Memory', *Culture and Psychology*, 8.1 (2002), 15–43, 21.

78. See material in D. Middleton and D. Edwards (eds), *Collective Remembering*. London: Sage, 1990.

79. D. Páez, N. Basabe, and J. L. González, 'Social Processes and Collective Memory: A Cross-Cultural Approach to Remembering Political Events', in J. W. Pennebaker, D. Páez, and B. Rimé (eds), *Collective Memory of Political Events: Social Psychological Perspectives*, Hillsdale, NJ: Lawrence Erlbaum, 1997, 147–74.

80. Ulster Unionist Party, *General Election Manifesto*, Belfast: UUP, 2017.

81. UUP, *Manifesto*, 2017.

82. Interview with Mike Nesbitt, 16 Dec. 2016.

83. See P. Connerton, *How Societies Remember*, Cambridge: Cambridge University Press, 1989; R. Samuel and P. R. Thompson (eds), *The Myths we Live by*, London: Routledge, 1990.

84. Interview with Howard Thornton, 20 May 2016.

85. UUP, *Manifesto*, 2017.

86. A. T. T. Smith, 'Relocating the British Subject: Ethnographic Encounters with Identity Politics and Nationalism during the 2014 Scottish Independence Referendum', *Sociological Review Monographs*, 65.1 (2017), 54–70.

87. See Cochrane, *Unionist Politics*.

88. See J. W. Foster (ed.), *The Idea of the Union. Statements and Critiques in Support of the Union of Great Britain and Northern Ireland*, Vancouver: Belcouver Press, 1995; M. Hall, *Beyond the Fife and Drum*, Belfast: Island Pamphlets, 1995; M. Hall, *The Death of the 'Peace Process'? A Survey of Community Perceptions*, Belfast: Island Pamphlets, 1997; M. Hall, *An Uncertain Future: An Exploration by Protestant Community Activists*, Belfast: Island Pamphlets, 2002.

89. R. Cohen, *Frontiers of Identity: The British and the Others*, London: Longman, 1994, 7.

90. R. Hanna (ed.), *The Union: Essays on Ireland and the British Connection*, Newtownards: Colourpoint, 2001.

7

Attitudes towards Other Parties

The replacement of Mike Nesbitt by Robin Swann after the double electoral trouble of 2017 signalled the end of the UUP's dalliance with an overtly cross-community approach. Swann abandoned the ambitious 'Vote Mike Get Colum' UUP–SDLP appeal with a return to unionist basics. 'Northern Ireland is not ready for that yet' was Swann's view. 'Vote Robin and you'll get an Ulster Unionist'. 'Ten years of DUP–Sinn Fein rule has put us back. It's them and us', he asserted.[1] This chapter analyses whether the UUP membership wants a 'go-it-alone' party or one which routinely builds bridges with other organizations.

Attitudes to the DUP

The UUP's fall from ascendancy within unionism has been difficult for many members to accept. The loss of power to Westminster direct rule was bitterly opposed in the early 1970s by many within the UUP, but amid the powerlessness, there was at least the consolation of remaining comfortably the lead party of unionism. Three decades after the loss of majoritarian Stormont dominance, the UUP suffered the indignity of being usurped electorally by the DUP, which went on to dominate a power-sharing axis with Sinn Féin. Since its inception, the DUP had been seen as a party of Paisleyite bombast, manifestly unfit for office. This attitude persists in some quarters. Members display little warmth towards their unionist colleagues. Table 7.1 indicates UUP members' attitudes towards other parties in the Northern Ireland Assembly (excluding People Before Profit).

As can been in Table 7.1, nearly three times as many UUP members dislike or strongly dislike the DUP as like or strongly like that party. There is more warmth towards the unionist militancy of Jim Allister's tiny TUV, often a thorn, if only a flesh wound, in the DUP's side. Views on the SDLP indicate the scale of ambition of the Nesbitt project in encouraging voting assistance down the ballot and cooperating as a coherent opposition in the Assembly. Whilst there

Table 7.1 UUP members' views of other parties (%)

	Strongly like	Like	Neither like nor dislike	Dislike	Strongly dislike
Democratic Unionist Party	1.3	18.1	26.9	36.3	17.4
Traditional Unionist Voice	4.4	30.0	32.7	24.2	8.7
Alliance Party	1.0	11.7	39.2	30.9	17.2
Green Party	0.7	8.7	44.1	27.5	19.0
Social Democratic and Labour Party	0.1	10.5	39.3	34.0	16.2
Sinn Féin	0.2	1.1	3.4	14.5	80.7

Table 7.2 UUP members' attitudes towards unity and pacts with the DUP

	%
I want the UUP and DUP to remain separate parties and not have electoral alliances/pacts	16.7
I want the UUP and DUP to remain separate parties but with electoral alliances/pacts for Westminster elections	18.4
I want the UUP and DUP to remain separate parties but with electoral alliances/pacts for Assembly elections	3.1
I want the UUP and DUP to remain separate parties but with electoral alliances/pacts for Council elections	1.0
I want the UUP and DUP to remain separate parties but with electoral alliances/pacts when it suits us	40.9
I want the UUP and DUP to merge	14.8
Other	4.9

is little deep hostility to the nationalist party, with indifference or mere dislike, rather than strong dislike, being the most common responses, there is very little empathy. The predictably hostile attitude towards Sinn Féin serves merely to remind of how the UUP membership was stretched in the Belfast Agreement in cementing obligatory coalitional power-sharing with republicans.

Despite the hostility towards the DUP, pacts with the unionist rival are accepted by many in the UUP, but only on the basis of UUP self-interest, as Table 7.2 shows.

The difficulty of course is that, in agreeing any pacts with the DUP, the UUP starts from by far the weaker negotiating position. Moreover, there may be limited utility to agreements. A Westminster election pact could not deliver Fermanagh and South Tyrone for the agreed unionist candidate in 2010, nor in 2017, and there is little value for either party in arranging pacts for other contests. Unionist unity would remain elusive if left to the members. Most members jealously guard the independence of their party. Despite the lack of clear policy differences, there are few takers for a merger of the two main unionist parties.

It is to be expected that party members are more partisan and exclusivist in their approach. Unionist voters take a more relaxed view. UUP and DUP voters are moderately sympathetic to election pacts, holding similar views, with a sizeable number of undecideds. At the 2017 Westminster election, 48 per cent of UUP voters and 50 per cent of DUP voters supported UUP–DUP pacts, with only 20 per cent of UUP voters and 21 per cent of DUP voters declaring opposition.[2] Support for electoral pan-unionism is thus greater among voters than party members.[3]

What motivates the UUP membership's disdain for the DUP, evident even in places such as Derry, where it might be expected that a unionist community apparently in retreat would be broadly united? UUP members in Northern Ireland's second city spoke of little cooperation between the two parties at council level or even informally between unionist representatives in the community and voluntary sectors.[4] Elsewhere, Colin McCusker, whilst acknowledging that the DUP has 'gone from being this very narrow, homogeneous group to a much broader church', highlighted historical enmity, recalling the 'abuse thrown at me from DUP people as a child...my dad [the former UUP MP Harold McCusker] would've been kicked and punched by DUP people'.[5] Former MLA, Adrian Cochrane-Watson, opined:

> I viewed the DUP as a bunch of idiots, a bunch of bigots—which they still are. They can wear nice suits, they can drive fancy cars—bigots, that's all they are. I've seen DUP members at council who, when we appointed a new officer, would whisper in my ear, 'is she one of us Adrian?' When I witness some of my former good friends now in political office in the DUP I laugh at them.[6]

Yet it is the perceived self-interest of the DUP, rather than that party's supposed bigotry, that provides by far the largest category of explanation (49 per cent) of why UUP members joined their party rather than the DUP. The view of the DUP as 'too extreme' comes second with 16 per cent, with the 'too religious' perception of the DUP the third largest category at 10 per cent, just ahead of the way the DUP 'do not represent my British values' at 9 per cent.

UUP MLA Roy Beggs argued: 'The DUP and Ian Paisley was a toxic brand from the viewpoint of the rest of the United Kingdom, and as such, if we were simply going to strengthen Ian Paisley and the DUP, you would be weakening the Union.'[7] The UUP still sees itself as more outward-looking than its unionist rival. According to former MP Danny Kinahan, 'Unionism is about the Union. The DUP is about little Ulster.'[8] One MLA argued that the DUP had been defined by its negativity: 'The DUP would be a natural fit for opposition, because that's all they do and that's all they did. They never had any ideas, you see.'[9]

Brand loyalty towards the UUP is considerable. Eighty-six per cent of members claim to have always voted UUP, with 84 per cent of members stating they have 'strong feelings of loyalty to my party'. Ten per cent have belonged to other parties, mainly Alliance or the DUP. Extensive and deep fidelity to the

UUP is a clear reason why unionist unity remains unlikely. As one UUP MLA put it:

I looked at the Democratic Unionist Party, and I just did not feel that they are representative of the people. Although they're the largest—it's a strange thing to say—I don't think they're representative of the people. I think, they're more to do with power as a collective, as opposed to representing what people really want, who are out there, and I mean, all demographics.[10]

A Londonderry focus group member lamented that 'the DUP is the party that split the unionists. You know, if they had come along and joined with us, we would've had one solid party. They split the unionists, split churches, split families, and all.' Another member of the same group insisted of the DUP: 'they're really for themselves, they're really for their members and they're not for the country at all'. A further comment from the group asserted the self-lessness of the UUP which:

put the country first. You know, they crippled themselves over the Good Friday Agreement, and they did put the country first, they put the people, and they put peace process ahead of any party political interests.[11]

Similar sentiments were offered in Coleraine:

the DUP are now doing exactly what the Ulster Unionists set out to do many years ago. I mean, if I were talking to Arlene Foster today…I would ask her what's so different now than when she ran away from Trimble? Because it wasn't different. She's implementing exactly what David Trimble [wanted] and the route he wanted to go down, as I see it, and she's doing it unashamedly now.[12]

A common reason for the antipathy towards the DUP is the feeling among UUP members that their party took all the initial risks in terms of power-sharing with Sinn Féin, before the DUP accepted the Belfast Agreement once it became the more popular unionist party on the back of the disquiet over the deal. Mark Cosgrove recalls the abuse aimed at supporters of the deal:

I was with my 7-year-old daughter waving a little yes flag outside Waterfront Hall Belfast and was confronted by a screaming Loyalist mob…I joined the UUP the following Monday…The mob literally terrorized my daughter and I thought we cannot go on with another thirty years of this type of bitterness and sectarianism.[13]

For one member, the UUP was:

the sacrificial lamb, the doing the right thing, despite the fact that it, electorally, was suicidal. But, it brought the peace that we have today. It was that decisiveness. It was that principled-ness that I do see as lacking from the DUP. They don't seem to be prepared to make decisions that would be good for the country, but bad for them. While, in history, we have been shown to do the opposite, even at great cost to the Party, but, I suppose, we can all sort of see the benefits in hindsight.[14]

155

The former MP Tom Elliott declared of the DUP's adoption of the Belfast Agreement:

> It makes me feel pretty peed off. As soon as they got to the top of the pile they had no problems embracing it [the Agreement] ... Where is the principle in that?[15]

The MLA Roy Beggs articulated a similar view:

> I'd love to get the thinking with those who flipped from the Unionist Party into the DUP, because of their objections to involvement with Sinn Féin. That is exactly where they are today. I would like them to explain what the difference is. Obviously, they have changed.[16]

A former MLA commented:

> Well, I was critical of aspects [of the Belfast Agreement], but I always believe that—particularly when many of those who jumped ship had a mandate as an Ulster Unionist, and yes, they went on to maintain that mandate under a different flag, being the DUP—I always believed that, when you're the member of a party, or a member of any organization, and particularly an organization that is allowing your voice to be heard, and it may not be going in a direction that you want, that you have to ... if you feel strongly and you're being given the opportunity to debate, to negotiate, to have your say ... I was given that opportunity, and I was very disappointed in certain former colleagues, who were strongly against the direction the party has moved, or was moving in. I look at them now, and I find in disbelief that these are the same people who came to my office for private meetings ... and I'm sitting now saying: 'But you're now sitting in government with Sinn Féin, and you were horrified that David [Trimble] would have wanted to sit with the SDLP, you know, a party with no links to paramilitarism, no links to terror, and yet, it was too big a step for you to take, you know, a relatively short period of time ago'. Yet, within nine years from that initial Belfast Agreement, to 2007, you're now inexplicably the best of friends with former godfathers of terror.[17]

According to Beggs, altruism conditioned the UUP:

> Ulster Unionists are not about getting power for ourselves. We have shown that, in fact, if you look at the Belfast Agreement, we acted not in our own Party's self-interest, not in individual self-interest, but we acted on community interest, and that is where we are. We want things to be better for the community, which we also strongly believe will be better for the Union in the long term. It's easy to look at short-term things, but we believe that it's important that we have a stable base of Northern Ireland in order to maintain the Union in the long term.[18]

Combating the DUP appears very difficult given the adoption of much of what the UUP attempted in 1998 and the changing nature of their rival: 'The DUP now are not the DUP when Paisley started, it's a totally different party' opined a Coleraine member,[19] views which were echoed across the Party, although the extent of the DUP's change and its genuineness is disputed. A Coleraine focus group member highlighted the problem of recapturing ground lost to the DUP:

> there's a lot of people out there who would be traditional Ulster Unionist voters . . . who have now gone to the DUP, because they felt the DUP didn't betray them, and didn't sell out. Even though, they're operating this system that we created. But that's a very difficult message to get to the electorate, you know, to go through all that and have to go through, 'Well, this is what we did.' And you know, the fact that Arlene stayed for five, six years after the Belfast Agreement, had no problem, and then effectively jumped ship when she's seen the opportunity arise. Now, that's very hard to go out to the electorate and then start going through the sequence of the events, and say, 'Well this is what we did right, and this is what we did wrong.' You know, you need a very clear message, which the DUP had.[20]

Many of the current differences and disagreements can be seen as having their roots in the DUP's rejection of the Belfast Agreement and subsequent acceptance of the vast bulk of the deal at St Andrews in 2006. The effects for relations within the unionist bloc and between the two major unionist parties endure, still resonating in everyday politics. Yet there is almost a grudging admiration for the chutzpah and strategic nous of the DUP. One UUP MLA observed:

> It stems back to the Belfast Agreement, and the DUP obviously mobilized themselves, you know, perfectly in attacking us. Politically, Peter Robinson outflanked and out-manoeuvred the Ulster Unionist Party at every chance. There's no doubting that he was a political strategist, and very good at what he was doing, and he made sure he was always one step ahead of the Ulster Unionist Party.[21]

There is some grudging respect for the succinct approach usually offered by the DUP, one UUP MLA commenting:

> what the DUP are very good at is getting a succinct, simple message and repeating it ad nauseam. You even saw that with 'Fair Deal' under Robinson. They are very good at that, and the Ulster Unionist Party is awful at it. If they produce a five-word strapline, we'll have ten points.[22]

Acknowledgement of DUP tactical acumen in the intra-unionist battle is not extended to admiration for how it conducts business. The top-down nature of the DUP is the source of much criticism from UUP members, articulated by one MLA.

> I see it [the DUP] very much so as a dictatorship. It's the party line, or it's, you know, it's the high line. You know, looking at some of the issues such as same sex marriage, they're using a Petition of Concern . . . you know, that their line is very much so the Party line. I had a number of dealings with DUP members through my involvement with the Assembly, and just didn't like what I was seeing and hearing, and I feel very much so that their seven/eight years in power, they've let the people down. I think it's time for change.[23]

This 'dictatorship' view of the DUP is seen as particularly offputting in terms of social and moral issues, as a UUP member in the Coleraine focus group claimed: 'Our party, there's conscience votes on same sex marriage and abortion, whereas the DUP take a very straight line, and I know there's DUP members who don't agree with that'.

Antagonism towards the DUP is heightened by what is seen as a sectarian carve-up of power with Sinn Féin. The change to the election of the First and Deputy First Minister in the St Andrews Agreement provided the clearest example. Cross-community voting was replaced by a system allowing the First Minister to be nominated by the largest party of the largest designation (the DUP) and the Deputy First Minister to be nominated by the largest party of the second largest designation (Sinn Féin). The First and Deputy First Minister rule change reflected a wider pattern according to Sandra Overend:

> When the DUP and Sinn Féin got to be the two largest parties, it was more, 'You have this. We have that. You have that. We have this.' It's more a divided out Northern Ireland, rather than an agreement to have a more shared future.[24]

Among younger UUP members, unfamiliar with the old Paisleyite and anti-Agreement DUP, criticism of the DUP tends more towards its inflexible approach on social issues. Yet the need for common cause on certain issues is acknowledged. A student UUP member argued:

> I think we've always kind of tried to work together. Like say, you know, whenever I was on Student Council, for example, there was the poppy debate going on, so, basically, there was a member of Sinn Féin on Council who wanted to ban the selling of the poppy. So, we would, like, work together on issues like that.[25]

There is also some geographical variation in attitudes to the DUP, one UUP councillor commenting that he found his fellow unionist councillors 'amicable, pleasant, not very religious. Some are Orange here in a religious way, but not aggressive, or in your face. So, we get on pretty well.'[26]

Most UUP members appear cognizant that any restoration of the UUP's onetime dominant status within unionism is, at best, a long-term ambition. Some UUP members conceded that the DUP leader Arlene Foster's appeal to the unionist core could be difficult to combat.

Attitudes towards other parties may also be shaped by constitutional issues and left–right perceptions of parties in Northern Ireland tend to be defined by views of the parties on the constitution. Social-class distinctions in part are much diminished within the unionist bloc. Whilst the DUP support base was once concentrated mainly among the loyalist working-class and rural evangelicals,[27] the expanded appeal of the party rendered social-class distinctions between the DUP and UUP largely redundant, albeit not quite extinguished.[28]

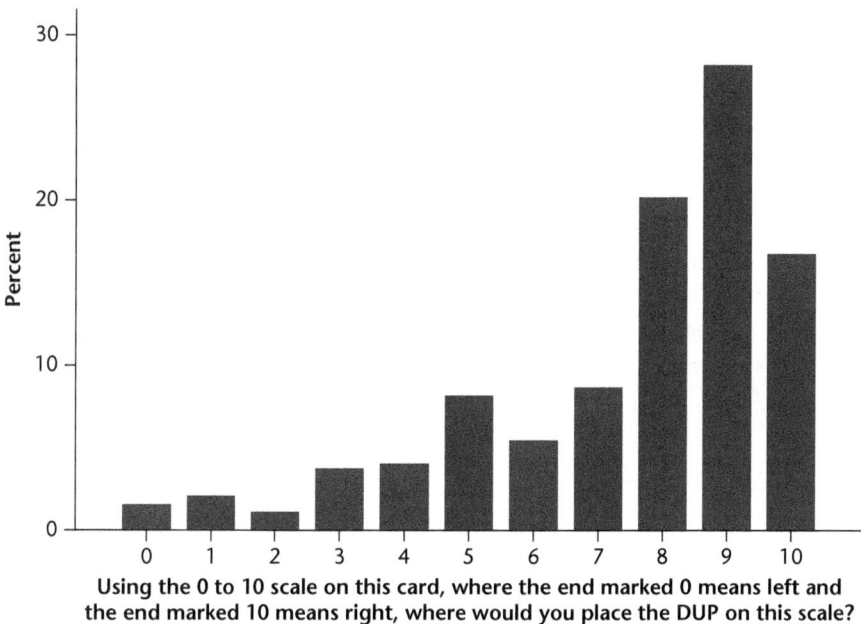

Using the 0 to 10 scale on this card, where the end marked 0 means left and
the end marked 10 means right, where would you place the DUP on this scale?

Figure 7.1 UUP members' perceptions of the DUP on a left–right scale

As Figure 7.1 shows, the DUP are seen by UUP members as substantially
further to the right. The median score is nine on a zero (far-left) to ten (far-
right) scale, whereas UUP members places their own party and themselves at
seven (see Chapter 4). The DUP is certainly right-wing on constitutional and
sovereignty issues and on some social and moral issues, but its economic
agenda tends to favour additional public spending, perhaps reflective of the
party's need to service a sizeable working-class loyalist constituency. Clearly in
UUP member perceptions, however, it is the DUP's right-wing tendencies that
are of greater salience.

UUP members see themselves as more reasonable than the DUP, offering
liberal or civic forms of unionism[29] more closely attuned to Britain than the
'insular Ulster nationalists' of the DUP.[30] A small number even flirted with the
short-lived NI21 party, which rejected pan-unionist pacts as sectarian. It
aimed at articulating a liberal form of unionism bereft of sectarianism and
designed to be cross-community but imploded quickly amid personality
clashes. NI21 'wanted a strong union, and that met one of my criteria. And
secondly, it was progressive thinking, so it didn't matter about what your
background was, what your religion was, it saw that everybody was an equal
and it would strive forward in maybe slightly more left of centre politics',

according to UUP MLA Doug Beattie, who nonetheless decided against entering politics via NI21 because 'it was too narrow a political party, and its leadership was a little bit too narrow ... a bit of an ego trip for people'.[31]

Despite often wanting to be seen as the liberal wing of unionism, one irony among the UUP membership is that criticism of the Traditional Unionist Voice is rare. UUP members appear to appreciate the propensity of its leader, Jim Allister, to criticize his former colleagues in the DUP, but there is also a widespread (and accurate) view that it is essentially a one-man band. Overall, pan-unionism is not a concept readily associated with UUP members. Long-standing antipathy towards the DUP is a more common trait than intra-unionist solidarity.

Attitudes to Sinn Féin

More predictably, Sinn Féin are the targets of derision and concern, because of their history of support for the IRA and political ambition of Irish reunification and ending Northern Ireland's UK status. At times, the language of some UUP representatives has appeared at least as strong as anything emanating from the DUP. One of the more graphic cases was Tom Elliott's reference to the 'scum of Sinn Féin' at his 2011 Assembly election count. Elliott, described his relationship with Sinn Féin as 'frosty' but stated 'you didn't have an option' regarding conducting business with republicans, defending his 'scum' comment as follows:

> I didn't regret saying it about those it was directed at. I did say after that if the ordinary nationalist community took offence, I apologized. It was quite difficult standing at the front and seeing someone booing and jeering you who you know has been responsible for the murder of several of your colleagues who you have carried the coffin of or walked behind the coffin and comfort their wife or mother.[32]

Even younger, ostensibly moderate, student UUP members defended Elliott's outburst, one insisting:

> he [Elliott] called individuals who were members of Sinn Féin, scum, which is perfectly fine if you know the individuals involved ... and their background and what they probably did too ... it wasn't calling the entire party scum, it was a sub-set of them. It probably wasn't the wisest way to phrase his comments, but, probably, you wouldn't say they were entirely inaccurate, either.[33]

A Coleraine focus group member summarized the perception of Sinn Féin articulated by many UUP members: 'They don't want Northern Ireland to succeed . . . They want a United Ireland, they want the whole thing to crumble, and I think they're gaining ground.'

Ex-MLA Jo-Anne Dobson 'much preferred working with the SDLP and Alliance' and had 'as little contact as possible' with Sinn Féin, whilst acknowledging, 'what do you do, if they have a mandate, and they're elected?'

Nonetheless, Sinn Féin rarely represent direct electoral competition to the UUP (the Fermanagh and South Tyrone parliamentary constituency is a notable exception). One UUP member claimed:

> I think there's some of the old, you know, Marxist crap, from the Shinners that you have to get through a wee bit, but I think when you get away from that, an awful lot of them are not actually as political as they want to pretend to be.[34]

Attitudes to Sinn Féin also vary considerably according to the personnel with whom a UUP representative was dealing, as a former MLA made abundantly clear shortly before Martin McGuinness's death:

> There's some of them I get on quite well with. You know, they're quite sociable, some of them. There's always a few that I despise, with passion, . . . because they have murdered members of my family and we will never forgive them. We know who they are. They've never been brought to justice. We know who they are, and they are active members of Sinn Féin. My wife had to move home because Special Branch came to her home and said, 'There's an IRA plot to murder your daddy, and you have to move now.' The current Deputy First Minister [Martin McGuinness at the time of interview] made a visit in the early '70s to my mother-in-law and father-in-law's home, in Shipley Street in Londonderry and he had a 9mm pistol in his hand, and politely asked them to leave the city of Londonderry. I think he's a murderer, and he's a terrorist! . . . You know, he put my family out of their homes, it may have been forty years ago, but he's not going to waltz about round here and talk peace, and [think] he's a great parliamentarian. This is a terrorist! This is a man who forced my wife's mother and father to leave home. This is members of his party who forced them. This is members who murdered my father's brother and his 9-year-old son, when he was taking his son to school, and they had targeted him every day. So, they knew he was taking his 9-year-old son in the car, taking him to school. So, if you think I'm going be nice to certain people who I know who done (sic) it, never in a month of Sundays.[35]

The antipathy to Sinn Féin relates to the experience that, despite the end of the IRA campaign, there remains a nasty aftertaste arising from perceived overlap between both wings of the Republican Movement. To ensure a good working relationship UUP MLAs have had to adopt a practical approach to working with Republicans, recognising the legitimacy of their political aspiration for a united Ireland by peaceful means. This works, of course, both ways: Republicans have to accept the UUP's right and desire to maintain the constitutional reality of Northern Ireland in the UK.

Student UUP members conceded that there were some attractive aspects of Sinn Féin policy, one commenting:

> I agree with Sinn Féin's education policy, with no 11-Plus, because I went to a secondary school and I got my A Levels at secondary school. In primary school, I was told, 'You're just going to secondary school,' and now I'm at Queen's. So, I don't think that the 11-Plus, or any of that matters.[36]

However, any empathy with Sinn Féin disappeared when issues strayed beyond domestic policies for Northern Ireland. Members of the Young Unionists felt scant warmth towards Sinn Féin nonetheless and failed to bond on issues affecting students. One recalled:

> There were elections the other week there, and the guy ... came in and it was in our politics lecture, and started going on about everybody wanting to vote for him, and then he went off with, 'Universities in the north of Ireland have been heavily hit,' and it switched me off. Because, he can't even say the country that he lives in's name properly. So, there was a lot of us sitting along, and we all sort of switched off as soon as he said that.[37]

Moreover, any left-leaning mini-bonding with Sinn Féin by young UUP members on social issues is overwhelmed by the (negative) perception among the bulk of the membership that the republican party is way to the left, as Figure 7.2 demonstrates.

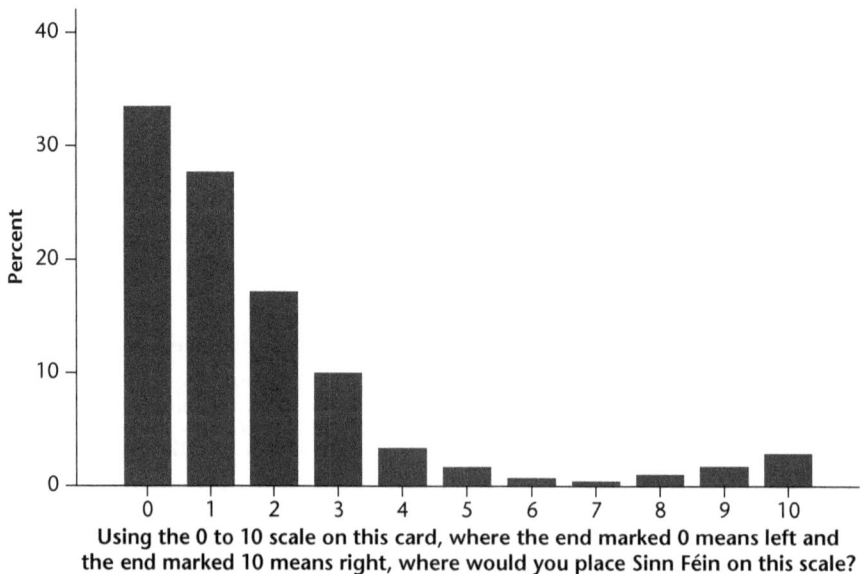

Figure 7.2 UUP members' perceptions of Sinn Féin on a left–right scale

The most common perception of UUP members is that Sinn Fein is a far-left party, again indicating a conflation between left–right economic and constitutional perspectives, Sinn Féin's ultimate ambition being the ending of Northern Ireland and the creation of a united Ireland. Sinn Féin's modern economic agenda, whilst certainly leftist and redistributive despite considerable toning down in recent years, is difficult to perceive as quite so 'far-left' as portrayed here.

Contempt for Sinn Féin is not extended towards the SDLP whose opposition to violence during the Troubles is acknowledged. Empathy has perhaps grown as the path of the SDLP has taken a similar course to that of the UUP, whose members tended to see harmonious UUP–SDLP relations, but too often united in irrelevance. As one councillor, put it, 'our relationship with the SDLP is extremely amicable, it's good, but we're in the same boat, really, as them'.[38]

Do UUP Members Vote across the Ethno-Sectarian Divide?

Beyond the commentaries on other parties presented here, where do UUP members transfer their votes in non-Westminster elections, all of which are conducted under the single transferable vote (STV) system? Table 7.3 indicates the probability of transfers (excluding 'don't knows') to the largest parties in Northern Ireland, bundling 'certain', 'very likely', or 'fairly likely' to give a lower preference vote as a likely endorsement and 'fairly unlikely' 'very unlikely', and 'no chance' responses as the reluctant categories.

Whilst a majority of UUP members are more likely than not to transfer to the DUP as the main party within unionism, the level of resentment towards that party is such the majority is slight. The marginally greater warmth towards the nationalist SDLP than the non-bloc aligned Alliance Party might also surprise and offers some support to the cross-community voting ideas tried out, unsuccessfully, under Mike Nesbitt's tenure as leader. Of UUP voters

Table 7.3 UUP members' likelihood of transferring lower preference votes to other parties

	'Certain', 'very likely', or 'fairly likely' prospect of receiving a lower preference transfer vote (%)	'No chance', 'very unlikely', or 'fairly unlikely' prospect of receiving a lower preference transfer vote (%)
Democratic Unionist Party	54.6	45.4
Alliance Party	35.5	64.5
Social Democratic and Labour Party	36.7	63.3
Sinn Féin	10.1	89.9

at the 2017 Westminster Election, 37 per cent avowed a willingness to vote for a candidate from across the sectarian divide, almost identical to the figure among party members likely to transfer a vote to the SDLP.[39]

Avowed willingness to transfer may not necessarily transfer to actual, but of identifiable transfers at the 2017 Assembly election, 24 per cent of the SDLP's haul came from the UUP, proving crucial for the nationalist party's successes in East Londonderry, Lagan Valley, and Upper Bann but only 10 per cent of the UUP's transfers came from the SDLP (admittedly helping win a seat in Fermanagh and South Tyrone) with 14 per cent coming from the DUP.[40]

What of calls for lower preference voting across the sectarian divide after registering initial preferences for the UUP? Where, if anywhere, did it resonate within his Party? A multivariate model (Table 7.4) shows which demographic categories are receptive or resistant to going over to the 'other side'. The dependent variable is the likelihood of giving a lower preference vote for the SDLP, with the three categories favouring the idea—'certain', 'very likely', or 'fairly likely', versus the three oppositional responses of 'fairly unlikely', 'very unlikely', and 'no chance'. In addition to gender as an independent variable, UUP members are placed in the following categories: aged 50 or under versus those aged 51+; level of education (degree, qualifications up to A level, or no

Table 7.4 Multivariate model of the propensity of UUP members to offer a lower preference vote to the SDLP

VARIABLES	(1) Voting SDLP—certain, very likely, fairly likely
Age 51+	−0.449**
	(0.189)
Male	−0.076
	(0.197)
Education	0.075
	(0.077)
Orange Order	−0.186
	(0.191)
Religiosity	0.440**
	(0.180)
Working class	0.123
	(0.177)
Constant	−0.693**
	(0.305)
Observations	717
Pseudo R-squared	0.0140

Standard errors in parentheses
** $p < 0.05$

qualifications); Orange Order membership; religiosity, with members divided into those attending church at least twice-monthly and those not; and self-identification as middle-class or working-class.

As indicated in Table 7.4, several independent variables have little explanatory power overall. However, older members are less likely to consider voting for the SDLP, while more religious members are more likely to do so. There are competing pulls here. The religious may particularly acknowledge the SDLP's consistent moral opposition to violence during the conflict, possibly explaining their relative warmth, but the oldest members of the UUP were politically socialized in an era of undiluted UUP majoritarian dominance, challenged by a civil rights movement which converted into the SDLP, perhaps accounting for their antipathy towards transfers to the nationalist party. Those not quite so old were politically acclimatized in an era where the UUP at least won the intra-communal battle and were not reliant upon SDLP favours, bought or sold.

Conclusion

Common perceptions of a strong sense of unionist unity need considerable qualification when the UUP membership is examined. Many members have lived through years of often ugly battles with the DUP and there is little warmth towards the UUP's rival. The sense of hostility has perhaps increased as the DUP has eclipsed the UUP, but it is of longer standing, dating back to a rejection of Paisleyism and deepened by the manner in which the DUP 'stole' the rewards arising from the Belfast Agreement.

Ultimately, unionist unity prevails on the basis of a shared constitutional position, rejection of Sinn Féin's republicanism, and reluctance to straddle the sectarian voting divide. Much of the intra-unionist rivalry owes more to political history and local electoral friction than clear policy differences between the DUP and UUP. The UUP has always held disdain for what it regards as the more vulgar DUP, which its members see as too right-wing and extreme but the membership is perhaps behind the curve. Unionists of all social classes have switched to the DUP and the DUP is not reliant upon UUP vote transfers for most of its election successes. As the DUP has prospered, many in the UUP membership have not lessened their wariness of their unionist rival. Few UUP members desire a merger of their party with the DUP, yet the case for two competing unionist parties has arguably never been weaker given the lack of contemporary distinctiveness.

Notes

1. Interview with Robin Swann, 14 Aug. 2017.
2. Northern Ireland General Election study 2017.
3. This was also confirmed via most membership interviews and expressed forcefully by e.g. the Young Unionists focus group, 10 Mar. 2016.
4. Derry focus group, 19 May 2016.
5. Interview with Colin McCusker, 3 Mar. 2016.
6. Interview with Adrian Cochrane-Watson, 11 Mar. 2016.
7. Interview with Roy Beggs, 28 Jan. 2016.
8. Interview with Danny Kinahan, 13 Apr. 2016.
9. Interview with Robert Butler, 10 Mar. 2016.
10. Interview with Doug Beattie, 16 Mar. 2016.
11. Derry focus group, 19 May 2016.
12. Coleraine focus group, 18 May 2016.
13. Interview with Mark Cosgrove, 4 Dec. 2016.
14. Omagh focus group, 30 May 2016.
15. Interview with Tom Elliott, 13 Apr. 2016.
16. Interview with Roy Beggs, 28 Jan. 2016.
17. Interview with Adrian Cochrane-Watson, 11 Mar. 2016.
18. Interview with Roy Beggs, 28 Jan. 2016.
19. Coleraine focus group, 18 May 2016.
20. Coleraine focus group, 18 May 2016.
21. Interview with UUP MLA 2016.
22. Interview with UUP MLA 2016.
23. Interview UUP MLA 2016.
24. Interview with Sandra Overend, 28 Jan. 2016.
25. Young Unionists focus group, 10 Mar. 2016.
26. Interview with Jeff Dudgeon, 20 May 2016.
27. S. Bruce, *God Save Ulster! The Religion and Politics of Paisleyism*, Oxford: Oxford University Press, 1986; G. Evans and M. Duffy, 'Beyond the Sectarian Divide: The Social and Political Consequences of Nationalist and Unionist Party Competition in Northern Ireland', *British Journal of Political Science*, 27.1 (1997), 47–81.
28. J. Evans and J. Tonge, 'Social Class and Party Choice in Northern Ireland's Ethnic Blocs', *West European Politics*, 32.5 (2009), 1012–30.
29. See A. Aughey, *The Politics of Northern Ireland: Beyond the Belfast Agreement*, Belfast: Blackstaff, 2005. N. Porter, *Rethinking Unionism*, Belfast: Blackstaff, 1996.
30. Omagh focus group, 20 May 2016.
31. Interview with Doug Beattie, 16 Mar. 2016.
32. Interview with Tom Elliott, 13 Apr. 2016.
33. Young Unionists focus group, 10 Mar. 2016.
34. Interview with Adrian Cochrane-Watson, 11 Mar. 2016.
35. Interview with Adrian Cochrane-Watson, 11 Mar. 2016.
36. Young Unionists focus group, 10 Mar. 2016.
37. Young Unionists focus group, 10 Mar. 2016.

38. Interview with Jeff Dudgeon 20 May 2016.
39. Northern Ireland General Election study 2017.
40. R. Barry, '2017 Assembly Election: Transferred Votes', Northern Ireland Assembly Research and Information Service Briefing Note, NIAR 25-2017, Belfast: Northern Ireland Assembly, 2017.

8

Liberal and Secular or Protestant and Orange?

Religion and the UUP

We considered Britishness and Northern Irishness as aspects of unionist political identity in a previous chapter. Now, we must consider the influence of Protestantism and Orangeism within the UUP. The chapter assesses the importance of religion for Party members and analyses the degree to which they think their faith ought to shape the political and social agendas of their organization. In exploring the extent to which the UUP 'does God' in terms of the breadth and depth of faith held by members, we assess the stances of members on key contemporary social and moral questions which have provoked considerable debate in Northern Ireland. We measure how the Protestant denominational characteristics of the UUP differ from its main political rival, the DUP, even if both parties are similar in their dearth of Roman Catholic members. We also consider why the formal alliance between the UUP and the Orange Order was severed in 2005. For the century following the formation of the Ulster Unionist Council (UUC) in 1905, the UUP and the Orange Order were bound together as a broad religious-political-ideological movement. We examine the legacy of that relationship. Are many members, politically socialized in an era of fraternal Orange–UUP relations, still 'deeply Orange' and what are the implications of that for party change? The chapter thus considers the lingering importance of Orangeism within the UUP. The survey data allow direct comparisons with the DUP throughout.

A Broad (Protestant) Church? Religious Affiliations

To begin with perhaps the least surprising finding, the UUP is overwhelmingly a Protestant party in respect of the affiliations of its members As Table 8.1 shows, the non-religious are rare specimens within the ranks, at 3.2 per cent,

Table 8.1 Religious affiliations of UUP and DUP members (%)

	UUP	DUP (2014)
Church of Ireland	43.4	17.7
Presbyterian	41.6	29.1
Methodist	6.9	4.2
Other Protestant	4.4	14.7
Free Presbyterian	0.1	30.5
Roman Catholic	0.2	0.6
Other religion	0.2	1.0
No religion	3.2	2.2

DUP figures from Tonge et al., *The DUP.*

and Roman Catholics are barely present, at 0.2 per cent. Church of Ireland and Presbyterian affiliations dominate.

The comparison with the DUP is included in Table 8.1 to highlight the contrast in terms of Free Presbyterians within the UUP. The UUP rejected the fundamentalist, Free Presbyterian brand with which the DUP was long associated for many years when led by Ian Paisley, founder of that church in 1951. Whilst Free Presbyterians are declining as a percentage of DUP membership, the legacy of Ian Paisley's use of the DUP as a political vehicle for his Free Presbyterian Church remains apparent. It remains a faultline between the two unionist parties. As the UUP former MLA, Danny Kennedy, put it, 'the Free Presbyterian Church . . . was a turn-off to mainstream Presbyterianism'.[1] The one UUP MLA brought up in the Free Presbyterian Church was critical of his former denomination:

> as a child, I didn't like what I heard from maybe a preacher. even as a child, a young Christian, I thought, wow, that's not really . . . it doesn't . . . I can't square that. It was a wee bit too much. Even if he's right, what he's saying, there's a hardness and a lack of humility, and a lack of humanity in what he's saying. For me, that's not what Christ is about, or being Christian was about. So, I sort of knew that that hard line wasn't for me.[2]

Whilst the Church of Ireland and Presbyterian percentages within the UUP are broadly in line with those found among Northern Ireland's Protestant population, the obvious disjuncture is in respect of the near-absence of Catholics. Indeed, Catholic under-representation is even more acute than that found within the DUP. A tiny 0.7 per cent of UUP members were brought up as Catholics, but this figure becomes even more miniscule in terms of those within the Party who are still Catholic. Bereft of Catholic membership, the UUP is similarly starved of Catholic votes. At the 2017 General Election, less than 1 per cent of Catholics voted UUP.[3] The stark lack of Catholics in the UUP is acknowledged by many members as unfortunate, but there is no clear plan to redress the problem of innate unionism not converting into support for, or membership of, unionist parties. Successive Northern Ireland Life and Times surveys have highlighted the apparent paradox of sizeable acquiescence among Catholics for the Union being juxtaposed with rejection of those parties who overtly back that Union. According to the 2016 such survey, 0 per cent of Catholics described themselves as unionists,[4] yet 41 per cent of Catholics believed that the best long-term solution for Northern Ireland was devolved government within the UK, a greater figure than the 35 per cent backing a united Ireland.[5]

The extent of Catholic unionism can be questioned. The 2017 Northern Ireland General Election study included a forced-choice border poll question between remaining part of the UK or becoming part of a united Ireland and only 14 per of Catholics preferred the UK option. However only a slight overall majority, 56 per cent, favoured unity,[6] indicating large numbers of waverers, or potential 'soft unionists', who might realistically be targeted by the UUP—but at present they will not touch the Party. Only 7 per cent of Party members disagree with the proposition that 'the UUP should be doing more to attract Roman Catholic members and voters', with 74 per cent agreeing more ought to be done. Two-thirds of Orange Order UUP members want more done to recruit Catholics, rising to 84 per cent among non-Orange members, but the near-void is not easy to tackle and elicits more resignation than action, as articulated by this UUP member:

> If you're a Catholic who lives in a Catholic area, who has got a good job, a nice car and is doing well and feels that his career and progress has been down to living in the United Kingdom, he's not going to go out and say, 'I think I'll go into the Ulster Unionist Party'. He wouldn't do it. He's going to have three or four neighbours in the road who disagree with him, or he thinks disagree with. So he's obviously not going to put his head above the parapet in case Joe Bloggs is going to give him a hard time.[7]

At 3.2 per cent, there are more UUP members of no religion than there are Catholics. That figure of 3.2 per cent is higher than the 0.9 per cent of members who state they were not brought up in any religion and even the UUP is not immune from the forces of secularism and movement from religion, which, at the younger end of the age scale, are making a difference to the type of UUP member. Among those aged under 35, 28 per cent of UUP members say they do not belong to a religion, higher than the overall 'no religion' figure for Northern Ireland of 17 per cent.[8] The figure for those aged 65 and over in the party is 0.3 per cent. The trend within the UUP is for movement away from religious affiliation per se among younger members, whereas the pattern among younger DUP members was the maintenance of religious affiliation, but with far lower membership of the Free Presbyterian Church.

Table 8.2 Regularity of religious attendance among UUP and DUP members (%)

	UUP	DUP (2014)
Once a week or more	45	59
2 or 3 times a month	18	16
Once a month	10	6
Several times a year	11	8
Less frequently	9	5
Never/no religion	7	6

Q. Apart from special occasions such as weddings, funerals, baptisms, and so on, how often do you attend services or meetings connected with your religion?
DUP figures from Tonge et al., *The DUP.*

Religious affiliation within the UUP remains important, but it is about believing as well as belonging. Most observe their Protestant faith, in that a large majority attend church at least once per month, as Table 8.2 shows, with the figures offering comparison with levels of observance within the DUP. It is perhaps also worth noting that the 45 per cent weekly church attendance figure of UUP members is nine times higher than that found among the British public.[9]

Whilst formal religious observance is slightly lower among UUP members compared to the DUP, regular religious services form a regular part of the lives of most members in both main unionist parties. According to Danny Kennedy, the UUP remains true to its roots: 'rural, conservative Northern Ireland, church-going, God-fearing, that's the structure of the Party where I am'. Kennedy's portrayal appears accurate and extends to many UUP voters, only 6 per cent of whom state categorically that 'they do not believe in God'.[10] Despite their high level of observance, UUP members are reluctant to portray themselves as overly religious. Only 19 per cent describe themselves as 'very religious', with the majority, 53 per cent, self-labelling as 'somewhat religious'. Almost one in five declare themselves 'not very religious' and a further 8 per cent state that they are 'not at all religious'. Again, these figures differ markedly according to age. Eighty-three per cent of the 65–74 age category describe themselves as either somewhat or very religious, but this falls to a mere 38 per cent among those aged under 35 ($p < 0.001$).

Having established that the UUP contains an overwhelming number of religious identifiers and a large volume of religiously practising members, the obvious question begged is whether those members want their party to be religious. Historically, the UUP was a more latently religious party which eschewed the overtly politicized Protestantism and fundamentalist Free Presbyterianism associated with the DUP. The UUP's 'religious' connection was to Orangeism, a broader cultural and political entity than that offered by a

Table 8.3 The perceived influence of faith and church upon the UUP and DUP, as seen by the respective party memberships

	UUP members' scaling of their party (%)	DUP members' scaling of their party (2014) (%)
0	2.6	1.1
1	2.3	0.3
2	2.3	1.9
3	6.0	2.7
4	5.9	3.2
5	18.2	7.6
6	17.3	11.6
7	21.2	18.1
8	14.8	24.1
9	5.3	16.5
10	4.3	13.0

Q. On a scale of 0–10, where 0 means no influence whatsoever and 10 means a very large amount of influence, how much influence do you think Faith and Church HAVE upon the UUP?
DUP figures from Tonge et al., *The DUP*.

Table 8.4 The desired influence of faith and church upon the UUP and DUP, as wanted by the respective party memberships

	UUP members' scaling of their party (%)	DUP members' scaling of their party (2014) (%)
0	10.1	6.5
1	3.9	2.2
2	4.3	5.1
3	5.4	4.3
4	4.7	2.4
5	13.4	11.6
6	8.5	8.1
7	11.3	7.8
8	16.2	14.3
9	7.8	10.8
10	14.3	27.0

Q. On a scale of 0–10, where 0 means no influence whatsoever and 10 means a very large amount of influence, how much influence do you think Faith and Church SHOULD HAVE upon the UUP?
DUP figures from Tonge et al., *The DUP*.

particular church. We thus asked UUP members two questions; one of perception, in terms of how religious a party they perceive theirs to be; and one of direction, how religious ought the UUP to be? Tables 8.3 and 8.4 indicate the spread of views on both questions—and provide a comparison with the DUP.

Table 8.3 indicates that UUP members see their party as quite considerably influenced by faith and church. Those believing otherwise, in scoring the party below five, amount to only 19.1 per cent of members, almost double the percentage of DUP members placing their own party in these low religion categories. Less than 10 per cent of UUP members place their party in the 'faith and church dominant' categories of nine and ten, whereas nearly one-third of DUP members put their organization in the highest categories. The overall picture is of one highly religiously influenced unionist party, the DUP, and another, the UUP, quite considerably influenced.

Table 8.4 indicates sizeable desire for the UUP to be a religiously oriented party, although this orientation is subject to differing interpretations, ranging from the modest religious leanings of a standard right-of-centre Christian Democrat party of the type still quite common in Europe, to a stridently Protestant vehicle, one for which Faith, Bible, and Orangeism are central planks. Nearly three-fifths of the UUP membership score the desirability of faith and church influence at six or more, although the DUP figure is higher, with more than two-thirds of its members wanting this considerable amount of influence and more than half opting for the top three categories of influence of eight, nine, or ten. Neither party has many adherents wanting to eschew faith and church. Those wanting religious influence to be low, at three or less, amount to less than one-quarter of the UUP's membership. There are, however, sizeable age differences within the UUP. Those aged below 35 do not want their party to be particularly influenced by faith and church, only 26 per cent giving a score of six or higher. Amongst the 65–74 age group, as a contrast, 71 per cent scored the desirability of faith and church influence at six or higher (significant at $p < 0.001$). The age effect is far less marked within the DUP. Half of DUP members aged below 35 place the desired amount of religious influence at eight or above, in line with older age categories. Overall, the UUP could still be viewed as a religious party, but it is a little more relaxed over faith and church than its unionist rival. Former leader Mike Nesbitt declared that his number on the zero to ten scale would be 'relatively low but the values are important. A lot of my values are Christian values, but I wouldn't say I was a great church man.'[11]

The common UUP argument is that its unionism is bound up far more in liberal 'British' values which owe nothing to a particular religion. The case for the union of Great Britain and Northern Ireland is articulated on a rational, contractual basis, with civic and liberal unionist arguments to the fore. Far from irreligious, the UUP nonetheless takes some pride in being seen as less religiously militant compared to how the DUP was long viewed. The UUP's historical associations are with the broader, less austere and sect-like denominations of the Church of Ireland and Presbyterian Church. It is a party which, as we have seen, does not attract Catholics, however, and has no clear plan to do so, but would regard such recruitment as desirable. Mixed marriages between Protestants and Catholics are hardly overwhelmingly endorsed, as Table 8.5 confirms.

Table 8.5 Attitudes to family 'mixed' marriages among UUP members (%)

Would mind a lot	25.1
Would mind a little	32.2
Would not mind	39.3
Don't know	3.4

Q. Would you yourself mind or not mind if one of your close relatives were to marry someone of a different religion?

There are big age differentials. 68 per cent of those aged 24 and under would not mind a mixed marriage, whereas only 24 per cent of those aged between 65 and 74 would be so sanguine (significant at $p < 0.001$). Orange Order membership appears particularly important regarding this question, with only 19 per cent of those belonging to the Orange Institution, which prohibits a member from marrying a Catholic, not minding a union beyond the Protestant faith. Marriage beyond the Protestant community is rare among UUP members. Less than 4 per cent are married to someone of a different religion (or have such a partner) whilst a further 3 per cent are coupled with someone of no religion. Whilst the communal homogeneity might be attributed to educational segregation, this would only be a partial explanation. Although 82 per cent of UUP members say that they were educated separately from Catholics, the 18 per cent who state that they attended a mixed or integrated school, educating both Catholic and Protestant children, is higher than what might reasonably be expected, given that integrated schools educate only 7 per cent of Northern Ireland's schoolchildren.[12] A majority (59 per cent) of UUP members would prefer to see a single integrated system of education, whilst 33 per cent support the retention of faith schools. The Party leader from 2012 until 2017, Mike Nesbitt, described mixed education as a 'virtual inoculation against sectarianism'.[13] Former MLA Adrian Cochrane-Watson insisted, 'The Catholic Church is the main obstacle to truly integrated schools in this country',[14] a not uncommon perception across the Party. A Londonderry UUP member argued that 'middle-class people, Catholic and Protestant, mix quite well. But, the working-class areas, there's a polarization. The only way to break that I think is through schools.'[15] A student focus group member opined:

> I know that Catholic education does perform quite favourably. I don't think there's a very large number of Catholic parents that want to do away with that. If they want to send their child to a Catholic school, they have that right. But, should the State have to support having a segregated system? We have handed over control of an entire sector to the Catholic Church. If they want to have control over their own schools, they can have that, but it shouldn't be within the State framework, as it is at the moment.

How Orange is the UUP?

Any transformation of the UUP into a modern civic unionist party, one whose case for the Union depended entirely on rational, contractual, and non-religious arguments, required divorce from the Protestant Orange Order. The link between the political and Protestant arms of unionism had been formalized via the role for the Orange Order within the Ulster Unionist Council (UUC) established in 1905.[16] There was hardly a queue of Catholics waiting to join the UUP—or vote for the Party—if the Orange Order left, so separation would not yield membership or electoral riches. It would, however, make the UUP of the twenty-first century look different from that of the twentieth, when the Order was highly influential within the Party, a major structural and political presence. Joint membership was the norm. Only three Cabinet members in the era of UUP majoritarian hegemony from the 1920s until the 1970s were non-Orange. From the 1920s until the 1970s, 95 per cent of UUP MPs at Westminster belonged to the Order.[17]

Although the Orange Order could help unite the UUP, it also infused unionism with a sectarian flavour which found little favour outside Northern Ireland and, increasingly, within its confines. The Orange perspective had been articulated clearly by the Grand Master of the Order during the 1960s, Sir George Clark, who opined that it was 'difficult to see how a Roman Catholic, with the vast difference in our religious outlooks, could be either acceptable within the Ulster Unionist Party, or, for that matter, bring himself unconditionally to support its ideals'.[18] As Walker illuminates,[19] there were occasional internal tensions between the Orange Order's perspective and that of some within the UUP, particularly over parading routes and funding for Catholic schools. However, such friction was subsumed within a broader Protestant-Orange unity which solidified cross-class unity to see off significant challenges, such as the labourist one posed by the Northern Ireland Labour Party.[20]

Friction between austere Paisleyite Free Presbyterian scripture and stricture associated with the DUP and Orangeism's somewhat more relaxed, if still strong, Protestantism, helped the UUP–Orange relationship to survive three decades of intra-unionist party rivalry from the early 1970s. The UUP–Orange relationship remained strong despite the Sunningdale Agreement's brief and ill-fated flirtation with devolved power-sharing and an Irish dimension, attempted by Brian Faulkner, a deal opposed by the Orange institution to which Faulkner belonged. Faulkner's immediate successors, Harry West and James Molyneaux, presided over comfortable UUP–Orange relationships. 'Ulster loyalists are fortunate they have the firm hand of James Molyneaux on the tiller' declared the *Orange Standard* in 1994.[21] The same outlet claimed a year later that 'no politician has been more respected'.[22] When however, the next UUP leader attempted to sell an ambitious revision of the Sunningdale Agreement, the historical Orange–UUP alliance was to become doomed.

The Orange–UUP alliance finally fractured over the tensions produced by the Belfast Agreement. It had been a divorce foretold. Even prior to the controversies attendant to that Agreement, a majority of Orange Order members favoured severance.[23] The 1998 deal proved the tipping point. David Trimble's election as UUP leader in 1995 was initially lauded by the Orange Order, of which Trimble was a member, as a 'masterly performance for unionism'.[24] Trimble had enjoyed a brief honeymoon period, when Grand Lodge had hailed his elevation to the leadership as a triumph of a 'cult figure among Portadown and Lurgan Orangemen . . . rock solid in his Protestant and Orange allegiance'.[25] Trimble had linked arms with Paisley to celebrate the Order being able to walk the Garvaghy Road in 1995 but the victory proved pyrrhic, with the Order banned from the road since 1998. Once elected leader, Trimble played down his Orange credentials:

> I have never been an active member of the Orange Order. I don't even own a bowler hat. The support I got from many in the Orange Order was nothing to do with Drumcree, everything to do with the fact that I set up the Ulster Society in 1985. This cultural body has much support in the Order and many of our meetings are in Orange halls.[26]

The Orange Order was greatly troubled by the Belfast Agreement, a deal which, the *Orange Standard* opined, 'no Protestant in good conscience could support'.[27] An anti-Agreement Orange Order meant trouble for the UUP leader. Orange delegates retained voting rights within the UUC and Executive Committee even if they were supportive of the DUP. Although the Orange Order leadership did not formally instruct its members to vote no to the Agreement, the messages of opposition were clear. For Grand Lodge, the Agreement, with its prisoner releases, policing changes, and unrepentant 'terrorists' in government, was immoral, a triumph of evil and wrongdoing over good. To these bitter criticisms were added 'Dublin interference', an 'undemocratically unaccountable Assembly', and the perception of a continuation of the 'Maryfield Secretariat and Anglo-Irish agreement in another guise'.[28] Orange opposition hardened; by the end of 2001, the Agreement was labelled 'disastrous for unionists'.[29]

It was the supposed immorality of the Belfast Agreement, more than the constitutional parts of the deal, upon which the Order focused its ire. Trimble was challenged for the party leadership in 2000 by the Grand Master of the Orange Order between 1971 and 1996, the Reverend Martin Smyth. Written off initially as a no-hope challenger, Smyth (who had polled a paltry sixty votes when one of the contestants in Trimble's 1995 leadership election) polled a hefty 43 per cent of the vote for his insurgency. Smyth was proud to declare his Orange credentials, having earlier cautioned the UUP against losing its Orange core vote in pursuing moderation and votes from across the divide. He argued in 1995 that risking Orange votes for Catholic ones was 'bad mathematics'.[30] In fact, there had been scant pursuit of Catholic votes or members and the severing of the Orange–UUP link could not be seen in that context. The UUC President, Josias Cunningham, made this clear in 1998, insisting that separation

> may make it easier for some of the Roman Catholic faith to identify with and join us. But this is not the reason why the matter has been under consideration for the last nine years. The thinking has been driven by an earnest desire to streamline and modernise our structure, so that we may establish effective discipline and cohesion which is difficult in the current federal structure.[31]

In 2000, Smyth garnered a strong vote from the Order's members, attracting more votes from Orange UUP members than the Party leader, whilst among non-Orange members of the Party, Trimble led by two to one.[32] An Orange versus non-Orange faultline was apparent within the UUP, with Orange Order members much more hostile to early prisoner releases and the Patten Report's reforms of policing than other UUP members. Whilst the UUP leadership could hardly expel its Orange brethren, a huge chunk of the party and providing many stalwarts, the status of the Orange Order as a distinctive policy-making vehicle within the UUP came under closer scrutiny. Whilst many individual memberships of the Orange institution would continue, Trimble wanted party dealignment. Conscious of the Order's position as a barrier to where he wanted to take his Party in terms of both outlook and structure and anxious to sell the Belfast Agreement, Trimble decided to remove what he saw as a barrier:

> We could see that roughly 75 per cent of party activists supported us, and opinion polls showed similar support [from] UUP voters. The problem lay with the Orange delegates. Historically the Orange delegates tended to be senior members of the Order and firmly loyal to the leadership. After the Agreement there was a movement to remove the delegates that supported the party and replace them [with] younger men who scarcely appeared except at the association AGMs and at requisited council meetings where they voted against the leadership.
>
> So, we decided that the subscription they would have to pay to the Party per Orange delegate, which had been for historical reasons just a nominal sum, would be brought into alignment with that paid by the constituency delegates. Unsurprisingly there was a reluctance to swell the party's coffers and a movement developed for the Orange Orders to disaffiliate from the party. This took some three years to happen.[33]

The Order's often rural and border-based, conservative membership had in times past provided ballast for the UUP leadership via its loyalty, but that was already dissipating when Trimble took office.[34] Compromises with Catholic nationalists were made more difficult by an organization which had a jaundiced view of the minority population. The majority of Orange Order members believed that 'most Catholics are IRA sympathisers'[35] and any power-sharing deal that offered the political representatives of the IRA an equal stake in government was always going to be a tough sell to the sceptical brethren. Trimble was determined to help break down old religious prejudices fuelled by arcane Orange rules. He made a point of paying tribute to Catholic unionists in his address to the UUP annual conference in 1996, attended Catholic funerals of Omagh bomb victims in 1998, and could point to pre-Troubles UUP leaders, all members of the Orange Order, having participated in Catholic services.[36]

Whilst it had many good and benign members, the Orange Order also attracted disreputable elements (sometimes band members not actually belonging to the Order) more associated with bigotry than Christianity at times and some within the UUP saw this as a barrier to the attraction of middle-class Unionist support. Parading issues at times appeared to usurp Protestantism and the values of the Reformed Church. This criticism was offered by a range of sources: a disillusioned former member of the Order,[37] journalists,[38] and academics.[39]

The Orange Order saved Trimble the bother of removing them, leaving the UUC voluntarily in 2005, by which time most of the Order's members were no longer voting for the Party to which Grand Lodge was affiliated. Making the UUP more attractive to Catholics was not prominent on the radar however; what mattered was the lack of mutual benefit to the arrangement. The Orange Order and the UUP leadership could see that the relationship was no longer beneficial for either grouping. Trimble regarded Orange delegates as trouble-some and the structure of the alliance anachronistic. The Orange Order saw little value backing a unionist party which had taken a course opposed by many Orangemen, who were switching political allegiance. Severance was backed by UUP and DUP supporters within the Order.

The resolution proposing ending the Orange–UUC link was tabled at a meeting of Grand Lodge, the Orange Order's ruling body, by a UUP backer, Edward Stevenson (later to become Grand Master of the Order) and supported by eighty-two votes to sixteen, with eleven abstentions. Two years after separation, only 24 per cent of Orange Order members dissented from the divorce although a majority were content for UUP meetings to be held in Orange halls and, among older Orange Order members, politically socialized in an era of cordial Orange–UUP relations, there remained greater warmth towards unionism's 'traditional' party.[40] Only 29 per cent of Orange Order members supported the Belfast Agreement and within three years of the deal more Orange Order members were supporting the DUP than the UUP

(49 per cent to 45 per cent) even though the UUP still led the DUP by 4 per cent at the 2001 Westminster election, the last time the UUP would hold a lead. By 2007, nearly two-thirds of Orange Order members expressed allegiance to the DUP, not the UUP.[41] Moreover, Ian Paisley was almost twice as popular as Trimble as preferred leader of unionism among Orange Order members. Whilst the UUP retained sizeable support among older Orange Order members and those in the middle class, support had ebbed in all other demographic categories.[42]

The large-scale political defections to the DUP, allied to the Order's anti-Agreement stance, were far more responsible for severance than Trimble's raising of Orange UUC subscriptions, although his move had increased the Order's ire. Many within the Order were aware of Trimble's motivations in demanding £12,000 a year from the Order for the right to have Orange delegates affiliated to the UUC. The Belfast Grand Master, Dawson Baillie, who also served on the UUP Executive, commented:

> It's payback time for the Orange Order. Back in 1998, we, as an institution, we could not advise our members to vote for the Belfast Agreement and David Trimble and his party have never forgiven us for that.[43]

Many of those loyal to both the Orange Order and the UUP endorsed severance. Colin McCusker, for example, highlighted how, regarding Orange delegate attendance at the UUC:

> some of those proposed to go . . . weren't even members of the party . . . they weren't paying their way or anything. So, I thought it was too loose an arrangement. We didn't have any control over it.[44]

McCusker's view of the desirability of severance was endorsed by many within the UUP, including the leader, Robin Swann, who believes that the Orange Order–UUP link 'became harmful—it was holding both back',[45] a view echoed elsewhere. A Coleraine UUP member praised the divorce:

> It was good for both parties, to be honest. Because the Ulster Unionist Party needed to shake off some of the older images of the party, and the Orange Order itself needed to get a distinct role within Northern Ireland society, a special post-Agreement programme. So, I think it was best for both parties really. It should've happened a bit earlier, maybe. I think it was a bit late in the day, and I know that there were earlier attempts to try and break the association, but, I think it was a good move.[46]

Others in the Coleraine group, also holding joint UUP–Orange Order membership, concurred:

> [The UUP–Orange link was] a good thing to shake that off, because it was abused. The Orange Order people turned up for the most contentious times, and it brought

about situations. I could tell you some hair-brained situations from when I was Secretary of the Constituency Association here. There were people turned up that we didn't know, they turned up at Council meetings in Belfast to vote against Trimble. So, it just had to be done.

They weren't even paying [UUP] members... it was because they were in the Orange Order, they were appointed at the local Orange Hall, and then they turned up at unionist meetings, and we never saw them...

You sometimes found, like, people who supported the DUP were delegates to our party and were coming to meetings just to attack the party.[47]

UUP Orangeman Mark Cosgrove offered a similar view:

The Orange Order was a party within a party. As a very minimum you should have had to have been a member of the Ulster Unionist Party as well as the Orange Order. Separation was something that had to be done to modernize the party. Some of the people I saw at those meetings did not subscribe to the values of the Ulster Unionist Party and openly supported other parties.[48]

The former UUP Assembly member (MLA) Danny Kennedy, a long-standing Orangeman, argues that the sharpness of intra-unionist rivalry was the cause of severance:

the relationship between the Ulster Unionist Party and Orangeism, whilst there was only one main, and prime unionist party, was... alright, or it was manageable. When there were two parties of an increasing, almost equal size, it was clear that something would have to give, and the separation was probably better.[49]

Kennedy had drafted a resolution urging separation at a UUP conference in the 1990s, seeing divorce as inevitable. Many party officials welcomed the ending of the link, one commenting:

From an administrative point of view—it did make things easier, because we were coming under fire because... we couldn't check the people that were coming through the Orange Order were party members, and a lot of people were saying to us, 'I know he's a member of another party', or, 'I know that he doesn't support what we do. What's he doing here?' It wasn't our call.[50]

Although the formal relationship between the UUP and the Orange Order was ended, individual membership of the Order remains common within the UUP: 35 per cent of UUP members also belong to the Orange Order. A further 9 per cent say they used to belong to the Order but are no longer a member, indicating a slippage of membership which is a problem for the Orange institution. Orange Order membership amongst different categories of UUP member and the comparison with the DUP are shown in Table 8.6.

As can be seen, there is little difference in the level of Orange Order membership between UUP and DUP ordinary members. However, whereas the DUP's Orange quota rises among elected representatives (a number of whom

Table 8.6 Orange Order membership within the two main Unionist parties (%)

	UUP	DUP (2014)
Councillors	27.2	54.2
MLAs	20.0	61.7
MPs	N/A	60.0
All members	35.4	34.6 (2014)

DUP membership figure taken from Tonge et al., *The DUP.*

Table 8.7 Orange Order membership held by UUP members, by period of joining the UUP

Period joined the UUP	Membership of the Orange Order
1998–current	27%
1967–1997	45%
1966 and earlier	64%

defected from the UUP and already held Orange membership) this is not the case within the UUP. The Orange proportions of both party memberships are sizeable.

There is a very sizeable difference in Orange membership according to age. Only 23 per cent of UUP members aged under 35 belong to the Order, whereas the majority (52 per cent) of those aged 65 and over belong. There is also considerable variation in the Orange Order membership period when a member joined the UUP, as Table 8.7 shows.

As is evident from the figure for those who joined the UUP in the pre-Troubles era, it was once the norm to hold joint UUP–Orange Order membership. Dual membership remained common, albeit declining, during the conflict. Since the end of the Troubles and the onset of the Belfast Agreement, most of those joining the UUP have not held Orange Order membership. What was once a symbiotic relationship between two organizations is no longer in existence and the majority individual choice of more recent UUP joiners has been to remain outside the Orange Order. A sharp tail-off in joint membership from new joiners began in the mid-1990s, prior to the Belfast Agreement. It is possible that the years of confrontations over the Orange Order's Drumcree parade may have deterred moderate unionists entering the UUP from Orange affiliation.

The formalities of divorce do not, of course, necessarily prevent the continuation of affection for a former partner and this seems true of UUP members and the Orange Order. As Table 8.8 demonstrates, a majority of UUP

Table 8.8 Attitudes towards the Orange Order among UUP members (%)

Strongly like	35.0
Like	28.7
Neither like nor dislike	26.3
Dislike	6.0
Strongly dislike	4.1

Q. Please describe how you feel about the following organization; the Orange Order.

Table 8.9 Attitudes to Orange Order parades among UUP members (%)

The Loyal Orders should be able to parade their traditional routes without restriction	41.0
The Loyal Orders should be able to parade their traditional routes if there is meaningful local engagement	24.3
The Loyal Orders should be able to parade their traditional routes if there is meaningful engagement leading to local agreement	26.4
The Loyal Orders should not be allowed to parade their traditional routes if they include nationalist areas	4.1
Other/Don't know	4.2

Q. Which of these comes closest to your view on the issue of Orange Order parades?

members feel warmth towards the Order and those with antipathy are a fairly small minority. Whilst a formal relationship between the two organizations had run its course, severance of the UUP–Orange link did not represent a major ideological shift away from Orangeism. Cultural, political, ideological, and religious bonds remain strong, transcending even the Trimble years of open political hostility and the Nesbitt era of a lack of interest in promoting Orange issues. Some non-Orange members of the UUP are also sympathetic about what they see as repeated attacks upon the Order. According to the MLA Robbie Butler, 'Orangeism has been demonized, and anything even remotely unionist, whether it's the parades, bonfires, and all those things, whether you agree with it environmentally, or not, they are part of the culture, and they've been demonized.'[51]

Behind the aggregate percentages however, there is evidence of less affection for the Orange Order among those who have joined the UUP since 1998, only half of whom claim any liking. This group is not particularly hostile either—only 13 per cent registered a dislike—but indifference appears quite common among more recent UUP joiners. Overall within the UUP, sympathy for Orange causes is sizeable. Many UUP members believe in unfettered Orange Order marching rights and a mere 4 per cent believe in their unqualified full steerage away from nationalist areas, but as Table 8.9 shows, the level of acceptance of the need for engagement with local nationalist communities over Orange parades exceeds that found in the strident category.

The level of stridency on parades is broadly comparable to that among DUP members, of whom 58 per cent wanted unrestricted parades and 5 per cent accepted full rerouting.[52] Orangeism retains its capacity to unify unionists who otherwise may endure sharp relationships. Perhaps unsurprisingly, Orange Order membership is an important variable among UUP members (as it was in the DUP). A majority (57 per cent) of UUP members also belonging to the Order favoured unrestricted marching rights compared to only 33 per cent of non-Orange members (significant at $p < 0.01$). Nonetheless, within the UUP there are sharp attitudinal differences according to age. Only 19 per cent of members aged under 35 advocate unfettered Orange parading rights, compared to half of those aged 65–74. There was a recognition of the need for sensitivity on parading from a large number of Orange interviewees. As one member of a large Antrim lodge put it:

> I would be very, very disappointed with my Orange lodge if we marched on the 12th of July and we offended many of my Catholic friends, many of my Catholic neighbours. The choice of our band, the choice of our behaviour, the choice of flags and symbolism, I think, are historically and culturally important to me, but they're certainly not offensive. I know many of my good, very close Catholic friends will come out and watch me and shout over at me on 12th July. That can be very different in Belfast.[53]

The UUP's support base is even more strident on parading issues than members. A majority of UUP voters at the 2015 general election declared support for unrestricted marching rights for the Orange Order, although at 53 per cent the level of stridency was below the 66 per cent offered by the DUP's voters.[54]

The willingness to engage in dialogue on parades held by a slight majority of UUP members does not translate into widespread backing for the Parades Commission, which attracted criticism even from those not associated with Orange causes. Mike Nesbitt declared:

> I do not think the Parades Commission is doing a great job. If you look at what happened in North Belfast there were riots and gunshots and the next year the paraders were punished . . . I don't get a sense that the Parades Commission got it.[55]

Unsurprisingly Nesbitt's critical perspective tends to be shared by Orange Order members, from the Party leader downwards. Robin Swann claimed that he 'met with hostility from the Commission . . . hostility I wouldn't have even met from those opposing the parades'. Asked whether parading would have been on the DUP's post-2017 election shopping list of demands placed upon the Conservative Government, Swann stated he was 'surprised it wasn't'.[56]

Colin McCusker complained of the Parades Commission:

I did try to engage with them and went to the trouble of going there and sitting in front of them and having all the questions…You just felt at the end of it they hadn't listened to a word you said…They just sort of ignore anything you've said and just do the usual ruling. I've seen the determinations where they've clearly just copied and pasted stuff.[57]

UUP MLA Roy Beggs complained that 'the ground rules, on which the police end up taking action, need to be changed, because they favour the objector, or someone who threatens violence'.[58] According to UUP Orangeman Tom Elliott, there was a need to end the 'nonsense of these determinations without explanation' and to stop the way the Parades Commission 'succumb to the violent argument'.[59] Even former UUP MP Danny Kinahan, often regarded as a moderate liberal, expressed concern that the Parades Commission 'live in a slightly different society and world, not in touch with someone who enjoys being in the Orange'.[60] A UUP student focus group, few of whom demanded unfettered Orange parading rights, criticized the lack of accountability of the Commission, in terms of appointments to serve on the body and in the lack of answerability to those affected by its determinations.[61] The Parades Commission was also criticized as surplus to requirements A Derry UUP member argued:

We can self-level this, or self-manage it, if we get responsible leaderships on all sides. Particularly, with them political people who would encourage people to get into a room and talk, you know. This, 'No, we're not going down there to talk to them,'…that's not going to stack up any longer. They're meeting, and they're sitting in government together, so why can't they go into a room and sit? I think the Parades Commission is a complication that we should be sifting out of the problem, and getting it down to local people.[62]

In determining what type of UUP member believes faith and church should be highly influential in the UUP and, likewise, which categories support unrestricted Orange Order parading rights, we use a logistic regression (Table 8.10). The first dependent variable is how much influence faith and church should hold in the UUP, dividing members into those who scored this at zero to five out of ten (i.e. opposed to, or lukewarm towards, the idea) and those who favoured such influence (grading this at six or above). The second dependent variable is that of those supporting unrestricted rights on Orange Order parades. The independent variables used are age, with UUP members divided into two categories (50 and under and 51 and over); gender; education (three categories: degree holders, up to A level, or no qualifications); Orange Order membership; the religiosity of members, divided between those who attend church weekly or at least two or three times per month and others

Table 8.10 Multivariate model of UUP members' views on (1) desired influence of faith and church on their Party and (2) Orange Order parading rights

	(1) Influence faith and church should have upon the UUP	(2) Unrestricted Orange Order parades
Age 51+	0.930***	0.775***
	(0.203)	(0.211)
Male	0.185	−0.330
	(0.210)	(0.213)
Education	−0.197**	−0.083
	(0.083)	(0.078)
Orange Order	0.808***	1.232***
	(0.201)	(0.194)
Religiosity	1.305***	0.431**
	(0.179)	(0.183)
Working class	−0.063	0.591***
	(0.196)	(0.183)
Constant	−1.106***	−1.534***
	(0.336)	(0.331)
Pseudo R-squared	0.182	0.117

Standard errors in parentheses
*** $p < 0.01$, ** $p < 0.05$

who attend church less regularly or never; and self-ascribed class status: middle- or working-class.

Several effects can be found in Table 8.10. Older members (aged 51 and above) are more likely to think that faith and church should have an important role in the UUP. The same applies to more religious members and Orange Order members. Education has the opposite effect: the higher the level of education, the less likely UUP members are to think faith and church should play a more important role. Self-ascribed social class and gender have no effect. In terms of effect size, the largest effect is that of religiosity. Very religious members (defined by frequency of church attendance) are 28 per cent more likely than less religious members to think faith and church should be more important. This is followed by the effect of age, as older members are almost 19 per cent more likely than younger members to think faith and church should be more important, a 43 per cent probability among those aged 18–50 versus 62 per cent among those aged 51 and over.

Regarding Orange Order parades, older members are more likely than younger members to oppose any restrictions on Orange Order parades. The same, unsurprisingly, applies to Orange Order members, compared to those UUP members who do not belong to the Orange Order who are more accepting of regulation. Working-class members and regular churchgoers are also more opposed to parading restrictions. Education and gender do not have a significant effect on this. What emerges from Table 8.10 is further indication of a generational divide between a conservative, religious, and Orange older UUP and a somewhat more liberal and less religiously inclined younger type of member.

Social and Moral Issues

The religious influences within the UUP contribute to the party's social conservatism on issues such as same-sex marriage and abortion, both still prohibited in Northern Ireland (abortion is permitted only in exceptional circumstances when the mother's life is at risk). The UUP is keen to stress that these issues are ones of conscience for members and elected representatives and are not subject to a party whip. The conscience aspect and more moderate tone tend to be highlighted as points of difference with the DUP, whose views came under considerable scrutiny after the 2017 Westminster election.

Nonetheless, UUP MLAs overwhelmingly opposed same-sex marriage in the five Assembly votes between October 2012 and November 2015. Only two of the UUP's thirteen MLAs voted in favour of liberalization (no DUP MLA supported change).[63] The November 2015 debate was followed by a narrow vote in favour of legalization, by 53 votes to 52, but the Assembly's parallel consent rules meant the measure came nowhere near to being passed, with only 7.5 per cent of Unionist MLAs backing change, way short of the 40 per cent required. Ordinary members appear more liberal on same-sex marriage compared to the UUP MLAs who served in the 2011–16 Assembly. Ironically, one MLA previously criticized for not welcoming same-sex couples to his bed and breakfast establishment,[64] and who voted against same-sex marriage, said he felt that petitions of concern 'had been misused in an inappropriate manner against the gay and lesbian community'.[65] Adrian Cochrane-Watson's earlier views caused controversy in 2010, when the UUP was in alliance with the Conservatives, the then UUP leader Reg Empey chosen as replacement contender in South Antrim.

During his penultimate conference speech as leader, in 2015, Mike Nesbitt wondered whether his party was 'on the wrong side of history' in opposing same-sex marriage. Nesbitt's public musing was greeted with silence in the hall. During his time as leader, Nesbitt acknowledged he was on the wrong side of his party's still oppositional sentiment and felt it would be too divisive for him to vote in favour of legalizing same-sex marriage. He duly abstained in the vote a few days after his 2015 conference speech but found his opposition

Table 8.11 UUP members' attitudes to same-sex marriage (%)

Strongly agree	15.2
Agree	14.1
Neither agree nor disagree	13.6
Disagree	21.3
Strongly disagree	35.6

'Same-sex marriage should be legalized in Northern Ireland.'

to the idea now 'untenable . . . if there was a vote tomorrow I would vote to change the law'.[66]

The membership survey data indicate that whilst a more liberal position on same-sex marriage is supported by a sizeable minority within the UUP, a slender overall majority of members prefer the status quo, as shown in Table 8.11.

UUP members appear grateful that same-sex marriage is a freedom-of-conscience issue, perhaps because strongly divergent views are therefore easily containable and there is difference from the DUP's approach. Some members took exception to Nesbitt's 'wrong side of history' comment as indicative of a leader being too critical of his own party: a 'terrible phrase to use' and the 'wrong phrase to use' were two responses,[67] but another insisted that it 'broke the ice' in encouraging change.[68] Danny Kinahan was the only UUP MLA to vote in favour of a Sinn Féin Assembly motion in favour of same-sex marriage, in 2015, prior to his subsequent (successful) campaign for the South Antrim parliamentary constituency that year.[69]

Many within the UUP struggle with the idea of same-sex marriage. Former MLA Sandra Overend argued:

I am against [same-sex marriage]. I see the problem in the schools, and when you talk about Mary was married, the assumption is that Mary was married to a man, and I just think, that the teachers are going have to start explaining to children of primary school age, 'Well, this Mary's not married to a man,' and, 'This Mary's married to a woman,' and, you know, with children, that explanation is going have to start earlier, to be politically correct. Not because, the child needs to know, it's just because the teacher is obliged to be politically correct. So, I don't know. It just creates a difficult environment.[70]

A UUP MLA commented:

I don't believe that if two guys want to get married, suddenly, that it's wrong, or anything. My first allegiance will be to the church, and I just have a fear that churches will be put in a position in terms of the holy matrimony, if you like, which I believe, fundamentally, there's a difference between holy matrimony and civil marriage, anyway.[71]

A UUP Executive member and councillor opined: 'I'm against same sex marriage because of what it says in the Holy Bible: "Marriage shall be between a man and a woman."'[72] The only area of apparent unanimity appeared to be in understanding why the UUP treats same-sex marriage as an issue for individual conscience. An elected representative participant in an Omagh focus group declared how 'if I was whipped to be anti-gay marriage...I would have trouble'.[73] Members of a Young Unionist focus group highlighted freedom of conscience as an important area of difference with the DUP (although the DUP has not formally whipped Assembly votes on same-sex marriage, not seeing the need), one highlighting how 'it would probably be the social issues' that marked the biggest area of difference:

> things like, say, gay marriage, the UUP would give you a free vote on that, which the DUP—I think they may be changing on that roughly...but they still haven't done it yet. Also, I wouldn't be so trusting of the DUP, because I still, ultimately, know the DUP was founded as a Christian party. You know, obviously, in the DUP book, they talk about it as being about Christian values and all that, while the UUP would sort of allow more secular people like me into the Party.[74]

Are the attitudes of UUP members far removed from the broader population in Northern Ireland? Overall, 54 per cent of voters at the 2017 General Election backed same-sex marriage, with 23 per cent opposed; the remainder were unsure. UUP members' attitudes diverge considerably from the views of nationalists who are mainly in favour. UUP members are somewhat more hardline on same-sex marriage than UUP voters, who were equally divided on legalization in 2017. Moreover, they are also tougher than DUP voters, who broke 44 per cent to 42 per cent in favour of legalization by 2017. Among UUP members, religious observance is a huge attitudinal marker. Only 19 per cent of regular churchgoers (attending at least monthly) support the legalization of same-sex marriage, with 67 per cent declaring opposition (opposition is even more extensive among weekly churchgoers). Among the small contingent of those holding no religion within the UUP, there is no opposition to same-sex marriage and among those who have a religion but never go to church, only 26 per cent are against such unions. Age is another big indicator. Sixty-four per cent of UUP members aged 35 or under back same-sex marriage with only 18 per cent opposed. In contrast, members aged 65 and older, many politically socialized in an era when homosexuality was still illegal in Northern Ireland, are mostly resistant to the idea, with 68 per cent opposed and only 24 per cent in favour.

Most UUP members do favour change to abortion laws. Again, this is a conscience issue for the party's elected representatives and not subject to whipped vote. Table 8.12 shows attitudes towards both the modest legalization proposals debated in recent years on legalization in exceptional circumstances and views on the bigger step, less prominent in Assembly debates but

Table 8.12 UUP members' attitudes to the legalization of abortion (%)

	Abortion should be legalized in cases of rape, incest, and foetal abnormality	Abortion should be permitted up to 24 weeks of pregnancy, subject to medical approval, in line with the law in England and Wales
Strongly agree	42.7	23.0
Agree	36.9	29.4
Neither agree nor disagree	10.1	17.3
Disagree	5.6	19.0
Strongly disagree	4.8	11.4

advocated by 'pro-choice' groups, to bring the law into line with that for England and Wales.

As can be seen, there is extensive support for a modest liberalization of abortion laws and also sizeable support for more sweeping legal reform. Attitudes towards abortion are one of the few social or moral arenas where age does not attain significance. 55 per cent of those aged 35 or under in the UUP support bringing Northern Ireland's abortion laws in line with those elsewhere in the UK and 57 per cent of those aged 65 and over also support this view. Religious impacts are also minimal. Whilst those attending church monthly are slightly less in favour of a twenty-four-week time limit than the party overall (47 per cent compared to 52 per cent) and more likely to be opposed (34 per cent to 30 per cent across the party) this does not reach statistical significance. UUP MLAs appear less keen on any change to the law than do members of their Party, only three supporting legal terminations in cases of foetal abnormality in the Assembly vote taken in 2016.

An anti-abortion MLA insisted he was 'pro-life, because I do believe that you have to be an advocate for the baby, for the unborn'.[75] Former MLA and ex-MP Tom Elliott argued that abortion law in Britain was 'much too liberal... There is a debate around fatal foetal abnormality but I wouldn't go any further.'[76]

The abortion issue is not one in which internal religious and age differentials are as evident, nor is there a sharp unionist versus nationalist binary. The issue clearly appears one of freedom of conscience and the party leadership appears keen to maintain that approach. There is, however, disjuncture between the resistance of UUP MLAs to allowing abortion in cases of fatal foetal abnormality and the support for change on this from the party members.

Conclusion

The UUP has long been keen to define its unionism in non-religious terms, viewing itself as more liberal in outlook than its overtly Protestant and, for a long time, Free Presbyterian, rival. Severance of the link between the Orange Order and the UUP can be seen as functional in reshaping the Party. Yet the Party's membership is not easily reshaped and the UUP remains a Protestant Party, whilst not wishing to operate only for a Protestant people. Diversity and inclusivity extends only to denominational choice of Protestant, rather than beyond that community. The elderly membership base is predominantly Orange, religious, and socially conservative, whereas the smaller, younger wing is more nominally religious (affiliated more than practising), much less Orange, and far less socially conservative.

The UUP's internal divisions between these two membership wings have been largely overlooked amid analysis of the DUP's religiously oriented social conservatism. This is understandable given the greater contemporary political relevance of the DUP, its ferocious religious history, and the capacity of the UUP to place moral issues within a freedom of conscience framework. Change within the UUP is also discernible but the pace is slow as its liberal and less religious section is modest in size. One of the UUP's biggest failings, given its keenness to articulate the rational rather than religious, the secular rather than scripture, regarding its case for the Union, is its failure to attract Catholics—as acute a problem in terms of non-membership as that found in the DUP. The UUP has, of course, also struggled to attract Protestants or the non-religious in recent years. The UUP leadership is hidebound by history in that the Orange Order's presence within the Party was as unappealing to Catholics as Paisleyite bombast. As that period recedes into memory and ought to be of little account to a new generation, the UUP could attempt to become truly the broad church it desires, but it faces a monumentally difficult task.

Notes

1. Interview with Danny Kennedy, 28 Jan. 2016.
2. Interview with Robbie Butler, 19 Oct. 2016.
3. ESRC Northern Ireland General Election survey 2017, available at <https://discover.ukdataservice.ac.uk/catalogue/?sn=8234&type=data%20catalogue> accessed Oct. 2017.
4. Northern Ireland Life and Times Survey, 2016, Political Attitudes, <http://www.ark.ac.uk/nilt/2016/Political_Attitudes/UNINATID.html> accessed Aug. 2017.
5. Northern Ireland Life and Times Survey 2016, Political Attitudes, <http://www.ark.ac.uk/nilt/2016/Political_Attitudes/NIRELND2.html>, accessed Aug. 2017.
6. ESRC Northern Ireland General Election survey 2017, available at <https://discover.ukdataservice.ac.uk/catalogue/?sn=8234&type=data%20catalogue> accessed Oct. 2017.
7. Interview with Colin McCusker, 3 Mar. 2016.
8. For the Northern Ireland-wide figure, see <https://www.theguardian.com/news/datablog/2012/dec/12/northern-ireland-census-2011-religion-identity-mapped>, accessed Aug. 2017.

9. *The Times*, 23 Dec. 2016, 8. 'Belief in God Slumps After Turbulent Year', citing YouGov survey, 18–19 Dec.

10. ESRC Northern Ireland General Election survey 2017, available at <https://dis cover.ukdataservice.ac.uk/catalogue/?sn=8234&type=data%20catalogue> accessed Oct. 2017.

11. Interview with Mike Nesbitt, 16 Dec. 2016.

12. Department for Education (Northern Ireland), <https://www.education-ni.gov.uk/ articles/integrated-schools> accessed Aug. 2017.

13. Interview with Mike Nesbitt, 16 Dec. 2016.

14. Interview with Adrian Cochrane-Watson, 11 Mar. 2016.

15. Derry focus group member, 19 May 2016.

16. D. Hume, *The Ulster Unionist Party 1972–1992*, Lurgan: Ulster Society, 1996; G. Walker, *A History of the Ulster Unionist Party: Protest, Pragmatism and Pessimism*, Manchester: Manchester University Press, 2004.

17. J. Harbinson, *The Ulster Unionist Party 1882–1973*, Belfast: Blackstaff, 1973.

18. E. Moloney, *Paisley: From Demagogue to Democrat?* Dublin: Poolbeg, 2008, 93.

19. Walker, *History of the UUP*.

20. See A. Edwards, *A History of the Northern Ireland Labour Party: Democratic Socialism and Sectarianism*, Manchester: Manchester University Press, 2009.

21. *Orange Standard*, Apr. 1994: 1. 'Nothing but an internal solution for Northern Ireland can be accepted'.

22. *Orange Standard*, Aug. 1995: 6. 'Government's betrayal of Unionism'.

23. E. Kaufmann, *The Orange Order: A Contemporary Northern Irish History*, Oxford: Oxford University Press, 2009.

24. *Orange Standard*, Oct. 1995, 5. 'Masterly performance for unionism'.

25. *Orange Standard*, Oct. 1995, 11. 'David Trimble: worthy champion of unionism'.

26. 'Standing by the Union'. David Trimble interviewed by Jonathan Moore, *Irish Post*, Feb. 1996, 12.

27. *Orange Standard*, May 1998, 1. 'No'.

28. *Orange Standard*, June 1998, 13. 'Grand Lodge says "No"'.

29. *Orange Standard*, Dec. 2001/Jan. 2002, 1. 'Agreement is disastrous for Unionists'.

30. Walker, *History of the UUP*, 253.

31. Letter to *Orange Standard*, July 1998, 7. 'Unionist Party debates'.

32. J. Evans and J. Tonge, 'Faultlines in Unionism: Division and Dissent within the Ulster Unionist Council', *Irish Political Studies*, 16 (2001), 111–31.

33. Interview with David Trimble, 30 June 2016.

34. For discussions of the UUP–Orange relationship and border unionism, see Kaufmann, *Orange Order*; H. Patterson and E. Kaufmann, *Unionism and Orangeism in Northern Ireland since 1945: The Decline of the Loyal Family*, Manchester: Manchester University Press, 2007.

35. J. W. McAuley, A. Mycock, and J. Tonge, *Loyal to the Core? Orangeism and Britishness in Northern Ireland*, Dublin: Irish Academic Press, 2011.

36. See H. McDonald, *Trimble*, London: Bloomsbury, 2002, 262–3, 293.

37. B. Kennaway, *The Orange Order: A Tradition Betrayed*, London: Methuen, 2006.

38. M. Jess, *The Orange Order*, Dublin: O'Brien, 2007.

39. D. Bryan, *Orange Parades: The Politics of Ritual, Tradition and Control*, London: Pluto, 2000; R. Dudley Edwards, *The Faithful Tribe: An Intimate Portrait of the Loyal Institutions*, London; HarperCollins, 2000; Kaufmann, *Orange Order*; Patterson and Kaufmann, *Unionism and Orangeism*.

40. McAuley et al., *Loyal to the Core?*, 143.

41. McAuley et al., *Loyal to the Core?*, 133.

42. J. Tonge, J. Evans, and J. McAuley, 'The Old Order Collapses? Why the Orange Order No Longer Supports the Ulster Unionist Party', paper presented to the Political Studies Association of Ireland annual conference, Limerick, 15–17 Oct. 2004.

43. *Orange Standard*, Mar. 2002, 9. 'Orange being "priced-out" of Ulster Unionist Party'.

44. Interview with Colin McCusker, 3 Mar. 2016.

45. Interview with Robin Swann, 14 Aug. 2017.

46. Coleraine focus group member, 18 May 2016.

47. Coleraine focus group members, 18 May 2016.

48. Interview with Mark Cosgrove, 4 Dec. 2016.

49. Interview with Danny Kennedy, 28 Jan. 2016.

50. Interview with Hazel Legge, 3 Mar. 2016.

51. Interview with Robbie Butler, 19 Oct. 2016.

52. J. Tonge, M. Braniff, T. Hennessey, J. W. McAuley, and S. A. Whiting, *The Democratic Unionist Party: From Protest to Power*, Oxford: Oxford University Press, 2014.

53. Interview with Adrian Cochrane-Watson, 11 Mar. 2016.

54. J. Evans and J. Tonge, 'Religious, Political and Geographical Determinants of Attitudes to Orange Order Parades', *Politics and Religion*, 10.4 (2017), 786–811.

55. Interview with Mike Nesbitt, 16 Dec. 2016.

56. Interview with Robin Swann, 14 Aug. 2017.

57. Interview with Colin McCusker, 3 Mar. 2016.

58. Interview with Roy Beggs, 28 Jan. 2016.

59. Interview with Tom Elliott, 13 Apr. 2016.

60. Interview with Danny Kinahan, 13 Apr. 2016.

61. Young Unionist student focus group, 10 Mar. 2016.

62. Derry focus group, 19 May 2016.

63. J. Evans and J. Tonge, 'Partisan and Religious Drivers of Moral Conservatism: Same Sex Marriage and Abortion in Northern Ireland', 2016, advance online access at <http://journals.sagepub.com/doi/pdf/10.1177/1354068816656665> accessed Aug. 2017.

64. See <http://www.belfasttelegraph.co.uk/news/politics/new-uup-mla-adrian-cochr anewatson-banned-gay-couples-from-his-bb-31328357.html> accessed July 2017.

65. Interview with Adrian Cochrane-Watson, 11 Mar. 2016.

66. Interview with Mike Nesbitt, 16 Dec. 2016.

67. Derry focus group, 19 May 2016.

68. Young Unionists focus group, 10 Mar. 2016.

69. Interview with Danny Kinahan, 13 Apr. 2016.

70. Interview with Sandra Overend, 28 Jan. 2016.

71. Interview with UUP MLA.
72. Interview with UUP councillor and Executive member, 20 May 2016.
73. Interview with UUP Omagh councillor, 19 May 2016.
74. Young Unionists focus group, 10 Mar. 2016.
75. Interview with Robbie Butler, 19 Oct. 2016.
76. Interview with Tom Elliott. 13 Apr. 2016.

9

Institutional Structures, Party Selection, and Spotty Tights

Women in the Ulster Unionist Party

> When the men make the tea at the Branch meetings, we'll know we're there.
>
> (Female UUP focus group, 2016[1])

Women have often been described as absent from a history of Ulster unionism.[2] The near invisibility of women in accounts of frontline party politics is not surprising given the established gender roles within unionism. These have steered men towards leadership positions whilst women's supportive roles were often an extension of their domestic responsibilities. However, reducing women's involvement in the UUP to the stereotype of 'tea-makers' is criticized for not fully capturing the significance of their contribution to the establishment or maintenance of unionism.[3] Unionist women have been as well organized as, but often separate from, their male counterparts and provided some of the first elected representatives in Northern Ireland. However, throughout the twentieth century the level of women entering the formal political arena in Northern Ireland remained far behind the rest of the UK, particularly within unionism.

Two decades on from the 1998 Belfast Agreement Northern Ireland had seen its first female First Minister and four of the five main parties at Stormont had been led by women. Despite this record, research into gender and women's political participation in Northern Ireland has demonstrated how the legacy of conflict continues to facilitate a unique political culture.[4] An examination of the UUP through a gendered lens not only highlights the role of women in the party and the factors influencing gender equality but is also revealing of intra-party organization and culture within a post-conflict context.

This chapter examines the supply and demand of female candidates in the UUP. Evidence is also drawn from several survey questions regarding the membership's views on gender discrimination, support for more women in Northern Irish politics, and measures to improve female political representation. The chapter begins by examining the historical background of unionism and the construction and evolution of gender roles throughout the twentieth century, from the establishment of the Ulster Women's Unionist Council (UWUC) and throughout the Troubles. Discussion then moves on to assess gender equality within the post-conflict context, particularly the relevance of institutional structures and political party cultures to female representation.

The Historical Background to Women in the UUP

The influence of religion and national identity on the segregation of Northern Irish society created a distinctive political culture that left little room for political agendas that cut across identities, such as gender equality. Within this context, women have maintained a political presence within unionism, yet there has been an enduring distinction between male and female political activity. Low levels of female participation in Northern Irish politics, particularly within unionism, can be traced back to traditionally established gender roles.

The prospects of Home Rule in the early twentieth century provided the catalyst for unionist women to become politically organized. The creation of the Ulster Women's Unionist Council (UWUC) in 1911 was in response to the third Home Rule crisis and the threat this posed to their civil and religious liberties. The establishment of the UWUC was primarily motivated by a resistance to Home Rule, where women had a very specific place as an auxiliary organization to the Ulster Unionist Council (UUC), seeking to work by means of 'gentleness, tact and quiet influence'.[5] Despite owning shared objectives, the UWUC were not integrated into the existing campaign efforts of their male counterparts, as, for example, women could not join the policy-making body of the UUC.

Urquhart describes the UWUC as having few intentions of influencing policy and no ambition to shake up the status quo.[6] Despite political engagement through fundraising, electioneering, and petitioning, there was no particular commitment to female suffrage. The UWUC combined political education and unionist values with domesticity, defining women's interest in 'family, housing, education and social services'.[7] These gender distinctions were typified in women not being able to sign the Solemn League and Covenant in 1912 but having a separate Declaration. Whilst the men of Ulster signed their name under a statement in the Covenant promising to 'use all means' necessary to resist Home Rule, the text of the women's Declaration was far more passive, expressing their 'desire to associate with the men of Ulster'.[8]

Despite the distinction between male and female activism, it would be a misrepresentation to assume women were passive actors within unionism. After women were granted the vote in 1918, the UWUC was given permission to organize as a separate entity and appealed for representation within the UUC. Yet, rather than encouraging newly enfranchised women to stand as elected representatives, it was deemed that 'the time was not ripe for this, and the essential thing in the first Parliament was to preserve the safety of the Unionist cause…and except in the case of outstanding qualifications, men candidates were preferable'.[9] Women were primarily viewed as voters rather than prospective parliamentary candidates.[10]

The creation of Northern Ireland in 1920 established a fifty-two-seat parliament at Stormont. From 1921 to 1969, twelve general elections took place in which a total of twenty women stood as candidates.[11] Over this forty-eight-year period, nine women were elected, including six unionists. Amongst these nine, the UUP's Dame Dehra Parker was the only woman to serve as a minister before the parliament was suspended in 1972. Parker served for three decades and originally stood against the advice of the UWUC. Parker's politics were described as instinctively unionist; when she claimed to speak for women, it was unionist women.[12] Despite an enduring dedication to the Union and the breakthrough of some remarkable women, gender constraints were to become a lasting feature of politics in Northern Ireland far beyond the Home Rule crisis and continue into the twenty-first century.

Gender Roles and the Northern Ireland Conflict

In order to discuss the role and position of women within the UUP, it is necessary to consider the wider influence of contested claims of sovereignty, rival ethno-national positions, and armed conflict in the construction of gender roles in Northern Ireland. As in other violent conflicts, thirty years of the Troubles in Northern Ireland helped define and reinforce clear gender roles based on essentialist constructions of femininity and masculinity.[13] This dichotomy emphasized women's role within the domestic sphere and as 'mothers of the new generation'.[14] Masculinity on the other hand was given strong, competitive, and protective (often through violence) characteristics. The consequence of this gender binary is the awarding of traits to women that do not suit the public sphere or political leadership.[15]

The participation of unionist women in the formal political arena may have been low throughout the twentieth century, yet their involvement at a grass-roots level was far more active. Whilst Ulster's loyal sons were by and large the politicians, judges, and civil servants, women tended to operate behind the scenes in support of male candidates and in the voluntary sector; unionist men and women occupied separate spheres.[16] Sectarian divisions also shaped women's lives in Northern Ireland to the extent that experiences differed between nationalists and unionists.[17] Women across communities were constrained by the conservative influences of churches on society, yet whilst Catholic women were able to capitalize on the equality agenda by tying women's rights to the broader 'tradition of struggle', Protestant women remained much less visible.[18] Ward explains that the centrality and domination of the constitutional question meant that feminism was a 'dirty word' within unionism.[19] As such, gender equality was outweighed by, and often viewed in conflict with, concerns over the security of the Union.

Gender in a 'New Northern Ireland'

The Northern Ireland peace process brought with it a possibility, and hope, that gender equality could be attached to the design and implementation of a 'new Northern Ireland'.[20] Yet, within the search for peace, which emphasized the importance of equality, gender was regarded a separate and a lesser priority than parity between communities.[21]

The power-sharing institutions set up under the peace process were designed to recognize and regulate the polarized positions of unionism and nationalism. With consociational features such as a power-sharing executive and weighted majorities, the recognition of ethno-national difference is vital to regulate against the domination of one group over another. Alongside the power-sharing structures, the peace agreement also affirmed the right of women to 'full and equal political participation'.[22] This was the first time in Northern Ireland's history that women's rights to political inclusion were formally recognized.[23] However, critics of consociationalism point towards the primacy given to ethnic or religious difference, which forces these cleavages to become the central axis around which all political affairs revolve.[24] The interaction between the legacy of the conflict, rival ethno-national positions, and political structures led to what Enloe refers to as a 'not now perspective', where primacy is given to communal unity to such an extent that approaching gender equality could undermine this cohesion.[25] Within a post-Agreement Northern Ireland, interests of gender remained subordinate to constitutional preferences.

Female UUP members reflected on the positive changes in Northern Ireland's political context since the Troubles. As one put it: 'You're not putting yourself in danger . . . it's actually okay to be in politics now.'[26] The violent period of the Troubles, which meant 'men would do more than women',[27] may have ended but assessments of gender equality within the 'new Northern Ireland' blames the desire of male actors to re-establish their pre-conflict prerogatives of domination, which continues to facilitate a highly masculinized political culture in Northern Ireland.[28] For Galligan, the legacy of 'armed patriarchy' has continued to define the political and cultural landscape.[29]

Institutional Structures: Women's Descriptive Representation

The dearth of female political representatives has been persistent through multiple levels of governance for Northern Ireland. At Westminster, the first Northern Irish woman to sit in the House of Commons was Patricia Ford (1953–5), followed by Patricia McLaughlin (1955–64), both from the UUP. After Bernadette Devlin (McAliskey), who represented Mid-Ulster from 1969 to 1974 having been elected on a 'Unity' label, Northern Ireland did not see another female MP elected until 2001, when Michelle Gildernew (Sinn Féin), Iris Robinson (DUP), and Lady Sylvia Hermon (UUP) were elected. The UUP lost their only MP in 2010 when Lady Hermon ran successfully as an independent candidate in opposition to the Party's electoral pact with the Conservatives. As a result, the two main unionist parties in Northern Ireland, the DUP and UUP, had no female MPs from 2010 until 2017, when Emma Little-Pengelly was elected for the DUP.

Local government is seen as a crucial site for the development of women's political careers and in providing the skills necessary to stand for higher office.[30] In 1989, female political representation at local level remained in single figures (9.2 per cent). This was led by Alliance (13 per cent) followed by Sinn Féin and the UUP (12 per cent), with the SDLP (9 per cent) and DUP (7 per cent) trailing behind.[31] By 2005, women made up one in five local councillors (20.3 per cent) with the two main unionist parties having the lowest percentages of female representatives at the local level (DUP, 19 per cent, and UUP, 13 per cent). In 2015 local government across Northern Ireland was restructured, reducing the number of councils from twenty-six to eleven. There has been criticism towards the lack of consideration for the effect of these reforms on women's representation in local councils amid difficulties in inserting gender equality into new governance structures.[32] Elections for these new 'super councils' took place in May 2014 with women accounting for 25 per cent of councillors, a gradual rise from 23.5 per cent in 2011. Variations still exist in the gender balance of councillors by party with the SDLP (39 per cent), Alliance (31 per cent), and Sinn Féin (30 per cent) leading in percentage terms and the DUP (23 per cent) and UUP (14 per cent) below average.[33]

In the broader context of women's representation in devolved institutions, Northern Ireland has fared below the performance of Wales and Scotland, where female representation from the first devolved election up to 2016 averaged 44 and 36 per cent respectively. As demonstrated in Figure 9.1, women's descriptive representation in Northern Ireland has been on a slow, but positive, trajectory, increasing from of 13 to 30 per cent between 1998 and 2017, giving an average of 20.6 per cent.

The legacy of conflict and variations in institutional architecture (voting system, consociational power-sharing) from Scotland and Wales means that Northern Ireland is often considered a 'place apart' from the rest of the UK. Female UUP members note that, despite some progress, Northern Ireland's legacy of the conflict has stilted the pace of change in comparison to the rest of the UK:

> England, Scotland and Wales, they have progressed...there was more women coming in to politics...But, there was that issue about women going into politics, the danger factor...so, that's why we're behind, I feel, that we're slower in catching up.[34]

The lower level of female representation is reflective of the unique social and political circumstances shaped by decades of conflict, giving Northern Ireland the accolade of 'bottom of the gender league tables' amongst the UK's devolved institutions.[35]

Beyond Northern Ireland, women's representation has been attributed to the influence of demand-side explanations of political representation such as structural barriers at party level (e.g. selection of election candidates) and systemic obstacles within the institutional architecture (e.g. voting system).[36] In order to consider the impact of these pressures on gender equality at party level, it is first necessary to consider broader institutional factors such as the

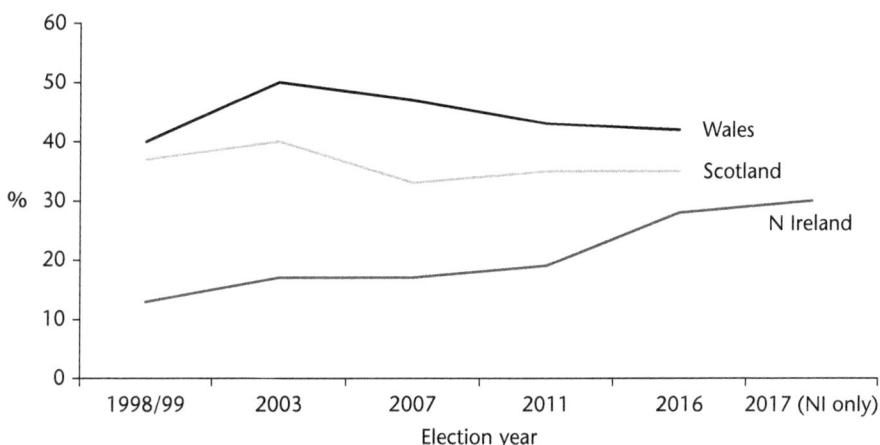

Figure 9.1 Female representation across devolved institutions 1998–2017 (%)

voting system, the size of the Assembly, and influence of ethnic bloc voting on the prospects for gender equality in Northern Irish politics.

First, in terms of the influence of institutional factors, the voting system of Single Transferable Vote (STV) in Northern Ireland is intended to facilitate ethnic representation and encourage the possibility of lower vote transfers across the ethnic divide. Multi-member constituencies (from 1998 to 2016 there were eighteen six-seat constituencies) means party selectors are more able to select multiple candidates per constituency without displacing an incumbent.[37] The voting system in Northern Ireland is considered friendlier to gender equality than First Past the Post's single-member constituencies which reduce the possibilities for selection. Against this, the regional list under the Additional Member System (AMS), used in Scotland and Wales, can almost guarantee female representation if the party places female candidates high enough on the list. As a result, the voting system of STV is considered mid-ranking in terms of facilitating women's descriptive representation. Therefore, the lack of gender diversity has been associated more with attitudinal issues within the parties rather than systemic failings of the voting system.[38]

Secondly, in 2016 the Assembly Members (Reduction of Numbers) Bill, cut the number of MLAs from 108 to 90. Concerns were raised that a reduction from six to five MLAs per constituency could make it more difficult for smaller parties and independent candidates to get elected. In terms of gender balance of the assembly, there were also concerns that this change could inhibit efforts to increase the number of female MLAs. Research by McGing and White in Ireland demonstrates the impact of variations in the number of elected representatives per constituency, which ranges from three to five, depending on population size. As district magnitude increases, so too does the percentage of female candidates, suggesting a link between the number of seats per constituency and greater gender diversity.[39] Within Northern Ireland, the connection between the reduction of seats per constituency and number of female candidates did not appear to have been considered by the Office of First and Deputy First Minister 'as part of its equality proofing of the legislation'.[40] These changes were intended to take place at the next scheduled Assembly contest in 2021, yet the unpredicted election in 2017 brought the reduction into effect earlier than planned.

The unexpected nature of the assembly election in March 2017 and the issues that surrounded it, such as the political fall-out over the Renewable Heat Incentive (RHI) scheme and the subsequent calls by Sinn Féin for Arlene Foster to step aside as First Minister, makes it difficult to judge the impact of the newly slimmed down assembly. Overall, the 2017 Assembly election saw a rise in the number of female MLAs from 28 per cent in 2016 to 30 per cent. Ahead in terms of gender diversity is Sinn Féin with eleven female MLAs, followed by the DUP with six. A reduction in the number of seats at Stormont did not seem to impact female candidate chances where standing for the two largest parties, with women in the DUP and Sinn Féin doing better than their male colleagues (see Table 9.1). The prominence of Arlene Foster and Michelle O'Neill leading the DUP and Sinn Féin respectively into the election helped raise the profile of women in the two parties. The SDLP managed to increase their number of female representatives from three to four, making up almost 40 per cent of the party's MLAs. Within the UUP the number of female MLAs dropped from four to one, the party losing high-profile representatives such as Jo-Anne Dobson and Sandra Overend. As demonstrated by the rate of candidate return in Table 9.1, women in the UUP have been disproportionately affected by a gradual reduction of seats since 1998.

A third systemic factor in women's descriptive representation in Northern Ireland is the impact that consociational power-sharing has on voting behaviour. The frozen nature of ethno-national identity and its determination of party preference means that electoral competition occurs within the separate ethnic blocs of unionism and nationalism. Because of the very low level of cross-communal voting, Sinn Féin and the SDLP have not had to respond directly to the electoral challenges posed by the DUP and UUP, and vice versa.[41] Therefore, unionism has not been exposed to electoral pressures from nationalist parties who have a far better track record in women's descriptive representation. Since devolution, unionism has been slower to address gender imbalance and from 1998 until 2011, the DUP and UUP had the lowest levels of female candidates.[42] Despite the progress made, until recently, unionist party cultures and structures were untouched by pressures to endorse more progressive gender policies.[43]

Within unionism, the DUP has steadily improved its descriptive representation of female MLAs and in December 2015 appointed Arlene Foster as the first female leader of the party and First Minister of Northern Ireland. Former UUP MLA Jo-Anne Dobson claimed this to be a positive move: 'I think it's

Table 9.1 Election of female candidates from the five main parties, 2017 Northern Ireland Assembly Election

	Female MLAs	Female candidates fielded by party (%)	Female MLAs elected as % of party total	Candidate rate of return (%)	
				Female	Male
DUP	6	21 (+9)	21 (+16)	75 (+50)	73 (+10)
UUP	1	25 (+17)	10 (+3)	17 (−33)	50 (−10)
Alliance	3	48 (+21)	38 (+21)	30 (+13)	45 (+9)
SDLP	4	38 (+15)	33 (+20)	50 (−)	62 (−4)
Sinn Féin	11	39 (+17)	41 (+13)	85 (+22)	80 (+35)

Authors' own calculations from <http://www.ark.ac.uk/elections>, accessed Aug. 2017. Figures in brackets show change from 1998.

great to see a woman in a powerful position, I do, definitely, and it's a step in the right direction.'[44] The coronation of Arlene Foster as party leader demonstrated further movement from the DUP's Free Presbyterian and male-dominated image. A UUP member expanded on this point: 'Arlene was the leader who would've pulled the most votes in, she is a woman, she's Church of Ireland, and she's an ex-Ulster Unionist. She certainly widened their appeal, slightly.'[45] The low level of female representation in the UUP contrasts with the rise of Arlene Foster in the DUP and sits uncomfortably for some who see this change as superficial, a UUP student member claiming, 'it's really just the same party with a different face . . . So, to me, I am actually disappointed she hasn't taken unionism forward . . . Ulster unionism takes unionism forward.'[46]

Despite having a female First Minister, the slow pace of change in women's descriptive representation within unionist politics has been placed with a continuation of embedded social norms and a division of labour that reinforces conservative attitudes towards defined gender roles.[47] Speaking to the Northern Ireland Assembly, shortly after Arlene Foster became First Minister, DUP MLA Edwin Poots commented, it would be the 'second most important job that she will ever take on. Her most important job has been, and will remain, that of a wife, mother and daughter.'[48] The assertion of such priorities demonstrates that, despite rising to the highest possible political position in Northern Ireland, gender roles and responsibilities have not dissipated.

The continuation of conservative family values, particularly within rural unionism, is highlighted by former UUP MP for Fermanagh and South Tyrone, Tom Elliott:

> Yeah, so I do actually think if the Assembly, and even councils, were more family orientated places, it would help encourage females. Now, people will say, and maybe you might say so, that that's even sexist saying that.[49]

In common with research findings in respect of the DUP, domestic responsibilities and a lower level of resources (time and money) form part of the supply-side explanations behind the low levels of women within the formal political arena.[50]

The membership survey asked several questions regarding the role of women in the UUP and public life more broadly and respondents were asked to grade their responses on a five-point scale (1 = strongly agree, 5 = strongly disagree). In response to the first statement around the existence of discrimination against women in public life, the majority of women agreed (56 per cent) whilst only a quarter of male respondents (25 per cent) supported the statement (Figure 9.2).

Despite more women recognizing the presence of gender discrimination in public life, female party members and elected representatives credited the UUP leadership with giving them encouragement and did not consider the

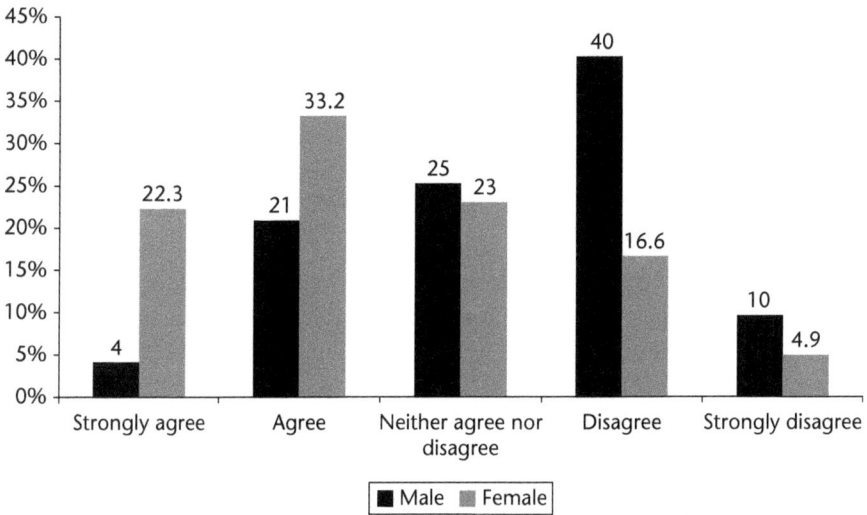

Figure 9.2 'There is discrimination against women in public life' (%)

party to have any structural barriers inhibiting gender equality. A female UUP member outlined her experience:

> I have found that in any position in the party, which has usually been behind the scenes, I have never had any problems with the men but I know a lot of women felt very nervous about putting their names forward, and it mostly was because they were married with children, and that's two jobs on its own, and it's not easy you know.[51]

The dearth of women at the senior levels of the UUP is therefore explained internally as a supply-side issue where women lack the confidence and resources (often due to family responsibilities) to put themselves forward.

In terms of discrimination, the representation of women in the media was highlighted in interviews and focus groups as a turn-off to women entering politics. Research on female politicians and the media in Northern Ireland highlights how elected representatives across all parties feel their outward appearance is the focus above anything they may say, where journalists are especially fascinated in them as 'gendered beings, in their style, their domestic arrangements, where they do their shopping and so on'.[52]

A *Belfast Telegraph* feature in 2015, which rated several parliamentary candidates' election posters (male and female), provides an example of this. Within the article the UUP's Jo-Anne Dobson was awarded the following description; 'that dazzling white smile, California tan and sun-streaked highlights could not be less representative of Northern Ireland folk', and 'see how the lip-gloss seems to catch the glow off her cheeks. She's a girly girl.'[53]

Asked about how she felt when the media described her in such a way, Dobson responded;

> Hate it! Hate it! Hate it! ... When I was supporting Mike [Nesbitt] for his leadership, I remember that day standing behind him at the front of Stormont, and the front page of the *Telegraph*, I think, the next day, was the fact that I was trying to undermine him by wearing spotty tights, not the fact that I was there supporting. So, it's twice as hard to succeed in this business if you're female.[54]

Whilst female elected representatives acknowledged that attitudes need to change, the issue was placed with politics and the media more broadly rather than based on their experiences within the UUP. The next section will consider the influence of intra-party structures and organization on the role of women within the UUP.

The Impact of Candidate Selection Procedures

Whilst institutional architecture may be important, so too is party architecture in understanding female representation. Kenny and Verge explain, 'We cannot fully grasp the relationship between state architecture and women's politics without a thorough understanding of political parties as complex organisations in their own right.'[55] Through their role as gatekeepers and deciding the make-up of candidates standing for election, political parties play a crucial role in shaping women's representation. As demonstrated in Figure 9.3, the gender equality scorecards vary hugely by party in Northern Ireland, with Sinn Féin out in the lead and the DUP improving its levels since

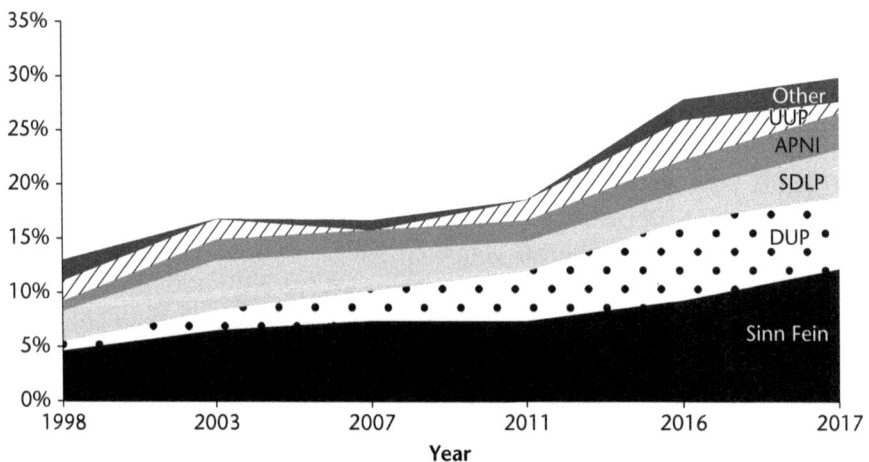

Figure 9.3 Breakdown of female MLAs by party 1998–2017 (%)

2011. This disparity is a reflection of each party's approach to candidate selection and intra-party culture.

Rather than pointing towards systemic institutional barriers, research into female representation in Northern Ireland has blamed the prejudices of party selection committees at local level, particularly within unionism.[56] Centralized structures of decision-making and selection give elites more power to select a higher number of female candidates and implement gender equality procedures, as long as they are willing to do so.[57] It is the high level of centralization within the DUP and Sinn Féin that has facilitated a higher return of women to Stormont in comparison to the UUP and SDLP, who have been more reluctant to introduce changes such as increased central control over candidate selection or (informal) quotas, although recent years have seen changes.

Whilst many unionists in Northern Ireland may struggle to differentiate the DUP from the UUP in policy terms, there are distinct and important variations between the parties that impact intra-party structures and culture. Such variations emanate from the different origins of the two parties. The formation of the DUP in 1971 was to protect Protestant values and defend Northern Ireland's place in the Union. Much of this appeal was also due to the evangelicalism espoused by the party and personified through the party's leader Reverend Ian Paisley. In terms of Paisley's leadership, some have likened the DUP to a religion in itself by having the common characteristics of 'worship and obedience of one man'.[58] Although the DUP dramatically moderated its position from 'no surrender' to sharing power with their 'arch enemies' in Sinn Féin following the St Andrews Agreement in 2006, strong leadership during and beyond Paisley's tenure has been central to the cohesion and electoral success of the party.

In contrast to the DUP, the UUP has a high level of decentralization within its structures. Although the autonomy enjoyed by the party's eighteen constituency associations has been much reduced over the last two decades, the legacy of previous autonomy is important and localism can still dominate candidate selection. The influence of the grass roots on procedures such as candidate selection is described as a positive for the UUP against its unionist rivals:

> To me, there is a total difference between the two parties. The difference is that we are very much ground level up. They are top down, total opposites. How authoritarian they are. Whereas we give our members an awful lot of say . . . it's very much that the members, and those that are paying annual subs to the party that have a big say. In the DUP, that's not the case, and it never has been the case. It's top down.[59]

On the other hand, the weaker influence of central party control, along with clear ideological factions that exist, has resulted in poor party discipline and mixed messages.

> I suppose the DUP have the luxury of being able to say, 'we're against Europe, against abortion, against same sex marriage...they [the DUP] put a very strict whip on themselves. We alternatively...had senior Assembly members and MPs voting to leave [EU], and you wouldn't get that in the DUP. So, we do offer this mixed message.[60]

Centralization can have a considerable impact upon the gender diversity of party candidates. The Assembly election in 2011 marked a shift towards the active promotion of female candidates in the DUP. Under the leadership of Peter Robinson, the DUP introduced a change in their selection process; in a constituency where the party is contesting more than one seat, the ruling body of the Party had the power over local associations to select the second candidate. In 2011 the DUP used this process of central selection to increase the number of DUP MLAs from two to five.[61] Whilst this may seem like only a minor increase on an already small figure (as shown in Figure 9.3), it demonstrates the intra-party barriers to female representation and how the party leadership can successfully implement structural modifications.

Research by Neil Matthews into candidate selection across Northern Ireland's political parties described the local constituency associations of the UUP prior to 2007 as 'independent little fiefdoms which essentially were controlled by a small group of men'.[62] A poor performance in the 2007 Assembly election forced a reassessment of selection processes, which introduced a greater level of central control. At constituency level, party members attend hustings with the prospective candidates and cast their vote at the end by secret ballot. After this process at a local level, two candidates go forward to a panel consisting of a central party Election Committee consisting of four party officers and three members from the relevant local association. At this stage, a final candidate is selected by a simple majority vote and ratified by the UUP Executive Committee.

Across interviews and focus groups there was a mixed response to the increased levels of centralization in the selection process and a debate existed about whether candidates should receive final approval from the constituency officers or party executive. For some, this change in procedure has resulted in variable results for candidate selection across local associations:

> the party changed it [candidate selection process]—and I have nothing against this—where they had to appear before a second selection panel...whereas it used to be local association that decided, and that was it, but it had to be endorsed by the leader...So, there is a problem in our mechanism and selection, how we're doing it, I think needs to be tidied up...Local Associations have been feeling really sore, because people have been brought in by the leader...it worked in some areas but didn't work in others.[63]

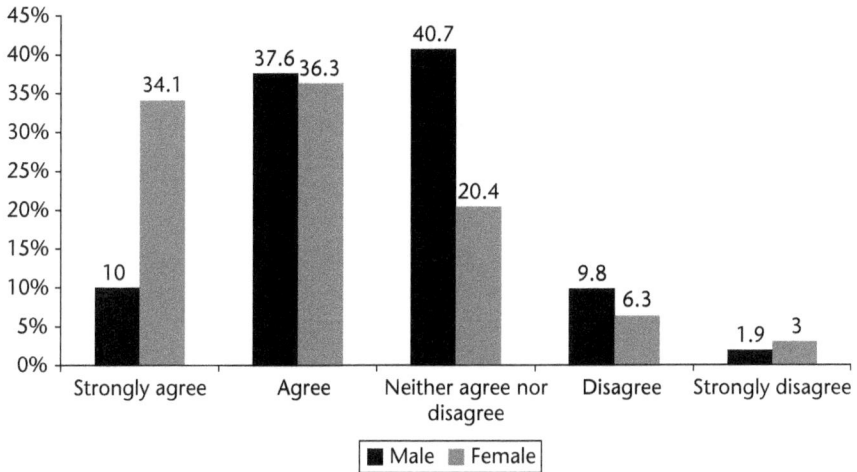

Figure 9.4 'Politics in Northern Ireland would improve if there were more women elected' (%)

In contrast to the DUP, the high levels of decentralization in the UUP has meant that local associations have enjoyed greater levels of autonomy. Whilst this allowed the membership more influence, it has not facilitated the same level of party unity and central party control found in the DUP.

Whilst disagreement exists internally over the levels of centralization in candidate selection there is support amongst UUP members for seeing more women in Northern Irish politics; more so than recorded amongst DUP members in 2014. As demonstrated in Figure 9.4 most (62 per cent) UUP members agree that politics in Northern Ireland would improve if there were more women. In response to the same question in 2014, 38 per cent of DUP members agreed.[64] Similarly to the DUP findings, there are significant gender differences with women more in support; in the UUP, 70 per cent of female party members agreed with this statement in comparison to 48 per cent of their male counterparts. The gap in support for this statement between DUP and UUP members suggest the role of the leadership and central selection is crucial for increasing the number of women in Northern Irish politics.

Female Representatives and Defending 'Women's Interests'

Substantive commitments on gender equality in the UUP are articulated through equal opportunities, particularly in the workplace and on issues such as equal pay. For example, the 1998 UUP manifesto supported 'access to training compatible with family responsibilities', and 'policies which promote the reconciliation of work and family life'.[65] Nearly two decades on, the 2017 Assembly election manifesto highlighted the need for affordable childcare, whilst other more controversial issues such as reproductive rights were not mentioned.[66] Two-thirds of UUP members strongly agree or agree that women are better placed than men to represent women's interests in politics and amongst female members this rose to over 75 per cent, as Figure 9.5 shows.

Such support for women's political presence in representing gendered interests were particularly voiced by female members in relation to abortion; 'I can't stand it when I hear men giving their views on abortion. I feel it's absolutely . . . nothing to do with men.'[67] The survey of party members highlighted that almost double the amount of UUP members agreed (55.2 per cent) than disagreed (28.3 per cent) that abortion should be in line with the twenty-four-week limit in the rest of the UK. In the case of rape, incest, and fatal foetal abnormality, 79 per cent agreed with the legalization of abortion, whilst 11 per cent disagreed. Despite this support amongst party members, former MLA Philip Smith described the opposition he encountered from being pro-abortion reform as well as being pro-EU and supportive of same-sex marriage, which 'for men of a certain age in their late 50s, 60s, those were your three strikes and you're out'.[68] Survey data from the 2017 general election survey demonstrate that on these 'three strikes' issues, there is divergence between

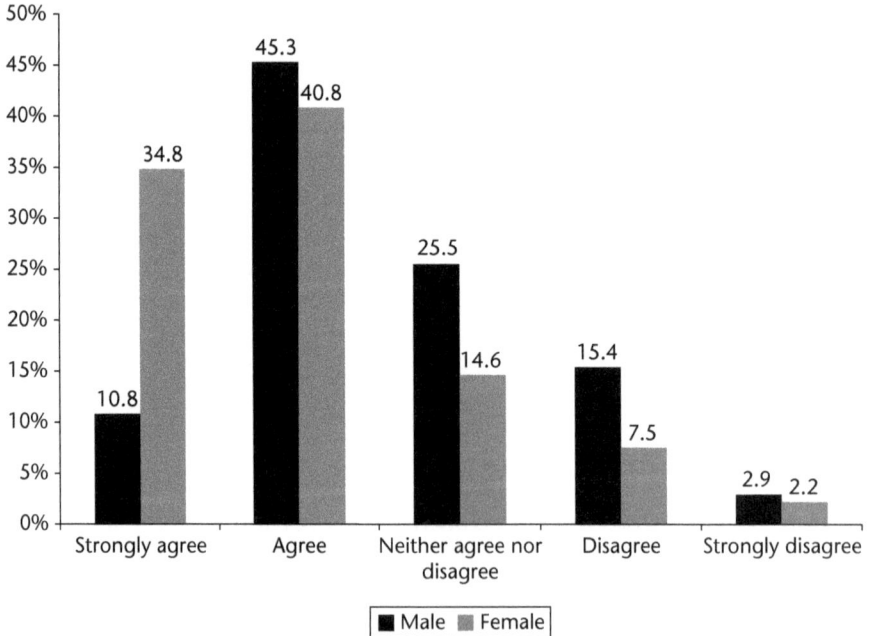

Figure 9.5 'Women are better placed than men to represent women's interests in politics' (%)

the political class and younger, more progressive voters, especially within unionism.[69] Philip Smith went on to outline his experience of the demographics trends behind these views:

> You could argue, according to research in Northern Ireland, public opinion is ahead of political opinion, certainly amongst unionism...[on the doorsteps] there were a few people that would've been pro-abortion reform, females, younger, but on the whole, it tended to be older men, and these were issues they came at you with. They were anti-abortion and anti-same sex marriage.[70]

Issues such as abortion remain controversial across the political spectrum in Northern Ireland, but for some members, the main concern is the reluctance of the party to debate these issues:

> I don't think being a woman in itself is an issue, but I think there is still a conservatism in addressing women's issues...this week Amnesty International came out with 71 per cent or 72 per cent of people support abortion, or limited abortion, and there was no real engagement with it, unless I have missed something, from our party, from women or men. These sort of issues that would affect women is where we are lacking.[71]

Amongst party members, particularly women, there is not only strong support to see more female elected representatives but also an acknowledgement that women's interests have been poorly represented.

Party solutions to the issues of gender equality and political representation across Northern Ireland have varied between exhortation and verbal encouragement to (informal) party quotas for candidate selection. For the UUP, efforts to improve the number of women in frontline politics have fallen on the end of the spectrum that values merit and informal mechanisms such as encouragement to promote female candidates internally. This approach is outlined by the party General Secretary:

> We are making a conserved effort to try and attract women into the Party, and I would hate to think that any of the women that are in the Party feel that they are treated any differently...I treat them as equals...If I spot talent, I spot talent, whether it's male or female.[72]

In discussions with members and elected representatives, the lack of women in the party was often described as a supply-side issue where women lacked the confidence to put themselves forward and were happy enough 'behind the scenes'. With responsibility for women's development in the Party, Sandra Overend, a UUP MLA from 2011 to 2017, launched the Dame Dehra Parker Programme in 2009. The programme, named after the first female Ulster Unionist politician elected to Northern Ireland's parliament in 1921, was 'designed to encourage more Ulster Unionist women to play a greater role in political activism and to become elected representatives'.[73]

Those involved in the Dame Dehra Parker Programme spoke positively of this support and they welcomed the opportunity to participate in training to develop skills such as public speaking. Philip Smith, who was also involved in the running of the programme, spoke of the positive impact within the programme's short lifespan:

> We've certainly had some success with both younger people and females at local government level. Hopefully that will start to percolate through. I think there is a development process there ... I don't know how long ago it was now, and it had a bit of success.[74]

Intentions to increase the number of women in leadership roles within the party and as elected representatives goes beyond party rhetoric and has led to skills-based programmes. However, there is an acknowledgement that, whilst gender equality is supported, in the past an understanding of how this can be approached has been lacking, as described by one female member:

> Everyone will say, 'Absolutely, I would love to see more women in the party, more young people in the party, more whatever.' I think there just isn't that understanding there of how to actually do that. I think that is where we are trying to make a change at the minute, is to gather that knowledge of our own current women membership, as well, and to find out what their views are on things.[75]

In terms of measures to improve the levels of female representation in the UUP, the use of quotas to ensure a fixed proportion of women candidates was only supported by just over one-fifth of party members. As shown in Figure 9.6, when broken down by gender, women were almost as likely to agree (35.2 per cent) as disagree (36.7 per cent) with the party having a fixed proportion of women candidates whilst male members were almost four times as likely to disagree than agree with the same statement.

In common with the DUP, the merit principle is the favoured method of selection within the UUP. The imposition of quotas is seen as 'blatant discrimination'[76] and 'detrimental'.[77] Some degree of contagion has been identified from the Irish Republic (party quotas) and Britain (Labour's use of all-women shortlists) in terms of political ideas and discourse around women's representation in Northern Ireland.[78] In February 2012, the SDLP Environment Minister Alex Attwood sought legal advice on his powers to legislate for gender quotas at local election level. No policy change emerged from this, but after the initial announcement a statement was released by the UUP placing the lack of female MLAs as an institutional, rather than party, problem;

> When Stormont begins to deliver for the people more women will become involved ... Currently the make-up of our Assembly isn't very diverse and this is because Stormont isn't relevant to many local people. We need to see more delivery and more common-sense government.[79]

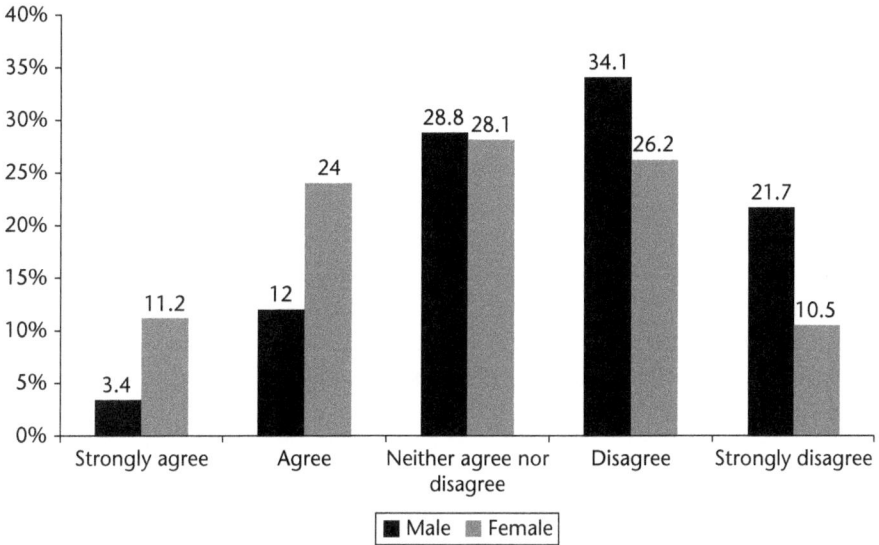

Figure 9.6 'The UUP should have a fixed proportion of women candidates' (%)

Negative sentiments towards positive discrimination were evident across all interviews with elected representatives and focus groups; quota systems were often cited as 'wrong for anything'.[80] Similarly to the DUP, opposition to quotas was expanded to include recruitment to the police:

> And quotas on the police, as well, you know, that was a discriminatory move as well. Because there were plenty of good people who went forward to take up jobs in the police and didn't get it because of this quota system. It could be the same within political parties. You could have excellent men who would lose out because we have to have 30 per cent women. On merit, if people have a fair and open mind, then that will work all the time.[81]

Quotas remain controversial, their deployment resisted by the UUP. The policy of 50-50 Roman Catholic and non-Roman Catholic recruitment used for police recruitment for a period of ten years, following the recommendations of the Patten Report[82] was labelled by the UUP leader, David Trimble, as shoddy and sectarian. Trimble argued that the 1998 peace agreement 'makes it unlawful for the police to discriminate against a person or class of person on the grounds of religious belief. The quota system will do just that.'[83] The UUP has retained its opposition to quotas in other spheres, notably that of gendered recruitment. The influence of Northern Ireland's violent past on the role of women is multifaceted. The legacy of the conflict has influenced the role of women in politics by shaping and reinforcing gender roles, whilst subsequent policies such as religious quotas in police recruitment have hardened opposition to the use of positive discrimination to facilitate gender equality.[84]

Conclusion: Who is Making the Tea?

Women's involvement in unionist politics has always been organized within gendered spheres. Traditionally, activities were in support of, but distinct from, the efforts of unionist men. In the twenty-first century, the distinct gender roles given to the men and women of unionism are still visible. Whilst women in the UUP are active and politically engaged, domestic responsibilities such as tea-making remain a way of some female members to reflect on the developments of gender roles within the UUP; 'it sounds a bit silly to boil things down to who makes the tea, but it is a wee bit symbolic you know'.[85]

Within the UUP there is clear support for seeing more women in politics. Across discussions with members and elected representatives, the lack of women in senior positions within the party was often described as a supply-side issue, where women lacked the confidence to put themselves forward and were happy enough 'behind the scenes'. Placing responsibility upon women themselves overlooks the impact of structural and cultural factors helping to explain the declining levels of female elected representatives in the UUP. The specific role and actions of political parties in facilitating the growth of female candidates becomes particularly apparent when the DUP appears to be (slowly) bucking the trend of unionism's poor record of women in elected politics.

Exploring the gender dynamics in the UUP has shone a light on the role of women but has also highlighted the importance of party cultures and structures in understanding political shifts in the 'new' Northern Irish politics. The high level of centralization and discipline within Sinn Féin and the DUP has not only allowed them to become the largest parties within nationalism and unionism respectively but has also facilitated the higher levels of gender equality amongst their elected representatives. Within the UUP, there is greater resistance to surrendering local autonomy and as a result lesser levels of central party control over candidate selection. The change in selection procedures within the DUP from 2011 onwards demonstrates the rewards that can be reaped in terms of female representation if a party's leadership are able, and willing, to select more women candidates. The rise of Arlene Foster to become Northern Ireland's first female leader is also symbolic of the DUP's deliberate attempts to modernize the image of the party in the face of their unionist rivals. Whether Arlene Foster would have been able to rise through the ranks of the UUP will never be known, but still a question worth asking.

Notes

1. Female UUP focus group, 22 Oct. 2016.
2. See D. Urquhart, *Women in Ulster Politics, 1890–1940: A History Not Yet Told*, Portland, OR: Irish Academic Press, 2000; P. Ward, *Unionism in the United Kingdom 1918–1974*, London: Palgrave, 2005; R. Ward, *Women Unionism and Loyalism in Northern Ireland: From 'Tea-Makers' to Political Actors*, Portland, OR: Irish Academic Press, 2006.
3. See L. Racioppi and K. O'Sullivan, '"This we will Maintain': Gender Ethno-Nationalism and the Politics of Unionism in Northern Ireland', *Nations and Nationalisms*, 7.1 (2001), 93–112.
4. See R. Wilford, 'Women and Politics in Northern Ireland', *Parliamentary Affairs*, 49.1 (1996), 41–54, 44; R. Sales, *Women Divided: Gender, Religion and Politics in Northern Ireland*, London: Routledge, 1997, 9; M. Braniff and S. Whiting, '"There's Just No Point Having a Token Woman": Gender and Representation in the Democratic Unionist Party in Post Agreement Northern Ireland', *Parliamentary Affairs*, 69.1 (2015), 93–114.
5. *Belfast News-Letter*, 24 Jan. 1911, quoted in D. Urquhart, 'Unionism, Orangeism and War', *Women's History Review* (online), 2016, advance access at <http://www.tandfonline.com/doi/pdf/10.1080/09612025.2016.1221292>, 2, accessed Oct. 2017.
6. D. Urquhart (2001) '"The Female of the Species is More Deadlier than the Male"? The Ulster Women's Unionist Council, 1911–1940', in A. Hayes and D. Urquhart (eds), *The Irish Woman's History Reader*, London: Routledge, 2001, 50–7.
7. Urquhart, 'Unionism, Orangeism and War'.
8. M. Coleman, *The Irish Revolution, 1916–23*, London: Routledge, 2013, 123.
9. UWUC Executive Committee minutes, 25 Jan. 1921: PRONI, D1098/1/2.
10. Ward, *Women Unionism and Loyalism*, 115–16.
11. R. Wilford, 'Women and Politics in Northern Ireland', *Parliamentary Affairs*, 49.1 (1996), 44.
12. Ward, *Unionism in the UK*, 168.
13. See J. Elshtain, 'Reflections on War and Political Discourse', *Political Theory*, 13.1 (1985), 39–57; J. Steans, *Gender and International Relations*, Cambridge: Polity, 2013, 99–100.
14. See L. Sjoberg and C. Gentry, *Mothers, Monsters, Whores: Women's Violence in Global Politics*, London: Zed, 2007.
15. Steans, *Gender and International Relations*, 99–100.
16. See Racioppi and O'Sullivan, 'This we will Maintain', 94; Urquhart (2000) *A History Not Yet Told*, 77–84.
17. Sales, *Women Divided*, 9.
18. Ward, *Women Unionism and Loyalism*, 14–15.
19. R. Ward, 'Gender Issues and the Representation of Women in Northern Ireland', *Irish Political Studies*, 19.2 (2004), 14.
20. Sales, *Women Divided*.
21. A. Grey and G. Neill, 'Creating a Shared Society in Northern Ireland: Why we Need to Focus on Gender Equality' *Youth and Society*, 43.2 (2011), 480–1.

22. K. Fearon, 'Whatever Happened to the Women? Gender and Peace in Northern Ireland', in: M. Cox, A. Guelke, and F. Stephen (eds), *A Farewell to Arms? From 'Long War' to Long Peace in Northern Ireland*, Manchester: Manchester University Press, 2000, 155.

23. Y. Galligan, 'Gender and Politics in Northern Ireland: The Representation Gap Revisited', *Irish Political Studies*, 28.3 (2013), 413.

24. See C. Murtagh, 'A Transient Transition: The Cultural and Institutional Obstacles Impeding the Northern Ireland Women's Coalition in it Progression from Informal to Formal Politics', *Irish Political Studies*, 23.1 (2008), 31.

25. C. Enloe, *Bananas, Beaches and Bases: Making Feminist Sense of International Politics*, Berkeley, CA: University of California Press, 2014, 120.

26. Female UUP focus group, 22 Oct. 2016.

27. Female UUP focus group, 22 Oct. 2016.

28. B. Hayes and I. McAllister, 'Who Voted for Peace? Public Support for the 1998 Northern Ireland Agreement', *Irish Political Studies*, 16.1 (2001), 73–93.

29. Y. Galligan, 'Women in Northern Ireland's Politics: Feminising an "Armed Patriarchy"', in M. Sawer, M. Tremblay, and L. Trimble (eds), *Representing Women in Parliament*, London: Routledge, 2006.

30. Y. Galligan and R. Wilford, *Women's Political Representation in Ireland*, in Y. Galligan, E. Ward, and R. Wilford (eds), *Contesting Politics: Women in Ireland, North and South*: Oxford: Westview, 1999, 136.

31. K. Cowell-Meyers, 'A Collarette on a Donkey: The Northern Ireland Women's Coalition and the Limitations of Contagion Theory', *Political Studies,* 59.2 (2011), 420.

32. Galligan, 'Gender and Politics in Northern Ireland', 417.

33. M. Potter and M. Kelly, *Local Elections 2014: Results by Party and Gender*, Research and Information Service Briefing Note, Belfast: NIAR, 333b-14, Paper 78/14, 18 June 2014.

34. Female UUP focus group, 22 Oct. 2016.

35. N. Matthews, 'Gendered Candidate Selection and the Representation of Women in Northern Ireland', *Parliamentary Affairs*, 67.3 (2014), 617–46.

36. See P. Norris, *Electoral Engineering: Voting Rules and Political Behaviour*, Cambridge: Cambridge University Press, 2004; P. Norris and J. Lovenduski, *Political Recruitment: Gender, Race and Class in the British Parliament*, Cambridge: Cambridge University Press, 1995.

37. Norris, *Electoral Engineering*.

38. House of Lords and House of Commons Joint Committee, *Draft House of Lords Reform Bill: Report Session 2010–12*, 3 (2012), 196.

39. C. McGing and T. J. White, 'Gender and Electoral Representation in Ireland', *Études Irlandaises*, 37.2 (2012), 33–48.

40. Northern Ireland Assembly, Research and Information Service Bill Paper Assembly Members (Reduction of Numbers) Bill, NIAR 7–16, 21 Jan. 2016, 8.

41. C. McGlynn, J. Tonge, and J. W. McAuley, 'The Party Politics of Post-Devolution Identity in Northern Ireland', *British Journal of Politics and International Relations*, 16.2 (2014), 274; P. Mitchell, 'Transcending an Ethnic Party System? The Impact of Consociational Governance on Electoral Dynamics and the Party System', in

R. Wilford (ed.), *Aspects of the Belfast Agreement*, Oxford: Oxford University Press, 2001, 44.

42. Y. Galligan and R. Wilford, 'Women's Political Representation in Ireland', in Y. Galligan, E. Ward, and R. Wilford (eds), *Contesting Politics: Women in Ireland, North and South*, Oxford: Westview, 1999.

43. K. Side, 'Women's Civil and Political Citizenship in the Post-Belfast Agreement Period in Northern Ireland', *Irish Political Studies*, 24.1 (2009), 71; M. Braniff and S. Whiting, 'Token Woman', 93–114.

44. Interview with Jo-Anne Dobson, 29 Jan. 2016.

45. Omagh focus group, 19 May 2016.

46. Young Unionist focus group, 10 Mar. 2016.

47. J. Tonge, M. Braniff, T. Hennessey, J. W. McAuley, and S. A. Whiting, *The Democratic Unionist Party: From Protest to Power*, Oxford: Oxford University Press, 2014, 209–11.

48. BBC News, 'DUP's Edwin Poots: Remarks on Arlene Foster "not sexist"', <http://www.bbc.co.uk/news/uk-northern-ireland-politics-35290537> accessed Aug. 2017.

49. Interview with Tom Elliott, 13 Apr. 2016.

50. See Tonge et al., *The Democratic Unionist Party*.

51. Female UUP focus group, 22 Oct. 2016.

52. K. Ross, 'Women Politicians and Malestream Media: A Game of Two Sides', Centre for Advancement of Women in Politics School of Politics, Queens University Belfast Occasional paper, 2003, <https://www.qub.ac.uk/cawp/research/media.PDF>, accessed Aug. 2017.

53. *Belfast Telegraph*, 'Election Posters: Which Northern Ireland Candidates are Topping the Poles?', <http://www.belfasttelegraph.co.uk/news/general-election-2017/election-posters-which-northern-ireland-candidates-are-topping-the-poles-31183952.html> accessed Aug. 2017.

54. Interview with Jo-Anne Dobson, 29 Jan. 2016.

55. M. Kenny and T. Verge, 'Decentralization, Political Parties, and Women's Representation: Evidence from Spain and Britain', *Journal of Federalism*, 43/1 (2013), 109.

56. Y. Galligan and K. Knight, 'Attitudes towards Women in Politics: Gender, Generation and Party Identification in Ireland', *Parliamentary Affairs*, 64.4 (2011), 585–611; N. Matthews, 'Gendered Candidate Selection and the Representation of Women in Northern Ireland', *Parliamentary Affairs*, 67.3 (2014), 617–46; Braniff and Whiting, 'Token Woman'.

57. Norris and Lovenduski, *Political Recruitment*.

58. E. Moloney and A. Pollok, *Paisley*, Dublin: Poolbeg, 1986, 274.

59. Interview with Howard Thornton, 20 May 2016.

60. Interview with Jo-Anne Dobson, 29 Jan. 2016.

61. See Tonge et al., *The Democratic Unionist Party*, 205–7.

62. UUP Representative, interview, July 2009, in Matthews, 'Gendered Candidate Selection', 628.

63. Interview with elected UUP representative 2016.

64. Tonge et al., *The Democratic Unionist Party*, 197–8.

65. Ulster Unionist Party Northern Irish Assembly Manifesto, *Together within the Union*, 1998, <http://cain.ulst.ac.uk/issues/politics/docs/uup/uup98.htm> accessed Aug. 2017.

66. Ulster Unionist Party Northern Irish Assembly Manifesto, *A Manifesto for Real Partnership: A Plan for a Better Northern Ireland*, Belfast, 2017, 19.

67. Female UUP focus group, 22 Oct. 2016.

68. Interview with Philip Smith, 20 Oct. 2016.

69. *Guardian*, 4 Aug. 2017, 'Northern Irish Unionist Parties Alienating Young Protestants, Study Says', <https://www.theguardian.com/uk-news/2017/aug/04/northern-irish-unionist-parties-alienating-young-protestants-study> accessed Aug. 2017.

70. Interview with Philip Smith, 20 Oct. 2016.

71. Female UUP focus group, 22 Oct. 2016.

72. Interview with Colin McCusker, 3 Mar. 2016.

73. Assembly and Executive Review Committee, *Stakeholder 'Call for Evidence' Paper on Review Women in Politics and the Northern Ireland Assembly*, <http://www.niassembly.gov.uk/globalassets/documents/assembly-and-executive-review-2011—2016/reviews/women-in-politics/submissions/ulster-unionist-party-submission.pdf> accessed Aug. 2017.

74. Interview with Philip Smith, 20 Oct. 2016.

75. Female UUP focus group, 22 Oct. 2016.

76. Interview with Adrian Cochrane-Watson, 11 Mar. 2016.

77. Interview with Hazel Legge, 10 Mar. 2016.

78. Y. Galligan, 'Persistent Gender Inequality in Political Representation, North and South', in Ó. Dochartaigh, K. Hayward, and E. Meehan (eds), *Dynamics of Political Change in Ireland: Making and Breaking a Divided Island*, Oxford: Taylor & Francis, 2016, 171.

79. Sandra Overend, 'Female Candidate Quotas a "Step Backwards for Equality"—Overend', available at <http://uup.org/news/587/Female-candidate-quotas-a-step-backwards-for-equality-Overend#.WXh66hPytAY> accessed Aug. 2017.

80. Interview with Howard Thornton, 20 May 2016.

81. Londonderry focus group, 19 May 2016.

82. Independent Commission on Policing, *A New Beginning: Policing in Northern Ireland* (The Patten Report), London: HMSO, 1999.

83. *Daily Telegraph*, 'Stop Patten's Sectarian Plans', 29 July 2000, <http://www.telegraph.co.uk/comment/4253433/Stop-Pattens-sectarian-plan.html> accessed Aug. 2017.

84. Braniff and Whiting, 'Token Woman'.

85. Female UUP focus group, 22 Oct. 2016.

Conclusion

The Future of the Ulster Unionist Party

Many of the ambitions of the UUP evident in the Belfast Agreement have been realized. The Party's interpretations of the deal proved correct.[1] The 1998 Agreement received popular endorsement and enshrined the principle of consent, confirming that Northern Ireland would remain part of the UK for as long as a majority within Northern Ireland's confines so chose. The Irish Constitution's territorial claim was removed and British legal sovereignty over Northern Ireland was conceded by Dublin. The North-South institutions presented no prospect of an embryonic all-Ireland government by stealth as was the case with the Sunningdale Agreement. The Irish dimension was matched by a British-Irish equivalent. The undisclosed elements of the Anglo-Irish Agreement were replaced by a British-Irish Intergovernmental Conference that was no longer secret to unionists. A new Northern Ireland Assembly restored some control to the region's elected representatives. The Agreement contributed substantially to the removal of the Provisional IRA and its weaponry from the scene. Violence largely subsided and a peace, albeit imperfect, took hold. Northern Ireland's police force commands greater acceptance than ever previously in the country's history. Relations between Protestants and Catholics improved in the first few years after the Agreement (before latterly declining again after the collapse of the Assembly in 2017). The Agreement was a constitutional victory for the UUP.

Yet, despite taking some of the political risks needed to fulfil these achievements, the UUP has failed to prosper in the subsequent decades. The emotional impact of prisoner releases, fears over the future of the RUC and the prospect of what many UUP members regarded as terrorists, with a private army, serving in Northern Ireland's government was almost overwhelming. The DUP ruthlessly exploited these concerns as a sell out only to supersede the UUP, while acquiescing in the Agreement's institutions, and then claiming the 'Union is safe'.

Ethnic tribune politics[2] and continuing communalism have marred the evident progress. The perceived stoutest defenders of their respective ethnic blocs fare best at the polls and the DUP and Sinn Féin are seen as the robust tribunes. Both of those parties have moderated their agendas but it is not their propensity to compromise that is the big feature of their electoral advertising. The result has been the maintenance of a politics of intercommunal rivalry, not joined-up government and rapprochement. The UUP's architect of the Belfast Agreement, David Trimble, argues that his desire for a 'pluralist parliament for a pluralist people' was, regardless of the ultimate fate of devolved power-sharing institutions, only partly created:

> in substance, yes, but the DUP are not actually making the best use of it, because they're still in a mode of feeling that they have to fight Sinn Féin and they have to demonstrate to their voters that they're fighting Sinn Féin. This is part of the reason why the administration is not working smoothly...The DUP feels that they have to be in competitive mode, rather than cooperative mode.[3]

The DUP's electoral logic is apparent. Unionist parties have historically thrived in offering robust opposition to nationalist parties and the mutual antipathy of the respective support bases remains intact. Such enmity remains difficult to dissipate. Trimble has effectively given up on the capacity of local parties to remove sectarian electoral politics, arguing that only the presence of UK-wide electoral politics can fulfil this aim. However, the idea does not find much broader favour within the UUP and might further narrow the Party's electoral ground.

The UUP's search continues for a sustained coherent strategy with which to prise support back from the DUP. A member of the Coleraine focus group insisted that the UUP 'need to be streetfighters now. If we're not willing to really take the fight to them [the DUP] now, we'll just slip into obscurity.'[4] This may be correct, but there needs to be a clear basis for the fight. A UUP elected representative even claimed, notwithstanding the two parties' different histories, 'personal ambition and career' now appeared at times to be the main reasons for the continuing existence of two separate unionist parties.[5] The markers which historically gave the UUP advantages over the DUP have disappeared. The UUP is no longer the party of the comfortable Protestant middle class, who now either vote DUP or abstain in contemporary elections. As the DUP stole the political clothes of the UUP, moving from belligerence to relative moderation, the UUP has struggled to respond. The DUP attempted to shed its overt sectarianism or Protestant fundamentalism, and the UUP's competitive advantage—as the representatives of the middle ground within unionism—declined to the point where the DUP's Deputy Leader, Nigel Dodds, could claim, albeit harshly, in 2017 that there was 'only one meaningful unionist party'.[6]

With the UUP marginalized it removed itself from a dysfunctional Northern Ireland Executive. As the DUP has shown, a small-sized party can thrive if its membership base is highly active. Whilst the UUP has many tireless activists, it also contains many inactive ones. Despite this the modern UUP, which played a key positive role in ending conflict, ought to now be more capable of extending its reach. According to the 2016 Northern Ireland Life and Times survey, the percentage of Catholics accepting Northern Ireland's place in the UK may be as high as 44 per cent, a sizeable pool to be fished.[7] Whilst the DUP, given its historical links to Free Presbyterianism and anti-Catholicism, could hardly appeal to Catholics, the data showing that the UUP has even less attraction surprises but reflect the sectarian reality of Northern Ireland's electorate. The DUP's attitude in government has been perceived by many nationalists as outright sectarian and the resulting polarisation of Northern Irish society has not been to the advantage of the UUP. Perhaps the greatest role the UUP can play, in the medium to long term, is presenting a brand of unionism that makes the Union an attractive option to non-unionists in a future border poll.

These problems highlighted, it should also be acknowledged that the UUP has changed considerably in recent times. Its internal organization, coherence, and discipline is much improved, although it still needs refinement, as the mixed messages from elected representatives during election campaigns have indicated. The integrationist tendencies of the UUP, a party once much more comfortable at Westminster—a 'Conservative border party' as one elected representative described it[8]—were adapted readily to accommodate devolution, about which the leadership was once very cautious. The UUP was prepared to abandon a largely token presence in the Northern Ireland Executive to move into Opposition. When devolved government failed again in 2017, the DUP's capacity to operate at Westminster was clearly shown. The UUP could only observe as the DUP's growth reaped reward amid the Conservatives' minority government reliance upon them following that year's General Election.

More positively for the UUP, the organization garners a very strong sense of loyalty from those belonging. A collective sense of belonging is important to the self-worth and self-concept of unionism and in that context party membership of the UUP plays an important role in expressing an individual's sense of security and stability. At the core of this construct of unionism is an understanding of Irish nationalism as the 'dangerous other' politically. Without disparaging nationalists and maintaining respectful disagreement, the UUP reinforces its inclusive sense of identity by excluding others through its major discourses and symbolism.

The UUP's primary tasks are to articulate a sense of unionist identity and offer a stout, reassuring defence—and advancement—of the Union which is unthreatening and welcoming to those who are not natural unionists. It is a vision not based upon appeals to the past or the defensive insecurities of an inbuilt demographic advantage. According to the MLA Steve Aiken, 'unionism cannot sell 1950s Britain as the argument for remaining part of the UK ... it appeals to a very small and narrow base'.[9] On this logic, the UUP offers a more coherent, sustainable and inclusive Britishness than its unionist rival:

> we have a more outward looking view [than the DUP]. We're not intolerant of others. We see very clearly that there is a different picture, and there's a different way of doing things. We're proud to be unionists. We're proud of the British connection. But you know, we live on an island with 4.5million people, or whatever it happens to be, and we need to get on, and there's a different approach ... I think it's much more a question about reasonableness. It's a question about reaching understanding and realizing that it's not a binary choice. I mean it's not black and white. There are elements of grey within it. When you're dealing with a party ... you know the DUP in particular ... the Ulster Unionist Party's more tolerant.[10]

Yet convincing a sceptical unionist electorate that the UUP is the superior custodian of unionist interests has proved tough. This has been made more difficult by the DUP's tinkering with the Belfast Agreement, at St Andrews, to ensure that the First Minister in Northern Ireland is elected by the largest party: a cynical decision to force unionist voters into opting for the DUP in order to prevent a Republican First Minister. The 2017 UK General Election also witnessed a similar channelling of votes towards the DUP to prevent Sinn Fein from winning Parliamentary seats.

The tactics of the UUP may need to extend beyond the hope that the DUP will implode, as even the failure of a disastrous renewable heating incentive scheme, over which it presided, failed to dent seriously the DUP's position among unionists. Whilst that scandal (and other sagas) may raise questions over the quality of governance or politics exercised by the DUP, concerns over those issues are insufficient reasons to vote for the UUP. There is no magic wand—no clear issue of difference between the UUP and DUP—which will revive UUP fortunes. The starkest distinction between the two parties since the Belfast Agreement concerned Brexit but the UUP readily accepted the referendum verdict, with its UK-wide perspective and concerns with national sovereignty of considerable import. But politics is also about trust and concerns about the competence of the DUP in governance allow for an alternative brand of unionism that can sustain the UUP and open up a flank to attack.

For almost all members of the UUP, Britishness remains central to their social identity and remains core to the expression of their worldview. Sharing a sense of Britishness, however, does not mean that those who self-designate as that category hold homogeneous views on all things. It does mean that the individuals share important characteristics and that events deemed relevant to the group also bear great significance for the individual member. Although less than 1 per cent of members chose Irish as their primary identity, the number of UUP members who recognized some degree of 'Irishness' in making up their self-identity was noteworthy. This complex relationship is constructed in oppositional terms to the politics of Irishness but is often expressed quite positively in cultural terms. While Britishness in this sense may act as a superordinate identity, within this category there are important differences in how UUP members construct the term.

The UUP's British unionism is less easy to distinguish from that offered by the DUPthese days. The distinctions are minor and of emphasis rather than serious divergence. Both parties now espouse a civic Unionism: in truth, however, the UUP always contained an element of an ethnic definition of unionism comparable to the DUP; but in the latter this was clearly dominant in the shape of Ian Paisley and the Free Presbyterian Church. The late DUP leader still casts a shadow over how his party is perceived by UUP members as an overtly sectarian entity and the unacceptable face of unionism.

In contrast the UUP perceives itself as a more liberal, pluralist body, one which owes nothing to a religious creed or cultural supremacy. Rather, the Britishness of the UUP is rational and non-sectarian. Although not accurate historically, traditionally, the UUP emphasized (and increasingly does) the civic and political bonds of citizenship as an integral part of the UK state, rather than espouse a DUP vision of unionism as an ethno-national community.

Civic unionism could have flourished in the context of the pluralist devolved political institutions created following the Belfast Agreement. These allowed for inclusive partnership government. Severance of the UUP's relationship with the Orange Order potentially allowed the chance for the UUP to articulate more clearly and boldly its liberal and civic versions of unionism.

For all the historical merits of these typologies, the distinctions, never absolute, are now far less clear-cut than might have once been the case. Both party memberships identify first as British; Northern Irish only later. Neither the UUP nor the DUP wants Northern Ireland to retreat into a sectarian laager. Both party memberships support devolved government within the UK and the UUP membership is as equally pro-devolution as that of the DUP.[11] Both parties have shared power with republicans and have been obliged to accept restrictions upon certain symbols of Protestant-Unionist-Britishness, including on flag displays and parades. Blurring of intra-unionist boundaries has been more of a process of DUP shifts than those emanating from the UUP. Paisleyite sectarian anti-Catholicism has long been displaced. The DUP's move from being a party of protest to one of power meant the displacement of bombast by a more restrained and professional outlook. The quiet diplomacy of the UUP's James Molyneaux may seem a long way from the DUP's fairly brazen acquisition of £1 billion for Northern Ireland from the struggling Conservative Government in 2017, in return for parliamentary support on key votes, but it is the DUP which is integrated into the Westminster system nowadays, not the UUP. In contrast, the UUP is confined to representation in Northern Ireland, mainly on local councils.

A struggle remains for the UUP leadership to establish a distinct discourse, aided by its membership, which will address the wider electorate, especially for those unionists who fear the rise of Sinn Féin. This book has shown how UUP members are very loyal to their Party (and their country) but often insecure over what the UUP has achieved. Although often proud of their party's achievements, desirous of progress, and supportive of friendly power-sharing relationships with nationalists, many such members feel unionists are in retreat, do not believe the relative peace is permanent, are sceptical of all-island economic and political links and are still suspicious of the recent actions of nationalists and wary of their long-term ambitions. When the UUP set aside those concerns for the greater good, they were punished by an opportunistic rival. Articulating the case that the UUP won the argument may be therapeutic but is not a future vote-gathering exercise. The UUP now needs to show how, by backing it, the Union would be safer, command wider acceptance, allow unionism to flourish and enjoy greater prosperity.

A context of a rising nationalist population and the loss of unionism's overall majority of seats, for the first time in Northern Ireland's history, in the 2017 Assembly election, place the issue of unionist unity on the agenda. If, as seems probable, Sinn Féin continues to eclipse the SDLP, can unionism afford to be divided between two parties (three if the Traditional Unionist Voice is included)? Intra-unionist rivalry increases the possibility of a Sinn Féin First Minister at the head of a devolved Northern Ireland government, a possibility many unionists might still refuse to countenance despite the reality that the position is co-equal with that of deputy First Minister. In Northern Ireland symbolism still counts for much. The UUP needs to present some evidence to the electorate that the UUP can win the intra-unionist contest without endangering unionism. The unionist electorate fears that electoral parity between the DUP and UUP could damage both, allowing Sinn Féin to become the largest party. Clear evidence of DUP failure will of course also assist the UUP, but the UUP needs agendas of its own.

A merger with the DUP would, however, be anathema to most UUP members. Only one in seven accept the prospect and it has been the first task of recent UUP leaders to reassure the base that an amalgamation with the DUP is not on the agenda. There is much enmity and historical baggage. UUP members see their party as selfless and view the DUP as selfish. Whilst there is far more that broadly unites than divides unionists, in the defence of the Union, support for Northern Ireland, Protestantism, and, to some extent, Orangeism, UUP–DUP relations have been characterized more by antipathy than empathy, other than for a brief period after the 1985 Anglo-Irish Agreement. The existence of two separate parties within a small community has more often been accompanied by antagonism than by a clear sense of pan-unionism.

The future of the UUP obviously rests on its capacity to win back the confidence of its electorate, while offering an inclusive, non-sectarian, and fresh unionism which is constitutionally robust—a unionism for all. It needs clear and cogent unionist messages, a strong leader, some points of distinction from the DUP, an attractive team of potential elected representatives, and an activist base capable of using modern campaigning techniques. There also needs to be greater consistency of messages.

It is far too soon to write the political obituary of the UUP. It has a deeply loyal membership prepared to weather lean times for their Party, enjoys resilient support, and internally now resembles a proper political party, not the loose conglomeration of feuding groups and autonomous associations it constituted at the beginning of the twenty-first century. The rapidity of the rise of the DUP itself indicates that no party is destined to be in the ascendancy in perpetuity and given the right set of circumstances and dynamic leadership, the UUP can revive. The Party suffered from perhaps the most acute fracture in unionist politics ever seen, over the Belfast Agreement. Therein lies the paradox for the UUP. At least partly thanks to the Party's efforts and sacrifices, Northern Ireland's future may be more secure, their party rather less so; a case of country before party.

Notes

1. Ulster Unionist Party, *Understanding the Agreement*, Belfast: UUP, 1998.
2. P. Mitchell, G. Evans, and B. O'Leary, 'Extremist Outbidding in Ethnic Party Systems is Not Inevitable: Tribune Parties in Northern Ireland', *Political Studies*, 57.2 (2009), 397–421.
3. Interview with David Trimble, 30 June 2016.
4. Coleraine focus group, 18 May 2016.
5. Interview with Jeff Dudgeon, 20 May 2016.
6. Nigel Dodds, speech to DUP Conference, La Mon hotel Belfast, 25 Nov. 2017.
7. Northern Ireland Life and Times Survey, *Political Attitudes*, 2016, <http://www.ark. ac.uk/nilt/2016/Political_Attitudes/NIRELND2.html#rel>.
8. Interview with Jeff Dudgeon, 20 May 2016.
9. Steve Aiken, 'What Unionism Ought to Do to Check Sinn Féin and Dublin', <http://eamonnmallie.com/2017/11/unionism-check-sinn-fein-dublin-dr-steveaiken>, Nov. 2017.
10. Interview with Steve Aiken, 19 Oct. 2016.
11. J. Tonge, M. Braniff, T. Hennessey, J. W. McAuley, and S. A. Whiting, *The Democratic Unionist Party: From Protest to Power*, Oxford: Oxford University Press, 2014.

List of Interviewees

Steve Aiken, 20 May 2017
Andy Allen, 4 March 2016
Doug Beattie, 16 March 2016
Roy Beggs, 28 January 2016
Robbie Butler, 30 October 2016
Adrian Cochrane-Watson, 11 March 2016
Mark Cosgrove, 4 December 2016
Jo-Anne Dobson, 29 January 2016
Jeff Dudgeon, 20 March 2016
Tom Elliott, 13 April 2016
Lord Reg Empey, 30 June 2016
Ross Hussey, 27 January 2016
Danny Kennedy, 28 January 2016
Danny Kinahan, 13 April 2016
Hazel Legge, 10 March 2016
Lindsay Millar, 4 March 2016
Colin McCusker, 3 March 2016
Mike Nesbitt, 16 December 2016
Sandra Overend, 28 January 2016
Jim Rodgers, 20 May 2016
Robin Swann, 25 February 2016 and 14 August 2017
Philip Smith, 30 October 2016
Howard Thornton, 20 May 2016
Lord David Trimble, 30 June 2016

List of Focus Groups

Young Unionists, 10 March 2016

Michael Palmer
Kris Dines
Sky Aughey
Andrew Wilson
Josh Lewy

Coleraine, 18 May 2016

Aaron Callan (now DUP)
Robert McPherson
William King
Tom Fleming
Gareth Bell

Londonderry, 19 May 2016

David Colhorn
Heather Hatrick
Barbara Hatrick
Willie Lamrock
Mary Hamilton
Heather White
Julia Kee

Female focus group, 22 October 2016

Lindsay Millar
Hilary Gibson
Lindsay Smith
Kay Clarke
Maureen Morrow
May Steele
Sky Aughey
Hannah Niblock

Author Index

Subject Index